The
BASIC
Handbook

An Encyclopedia of the BASIC Computer Language
by
David A. Lien

COMPUSOFT PUBLISHING
A Division of CompuSoft, Inc.
P.O. Box 19669 ● San Diego, California 92119 U.S.A.

International Standard Book Number: 0-932760-00-7
Library of Congress Catalog Card Number: 78-64886   94688

Printed in the United States of America

Preface

With the roots of the BASIC language now firmly established throughout the world, it is necessary to make its many dialects understandable so programs can be transported between different computers. After you've found just the program you've been looking for, you know how frustrating it is only to discover that it won't RUN on **your** computer. This HANDBOOK addresses that problem by discussing in detail every commonly used BASIC Statement, Function, Operator and Command.

For the most part, BASIC words mean the same thing to every computer which recognizes them. If a computer does not possess the capabilities of a needed or specified word, there are often ways to accomplish the same function by using another word, or combination of words.

That's where The HANDBOOK comes in. It helps you get the most from your computer, be it a "bottom-of-the-line" micro, or an oversized monster.

Have fun computing!

Dr. David A. Lien
San Diego − 1978

Personal Acknowledgements

In a book of this scope and complexity, there are far too many contributors, direct and indirect, to identify by name. In fact, most are unknown, but the fruits of their intensive labors are documented in this *Handbook*.

Much credit is due fellow computer fancier, Ham radio operator and technical writer, Dave Waterman of Alpine, California. He assisted as a researcher, tester and "rough writer".

Dave Gunzel of Ft. Worth, Texas was the designer and Editor. Since he is one of the best in the business, he kept the irrepressible author on a short leash, and the book turned out the way you see it.

Dr. Lance Leventhal, fellow pioneer in this exciting business, was visionary enough to concur that this book had to be written, and could be, and provided the needed encouragement.

The cover photo is by James R. Ney.

Many others reviewed early copies of the manuscript outline, and their helpful suggestions turned the germ of an idea into a book.

They include:

Mr. Harold Ehler, Head of Computer Operations, R.J. Fisher Construction Co., Fresno, CA.

Prof. W.E. English, W6WYQ, Chairman, Engineering & Technology Dept., Cuesta College, San Luis Obispo, CA.

Mr. Jacob Konen, Systems and Programming Supervisor, Grossmont College, El Cajon, CA.

Prof. David Lunsford, Mathematics and Computers, Grossmont College, El Cajon, CA.

Dr. Donald Martin, Director of Engineering Services, KPBS-TV/FM, San Diego State University, San Diego, CA.

Dr. Ed Thorland, Computer Center Director, Luther College, Decorah, Iowa.

Mr. Charles Zappala, WA6VZR, Technical Writer, Tel-tone Corp., Bothell, WA.

Introduction

While preparing this *Handbook*, a number of assumptions and ground rules were established. Without them, the job would never have been completed and no one would benefit from the accumulation of information. Those assumptions and ground rules are listed here so you might better understand where the *Handbook* is "coming from".

1. Users of the language are exceedingly frustrated by not being able to take a BASIC program from another computer or a magazine article and make it work on their computer. Top priority will be given to that information which will help users solve this "incompatability" problem.

2. There is a large central core of BASIC words which are shared by all manufacturers. A thorough treatment of that core is more important than extended discourse on lesser used and obscure special-purpose BASIC words.

3. To the extent that time and space allow, lesser used BASIC words will be covered, but like the expanding universe theory, BASIC keeps expanding. We can only chase it — but never catch it all.

4. BASIC is used on all sizes of computers, Micros, Minis and Maxis. Size is unimportant, since some smaller computers have vastly superior BASIC capabilities. Emphasis shall therefore be on the language, not the size of machine.

5. The *Handbook* will be an Encyclopedic type reference work — not a dictionary or a textbook. It will be a precise and definitive reference which can accompany a good BASIC text, but not try to replace it.

6. To make the *Handbook* easy to use, it will be divided into logical sections, and a uniform method of dealing with each BASIC word will be followed.

7. It's not as important to identify whose version of BASIC does what, as it is to make a given program run on a given computer, *if at all possible.* Tying specific capabilities to specific manufacturers will therefore be given low priority.

8. Large computers typically use compilers; small ones typically use interpreters. Since it makes little difference to the language itself, we will use the words **interpreter** and **compiler** interchangeably.

9. Each BASIC word will be treated clearly and concisely. To avoid wasting trees for excess paper, duplication will be minimized by referring the reader to other related words.

10. The *Handbook* is important enough to users that they will readily (and hopefully, gently) point out errors, omissions and variations which might not be covered in this edition. We can pick up those changes and additions in future editions.

11. There is very little uniformity in control of peripheral devices, such as disks, tapes and printers. The words that are required and used extend far beyond the original scope of Dartmouth BASIC. To attempt to include them at this point would be premature.

12. The *Handbook* is not a substitute for the manufacturer's manual which accompanies each computer. It is a supplement.

Some Thoughts about the BASIC Language

A computer is just a box of switches, not very different from the on/off switches which control household light bulbs. Each of the thousands of switches is either ON or OFF at a given time. By making up a "code" whereby the on/off status of each switch means something, an extensive (but not very complicated) system of holding and processing information can be created.

Unfortunately, computers can only hold, process and communicate information in the form of "switches" being either ON or OFF. To most of us that's like a tough foreign language. That "computer language" is now taught in many schools and colleges.

For most of us mere mortals, however (or those of us in a hurry), it is much more efficient to hire an **interpreter** to translate back and forth between this strange ON/OFF computer language and English. That way, we can talk directly to the interpreter, let the interpreter talk to the computer, let the computer talk back to the interpreter, and then the interpreter talks back to us. This might seem tedious and inefficient, but modern computer interpreters work so fast they are effectively "invisible" between us and the computer (and nothing is lost in translation but a few millionths of a second).

We say the computer "talks" in **machine language**. We talk in English. Our interpreter isn't content to just do its job and not fuss about it, it wants to be called a **language** too. (These days, everybody's got to have a fancy title that no one can really pin down!) The most common interpreter language is named BASIC. BASIC stands for Beginners All-purpose Symbolic Instruction Code. Our interpreter's language is BASIC, and we hide it right *inside* the computer. Pretty sly — using part of the computer to act as its own interpreter.

Early computers were almost entirely preoccupied with interpreting, when forced to communicate in the English language, (leaving little capability for doing anything useful). Changes in technology have brought prices down to where even today's "small" computers are large enough to easily do the interpreting, with room and power to spare for *real* computing.

Development of the BASIC language at Dartmouth College in 1963 by Professors Kemeny and Kurtz was an important breakthrough, making it possible for us ordinary folks to use computers. That was why it was developed, and because it's so easy to learn and use, it is the most popular computer language.

There are a number of other computer "languages" which act as interpreters, but most are so complicated that you have to learn them like a foreign language. Even so, they are still much simpler than machine language.

The BASIC language is incredibly simple compared to the entire English language. Its vocabulary is very limited, several hundred words at most, compared to hundreds of thousands of English words. Unlike English, it has to be used with great precision — *no sloppiness is allowed.* The computer is just a dumb box of parts that does as it's told, but hasn't the good sense to come in out of the rain.

BASIC was once looked down on by elitists as a simple-minded computer language of the unwashed masses, and, tho phenomenally powerful, not worthy of respectability. *(So was the Volkswagen.)* More computers now speak BASIC than any other computer language. Because of BASIC's simplicity, computer programming (and thereby control) has escaped the grasp of just a select few.

Because we have to "speak" BASIC clearly and concisely to the Computer, there are a few simple ground rules we must know. They include:

1. Each message we send to the computer must be typed on one line, and that line must have a number. For Example:
   1Ø PRINT "HELLO THERE DUMB COMPUTER!"
   The computer reads our message from the smallest line number to the largest, acting on each one as it goes.

2. Letters of the alphabet are used just as in regular mathematical equations. If more than the 26 letters are needed, each letter can be followed by a single number (e.g. B7), making available 260 additional "variables." In some versions, 2 or more letters can be combined to give a variable a name (e.g. "UP" or "ANGLE" or "IRVING", etc.).

3. The computer responds to specific commands like RUN, STOP, LIST, etc., after we type those simple English words.

4. A computer "program" is a whole set of messages in the form of a LISTing of numbered lines.

5. The standard rules of mathematics generally apply to solving equations. The standard symbols also apply, with the exception of multiplication, where * is used instead of "x". Trigonometry, Matrices and Arrays, and other advanced operations can be performed with relative ease.

If these and other simple rules were universally true, there would be no need for *The BASIC Handbook.* However, as computers developed in laboratories around the world, over a hundred variations or "dialects" of BASIC also developed.

These dialects have much in common, but there are enough differences that non-trivial programs written for one computer will seldom run on another without modification.

The efforts of the ANSI (American National Standards Institute) and NBS (National Bureau of Standards) towards standardization of at least a common language core will probably be the major factor in some day having a Standard BASIC. Failing that, the immutable laws of the free market will determine which version of BASIC survive.

Caution:

When you come across "standard" English words or abbreviations in computer programs, don't automatically assume they are BASIC words (the program might be in another computer language). A word to the wise . . .

BASIC not only changes from manufacturer to manufacturer, it changes from a given manufacturer with time. Features are added, changed and dropped, often without notice. That's why two apparently identical computers may not always work exactly the same.

How To Use This Handbook

The information about each BASIC word is broken into a number of parts. Study this example carefully to better understand what to expect from your *Handbook*.

① **The WORD itself:** It is a word found in a BASIC program, or used to control one. Words which are used for overall system monitor purposes, editor languages, and other computer languages are **not** part of *The BASIC Handbook*.

② **ANSI Standard notation:** If the word "ANSI" appears here, it means that the word is part of the proposed National Bureau of Standards American National Standards Institute minimum BASIC vocabulary. Although adoption was not official as of press time, any changes in the proposed Standard are expected to be minor.

③ **Word Category:** BASIC words are divided into 4 categories:

Commands: which tell the computer to do something with a program, like RUN, LIST, etc. Some computers allow commands to be imbedded in a program, thus also serve as a Statement.

Statements: words which actually appear within a program, and comprise the detailed instructions on which the computer makes its decisions and performs its duties. Example:

>   PRINT A,B,C

Functions: words which call forth pre-programmed machine-level "micro-programs". They perform relatively complicated "functions" such as finding a trigonometric value, a square root, etc., serving as part of a larger statement. Examples:

>   LET X = TAN(Y)   PRINT LOG(A)

Operators: non-word characters which perform in special comparative or modifying capacities. Examples: comma, colon, equal sign, etc.

In *The BASIC Handbook*, Commands, Statements and Functions appear in alphabetical order. Operators, not lending themselves to alphabetizing, appear in a separate section at the back.

④ **Introductory and Descriptive remarks** about the WORD, telling what it is and what it does. May include special notes relating to brands of computers which predominantly or exclusively use the word.

⑤ **TEST PROGRAM:** Allows user to enter a brief program into a computer to see if its interpreter or compiler recognizes the word and makes use of it.

⑥ **SAMPLE RUN:** Shows how the computer might be expected to respond to the TEST PROGRAM. Results will vary slightly from machine to machine, but the general pattern should not vary widely from the sample run.

⑦ **HELPFUL HINTS:** Sometimes there are programming techniques which greatly simplify achieving a high level of simplicity and/or reliability. They are noted here.

⑧ **IF YOUR COMPUTER DOESN'T HAVE IT:** Gives alternate ways to accomplish the same objective using other BASIC words, when possible . . . and it isn't always possible. In the case of functions, a sub-routine is usually included which is able to circumvent the absent intrinsic function. In the case of statements (especially PRINT), a simple re-writing of part of a program using other words and techniques allow program execution with the same or somewhat diminished results.

⑨ **VARIATIONS:** Variations in usage of the WORD; that is, how the WORD **itself** might be used differently by different computers. (Not variations in how the desired results might be achieved with other words.)

⑩ **ALSO SEE:** Rather than spend an inordinate amount of space duplicating information, words are sometimes "clustered" around a central word, and that central word is discussed in great detail. Related words then treat their specific purpose only, referring to other words for more detail as desired.

The FIX function is used to remove all numbers to the right of the decimal point. Its operation is similar to the ④ INT function except FIX does not round negative numbers down.

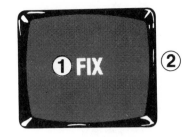

Function ③

Example: 1Ø PRINT FIX(3.6)
          2Ø PRINT FIX(-3.6)

prints the numbers 3 and -3. While

          1Ø PRINT INT(3.6)
          2Ø PRINT INT(-3.6)

prints the numbers 3 and -4.

FIX is capable of handling any number, large or small, within the limitations of the computer's interpreter.

⑤ **TEST PROGRAM**

```
1Ø REM 'FIX' TEST PROGRAM
2Ø N=-12.3456
3Ø A=FIX(N)
4Ø PRINT "FIX PASSED THE TEST IF ";N;"IS CHANGED TO ";A
99 END
```

⑥ **SAMPLE RUN**

```
FIX PASSED THE TEST IF -12.3456 IS CHANGED TO -12
```

⑦

⑧ *IF YOUR COMPUTER DOESN'T HAVE IT*

If your interpreter does not have the FIX function capability, but has the ABS, INT and SGN functions, then line 3Ø in the TEST PROGRAM can be replaced with:

```
3Ø A=SGN(N)*INT(ABS(N))
```

⑨ **VARIATIONS IN USAGE**

None known.

⑩ **ALSO SEE**

INT, ABS, SGN

A. is used in the TRS-80 Level I and other variations of Palo Alto Tiny BASIC as an abbreviation for the ABS (absolute) function.

For more information see ABS.

Function

TEST PROGRAM

```
1Ø REM 'A. (ABS)' TEST PROGRAM
2Ø X=A.(-1ØØ)
3Ø PRINT "'A.' PASSED THE TEST IF";X;
4Ø PRINT "IS PRINTED AS A POSITIVE VALUE."
99 END
```

SAMPLE RUN

'A.' PASSED THE TEST IF 1ØØ IS PRINTED AS A POSITIVE VALUE.

VARIATIONS IN USAGE

A. is also used in the Level I Basic as an abbreviation for the function AT, when used in PRINT statements.

For more information see AT.

TEST PROGRAM

```
1Ø  REM "A. (AT)" TEST PROGRAM
2Ø V =A.(-2Ø)
3Ø  PRINT A.V;"A. PASSED THE 'AT' TEST."
99 END
```

SAMPLE RUN

A. PASSED THE 'AT' TEST.

The function ABS must be used instead of A. to **print** absolute values. A. used after PRINT is always executed as the function AT.

ALSO SEE

ABS, AT, @

The ABS function gives the absolute value of a number or numeric variable. A number's absolute value is its value without a + or − sign.

A
N
S
I

Function

Example: **PRINT ABS(-1∅)** prints 1∅.

ABS is capable of handling any number, large or small, within the limitations of the computer's interpreter.

TEST PROGRAM

```
1∅ REM 'ABS' TEST PROGRAM
2∅ X=35
3∅ PRINT "ABS PASSED THE TEST IF";
4∅ PRINT ABS(-435.28);
5∅ PRINT ABS (-.∅3245);
6∅ PRINT ABS (-X)
7∅ PRINT "ARE ALL PRINTED AS POSITIVE VALUES."
99 END
```

SAMPLE RUN

```
ABS PASSED THE TEST IF 435.28  .∅3245  35
ARE ALL PRINTED AS POSITIVE VALUES.
```

Some interpreters also allow the ABS function within arithmetic operations. This feature can be used in programs which require a positive value from math operations that would otherwise produce a negative value.

The entire math operation following ABS must be enclosed in parentheses.

TEST PROGRAM

```
1∅ REM 'ABS' MATH OPERATION TEST PROGRAM
2∅ A=18
3∅ B=58
4∅ PRINT "THE ABSOLUTE VALUE OF";(A—B)/2;"IS";ABS((A—B)/2)
99 END
```

SAMPLE RUN

```
THE ABSOLUTE VALUE OF -2∅ IS 2∅
```

ABS

IF YOUR COMPUTER DOESN'T HAVE IT

If ABS is not intrinsic to the computer, it can easily be simulated by the following sub-routine:

TEST PROGRAM

```
10 REM 'ABS' SUBROUTINE TEST PROGRAM
20 PRINT "ENTER A NEGATIVE NUMBER";
30 INPUT X
40 GOSUB 30000
50 PRINT "THE ABSOLUTE VALUE OF ";X;"IS";Y
60 GOTO 20
30000 REM * ABS(X) SUBROUTINE * INPUT X, OUTPUT Y
30010 IF X >=0 THEN 30040
30020 Y=X*-1
30030 RETURN
30040 Y=X
30050 RETURN
30999 END
```

SAMPLE RUN *(using -35.5)*

```
ENTER A NEGATIVE NUMBER? —35.5
THE ABSOLUTE VALUE OF -35.5 IS 35.5
ENTER A NEGATIVE NUMBER?
```

VARIATIONS IN USAGE

None known.

AND is used in FOR-NEXT statements as a "logical math" operator.

For example, IF A=8 AND B=6 THEN 8∅ reads; if the value of variable A equals 8 **AND** the value of variable B equals 6, the IF-THEN condition is met and execution continues at line 8∅.

Operator

TEST PROGRAM #1

```
1∅ REM LOGICAL 'AND' TEST PROGRAM
2∅ A=8
3∅ B=6
4∅ IF A=8 AND B=6 THEN 7∅
5∅ PRINT "AND FAILED THE TEST AS A LOGICAL OPERATOR"
6∅ GOTO 99
7∅ PRINT "AND PASSED THE LOGICAL OPERATOR TEST"
99 END
```

SAMPLE RUN

```
AND PASSED THE LOGICAL OPERATOR TEST
```

A few computers use the AND operator to "logically" compare strings.

For example, IF A$="A"AND B$="B" THEN 8∅ reads, if the string variable A$ is equal to (or "the same as") the letter A **AND** the string variable B$ is to the letter B, the IF-THEN condition is met and execution continues at line 8∅. For more information see the operators + and *.

TEST PROGRAM #2

```
1∅ REM 'STRING LOGICAL 'AND' TEST PROGRAM
2∅ A$="A"
3∅ B$="F"
4∅ IF A$="A"AND B$ >"B"THEN 7∅
5∅ PRINT "'AND' FAILED THE TEST AS A LOGICAL OPERATOR"
6∅ GOTO 99
7∅ PRINT "'AND' PASSED THE STRING LOGICAL OPERATOR TEST"
99 END
```

AND

SAMPLE RUN

'AND' PASSED THE STRING LOGICAL OPERATOR TEST

Some computers use the logical operator AND to determine if the conditions are met in two relational operators. When the condition of both operators is met, AND returns the number -1. When the condition of the AND operator is not met, AND returns a $\emptyset$.

For example, **PRINT A=4 AND B=8** if A equals 4 AND B equals 8 the computer will print the number -1. If either condition is not met, the computer prints a $\emptyset$.

TEST PROGRAM #3

```
1Ø REM 'AND' LOGICAL TEST PROGRAM
2Ø PRINT "ENTER A NUMBER FROM 1 TO 1Ø";
3Ø INPUT A
4Ø B=A > 4 AND A < 11
5Ø IF B=-1 THEN 8Ø
6Ø PRINT A;"IS NOT GREATER THAN 4 AND LESS THAN 11"
7Ø GOTO 2Ø
8Ø PRINT A;"IS GREATER THAN 4 AND LESS THAN 11"
99 END
```

SAMPLE RUN *(typical)*

```
ENTER A NUMBER FROM 1 TO 1Ø? 2
  2 IS NOT GREATER THAN 4 AND LESS THAN 11
ENTER A NUMBER FROM 1 TO 1Ø? 8
  8 IS GREATER THAN 4 AND LESS THAN 11
```

The AND operator is used by a few computers to compute the binary logical **AND** of two numbers using Boolean algebra.

Without presenting a complete course in Boolean algebra, . . . it compares two binary bits to determine whether **both** are a binary "one". When both ANDed bits are a binary one, the computer answers with a $\emptyset$.

For example:

```
1 AND Ø = Ø
Ø AND 1 = Ø
1 AND 1 = 1
```

AND

Therefore, when the computer ANDs one number with another, each number's bit value is logically ANDed with the other number's bit value, producing a third number.

For example

	DECIMAL		BINARY
	3		$\emptyset\emptyset11$
(logical)		AND	
	5		$\emptyset1\emptyset1$
=	1		$\emptyset\emptyset\emptyset1$

In this example only the first (right hand) bit in each number is a binary one, so the resultant number is a decimal 1 (binary $\emptyset\emptyset\emptyset1$).

TEST PROGRAM #4

```
1Ø REM 'AND' BINARY LOGIC TEST PROGRAM
2Ø PRINT "ENTER A VALUE FOR X";
3Ø INPUT X
4Ø PRINT "ENTER A VALUE FOR Y";
5Ø INPUT Y
6Ø A=X AND Y
7Ø PRINT "THE LOGICAL 'AND' VALUE OF";X;"AND";Y;"IS";A
8Ø GOTO 2Ø
99 END
```

SAMPLE RUN *(using 6 and 1Ø)*

```
ENTER A VALUE FOR X? 6
ENTER A VALUE FOR Y? 1Ø
THE LOGICAL 'AND' VALUE OF 6 AND 1Ø IS 2
ENTER A VALUE FOR X?
```

VARIATIONS IN USAGE

None known.

ALSO SEE

*, +, =, < , > , < >

The ASC function converts a character or string variable to ASCII integer code.

For example, **PRINT ASC("A")** prints 65, the ASCII code for the letter A. **PRINT ASC(A$)** prints the ASCII code of the first character in string variable A$.

Function

TEST PROGRAM

```
10 REM 'ASC(CHARACTER)' TEST PROGRAM
20 PRINT "THE ASCII CODE FOR LETTER A IS";
30 PRINT ASC ("A")
40 IF ASC("A")=65 THEN 70
50 PRINT "ASC FAILED THE TEST"
60 GOTO 99
70 PRINT "ASC PASSED THE TEST"
99 END
```

SAMPLE RUN

```
THE ASCII CODE FOR LETTER A IS 65
ASC PASSED THE TEST
```

The next program tests the ASC function with a variable.

TEST PROGRAM

```
10 REM 'ASC(STRING VARIABLE)' TEST PROGRAM
20 PRINT "TYPE ANY LETTER, NUMBER, OR CHARACTER";
30 INPUT A$
40 PRINT "THE ASCII CODE FOR ";A$;" IS";ASC(A$)
99 END
```

SAMPLE RUN *(using H)*

```
TYPE ANY LETTER, NUMBER, OR CHARACTER? H
THE ASCII CODE FOR H IS 72
```

Some computers which incorporate the ASC function can *accept* character strings longer than one character, but only the first character is evaluated and converted to ASCII code. To test for the ASC string limit, use the second Test Program and INPUT progressively longer strings until an error message appears.

VARIATIONS IN USAGE

Some interpreters (e.g. MAXBASIC) use the format ASC(A$,X) which prints the ASCII code of the first X characters contained in A$.

ALSO SEE

CHR$, Appendix A for the ASCII code.

The ASN(n) function is used by the TEKTRONIX 4051 BASIC to compute the ARCSIN **in Radians** (not in **degrees!**) of the ratio n. A radian is approximately 57 degrees.

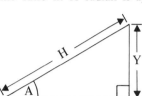

Function

Arcsin (ASN) is defined as the angle (A) created for a certain **ratio** of the length of the side opposite it (Y) to the length of the hypotenuse of the right triangle.

        A=ASN(Y/H)

The opposite of ASN is SINE (SIN). The SINE of an angle is the ratio of the length of the side opposite the angle to the length of the hypotenuse of the right triangle.

        SIN(A)=Y/H

TEST PROGRAM

        10 REM 'ASN' TEST PROGRAM
        20 PRINT "ENTER A RATIO OR SINE VALUE";
        30 INPUT N
        40 W=ASN(N)
        50 PRINT "THE ANGLE WITH THE Y/H RATIO OF";N;"IS";W;"RADIANS"
        30999 END

SAMPLE RUN *(using .5)*

        ENTER A RATIO OR SINE VALUE? .5
        THE ANGLE WITH THE Y/H RATIO OF .5 IS .52359 RADIANS

To convert values from radians to degrees, multiply the angle (in radians) times 57.29578.

Example, `D=ASN(A)*57.29578` To convert values from degrees to radians, multiply the angle (in degrees) times .0174533.

Example, `R=A`*(angle expressed in degrees)* `*.0174533`.

If your interpreter has the ATN (ARCTANGENT) and SQR (SQUARE ROOT) capability, but does not have ASN, substitute ATN(X/SQR(-X*X+1)) for ASN.

If your interpreter does not have ASN or ATN and SQR capability, the following sub-routine can be substituted:

```
30000 GOTO 30999
30530 REM * ARCSIN SUBROUTINE * INPUT S, OUTPUT W
30535 REM ALSO USES VARIABLES X AND Z INTERNALLY
30540 X=S
30545 IF ABS(S) < =.707107 THEN 30600
30550 X=1-S*S
30555 IF X < 0 THEN 30558
30557 GOTO 30560
30558 PRINT S;"IS OUT OF RANGE"
30559 STOP
30560 W=X/2
30565 Z=0
30570 Y=(X/W-W)/2
30575 IF Y=0 THEN 30597
30580 IF Y=Z THEN 30597
30585 W=W+Y
30590 Z=Y
30595 GOTO 30570
30597 X=W
30600 Y=X+X*X*X/6+X*X*X*X*X* .075+X*X*X*X*X*X*X*4.464286E-2
30605 W=Y+X*X*X*X*X*X*X*X*X*3.038194E-2
30610 IF ABS(S) > .707107 THEN 30620
30615 GOTO 30625
30620 W=1.570796-W
30630 RETURN
```

To use this subroutine with the TEST PROGRAM for finding the ARCSIN (in RADIANS) of a ratio (SINE), make the following TEST PROGRAM changes:

```
35 S=N
40 GOSUB 30540
```

To make the ARCSIN subroutine express the angle in DEGREES, add the following line to it:

```
30625 W=W*57.29578
```

VARIATIONS IN USAGE

None known.

ALSO SEE

SIN, ATN, SQR, COS, TAN

The AT function is used with PRINT statements (TRS-80 Level I BASIC) to indicate the PRINT statement's starting location. The AT function value may be a number, numeric variable, or mathematical operation. A comma or semi-colon must be inserted between the AT value and the string.

Function

For example:

```
1∅ PRINT AT 42∅, "HELLO"
2∅ PRINT AT (42∅); "HELLO"
```

Both lines print the word "HELLO" AT location 42∅. The parentheses are optional.

TEST PROGRAM

```
1∅ REM 'AT' TEST PROGRAM
2∅ PRINT AT 128,"2. IF THIS LINE IS PRINTED AFTER LINE 1."
3∅ PRINT AT ∅."1. THE 'AT' FUNCTION PASSED THE TEST"
4∅ GOTO 4∅
99 END
```

SAMPLE RUN

```
1. THE 'AT' FUNCTION PASSED THE TEST
2. IF THIS LINE IS PRINTED AFTER LINE 1.
```

The TRS-80 has 1∅24 PRINT AT locations (∅ to 1∅23). If an AT value smaller than zero or larger than 1∅23 is used, the computer automatically calculates the difference between the out-of-range number and 1∅23 for the AT value.

For example, **PRINT AT 1∅34 "HELLO"** prints the word HELLO at location 1∅ (don't forget to count zero as one location).

TEST PROGRAM

```
1∅ REM 'AT OVERFLOW' TEST PROGRAM
2∅ PRINT AT 192,"'AT' (OVERFLOW) PASSED THE TEST"
3∅ PRINT AT 1248,"IF ONLY ONE LINE IS PRINTED."
99 END
```

SAMPLE RUN

```
'AT' (OVERFLOW) PASSED THE TEST IF ONLY ONE LINE IS PRINTED."
```

AT

The following program tests the interpreter's ability to use numbers, numeric variables, or mathematic operations in the AT function.

TEST PROGRAM

```
1Ø REM 'AT VALUE' TEST PROGRAM
2Ø FOR X=1 TO 15
3Ø PRINT X
4Ø NEXT X
5Ø PRINT ATX*28+4,"'AT' PASSED THE TEST IF THIS IS LINE #8.";
6Ø GOTO 6Ø
99 END
```

SAMPLE RUN

```
1
2
3
4
5
6
7
8 'AT' PASSED THE TEST IF THIS IS LINE #8.
9
1Ø
11
12
13
14
15
```

DIFFERENT WORD FOR AT

The @ operator is used by some computers (e.g. the TRS-80 Level II BASIC) for the AT function. See @ for specific constraints.

ALSO SEE

@, PRINT, TAB

ATAN(n) is used in the Motorola BASIC to compute the ARCTANGENT in **Radians (not in degrees)** of the ratio n. A radian is approximately 57 degrees.

For more information see ATN.

Function

TEST PROGRAM

```
1Ø REM 'ATAN' TEST PROGRAM
2Ø A=ATN(2)
3Ø PRINT "THE ANGLE WITH THE Y/X RATIO OF 2 IS";A;"RADIANS"
99 END
```

SAMPLE RUN

THE ANGLE WITH THE Y/X RATIO OF 2 IS 1.1Ø715 RADIANS

To convert values from radians to degrees, multiply the angle (in radians) times 57.29578. Example, D=ATAN(A)*57.29578. To convert values from degrees to radians, multiply the angle (in degrees) times .Ø174533. Example, R=A(angle expressed in degrees)*.Ø174533.

IF YOUR COMPUTER DOESN'T HAVE IT

See the special subroutine in ATN.

VARIATIONS IN USAGE

None known.

ALSO SEE

ATN, TAN

The ATN(n) function computes the ARCTANGENT **in Radians (not in degrees!)** of the ratio n. A radian is approximately 57 degrees.

Function

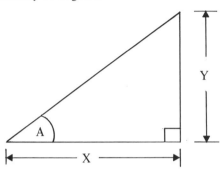

ARCTANGENT (ATN) is defined as the angle (A) required for a certain **ratio** of the length of the side opposite it (Y) to the length of the side adjacent to it (X). ATN means literally "The Arc (angle) of the Tangent (ratio)."

    A=ATN(Y/X)

The opposite of ATN is Tangent (TAN). The Tangent of an angle is the **ratio** of the length of the side opposite it to the length of the side adjacent to it.

    TAN(A)=Y/X

TEST PROGRAM

```
1Ø REM 'ATN' TEST PROGRAM
2Ø PRINT "ENTER A RATIO OR TANGENT VALUE";
3Ø INPUT N
4Ø A=ATN(N)
5Ø PRINT "THE ANGLE WITH THE X/Y RATIO OF";N;"IS";A;"RADIANS"
3Ø999 END
```

SAMPLE RUN *(for input of 2)*

```
ENTER A RATIO OR TANGENT VALUE? 2
THE ANGLE WITH THE X/Y RATIO OF 2 IS 1.1Ø715 RADIANS
```

To convert values from radians to degrees, multiply the angle (in radians) times 57.29578.

Example: `D=ATN(A)*57.29578`

To convert values from degrees to radians, multiply the angle (in degrees) times .Ø174533.

Example: `R=A`(angle expressed in degrees)`*.Ø174533`

IF YOUR COMPUTER DOESN'T HAVE IT

If your interpreter does not have the capability of finding the ATN (Arctangent), the following subroutine can be substituted.

The subroutine program you'll find under SGN **must** be added to this one to make it work (saves space not to duplicate it here).

```
30000 GOTO 30999
30660 REM * ARCTANGENT SUBROUTINE * INPUT X, OUTPUT A (RADIANS)
30670 REM ALSO USES B AND T INTERNALLY
30680 GOSUB 30805
30690 X=ABS(X)
30695 C=0
30700 IF X >1 THEN 30710
30705 GOTO 30720
30710 C=1
30715 X=1/X
30720 A=X*X
30725 B=((2.86623E-3*A-1.61657E-2)*A+4.29096E-2)*A
30730 B=((((B-7.5289E-2)*A+.106563)*A-.142089)*A+.199936)*A
30735 A=((B-.333332)*A+1)*X
30740 IF C=1 THEN 30750
30745 GOTO 30755
30750 A=1.570796-A
30755 A=T*A
30760 RETURN
```

To use this subroutine with the TEST PROGRAM for finding the Arctangent (in Radians) of a ratio (Tangent), make the following TEST PROGRAM changes:

```
35 X=N
40 GOSUB 30680
```

To make the Arctangent subroutine express the angle in Degrees, add the following line to it:

```
30760 A=A*57.29578
```

VARIATIONS IN USAGE

Some (rare) interpreters convert everything to degrees automatically.

ALSO SEE

TAN, ATAN, ASN, SIN, COS

ATN

A TRICK

This is very important! Most computers only have an ATN as their "inverse trig function". ARCCOS and ARCSIN are rarely found. This leaves ATN as the only "window" through which all angles can be calculated and returned to the "outside".

Now obviously, if ATN is to be used, the TAN must be known, or able to be determined, and that may be easier said than done. The following formulas will enable you to convert any ratio to TAN, and from there to the angle itself, via ATN.

$$TAN = 1/COT \qquad TAN = \sqrt{\frac{1 - COS^2}{COS^2}} \qquad TAN = \frac{1}{\sqrt{\dfrac{1 - SIN^2}{SIN^2}}}$$

$$TAN = \frac{1}{\sqrt{CSC^2 - 1}} \qquad TAN = \sqrt{SEC^2 - 1}$$

The AUTO command provides automatic insertion of program line numbers. The starting line number and the incremental value between lines can be specified in the AUTO command. For example, **AUTO 1ØØ,5** sets the first line number at 1ØØ and increments each successive line number by 5.

If the starting line number and increment value are not specified in the AUTO command, the computer automatically sets the first line number at 1Ø and increments the line numbers by 1Ø.

Command

If the AUTO command generates a line number that is already in use, an asterisk may appear following the number. This cautions the programmer that information typed into the computer at that line number will erase existing statements. The AUTO feature may be turned off to prevent this from happening. To turn off the AUTO feature, some computers require pressing the BREAK key, while others require typing a control C.

TEST PROCEDURE

To test the computer's AUTO feature, type the AUTO command and press the ENTER key (RETURN on some keyboards). If the line number 1Ø is printed followed by a prompt, then the computer successfully passed the AUTO command test.

Press the ENTER key again. The computer should print another line number increased in value by 1Ø.

Type the command **AUTO 1Ø,5** and enter this program.

```
1Ø REM 'AUTO' TEST PROGRAM
15 PRINT "THE NEXT LINE NUMBER SHOULD INCREASED BY 5"
2Ø PRINT "PRESS THE BREAK KEY TO STOP THE AUTO FEATURE"
99 END
```

After the AUTO feature is stopped with the BREAK key, line numbers out of sequence can be entered (e.g. line 99).

Again enter **AUTO 1Ø,5** and line 1Ø should be printed, followed by an asterisk, indicating information is presently stored at line 1Ø. New information can be typed in at this point or the original information can be saved by pressing the BREAK key.

List the program to check the contents of each line.

VARIATIONS IN USAGE

None known.

ALSO SEE

BREAK, LIST

The BASE statement is used in some computers (e.g. those with Control Data BASIC Version 3) to define the BASE (lowest) variable array element value as Ø or 1.

For example:

```
1Ø BASE Ø
2Ø DIM A(5)
```

Statement

A
N
S
I

The BASE Ø statement defines this array as a six element array [A(Ø) to A(5)].

Many computers automatically allow array elements 1 to 1Ø (1Ø elements) without prior DIMensioning. The BASE statement allows this range to be changed from the normal 1Ø elements (1 to 1Ø) to 11 elements (Ø to 1Ø), and back again.

Only one BASE statement may be used in a program and it must be executed before DIM statements and before array variables are manipulated.

TEST PROGRAM

```
1Ø REM 'BASE' TEST PROGRAM
2Ø BASE Ø
3Ø DIM A(5)
4Ø FOR X=Ø TO 5
5Ø A(X)=X
6Ø NEXT X
7Ø FOR X=Ø TO 5
8Ø PRINT A(X);
9Ø NEXT X
1ØØ PRINT "THE BASE STATEMENT PASSED THE TEST"
999 END
```

SAMPLE RUN

```
Ø 1 2 3 4 5 THE BASE STATEMENT PASSED THE TEST
```

A few computers (e.g. those using MAXBASIC) allow more than one BASE statement in a program and allow the BASE value to be defined at any integer value.

For example:

```
1Ø BASE 5
2Ø DIM A(1Ø)
```

The BASE 5 statement defines this array as a six element array [A(5) to A(1Ø)].

BASE

TEST PROGRAM

```
10 REM 'BASE' TEST PROGRAM
20 BASE (3)
30 DIM A(5)
40 FOR X=3 TO 5
50 A(X)=X
60 NEXT X
70 BASE (0)
80 FOR X=0 TO 2
90 A(X)=X
100 NEXT X
110 FOR X=0 TO 5
120 PRINT A(X);
130 NEXT X
140 PRINT "THE BASE STATEMENT PASSED THE TEST"
999 END
```

SAMPLE RUN

```
0 1 2 3 4 5 THE BASE STATEMENT PASSED THE TEST
```

VARIATIONS IN USAGE

ANSI BASIC includes the OPTION statement.

ALSO SEE

DIM, OPTION

BREAK is used in a few computers (e.g. the Harris BASIC-V) to direct one or more program lines to stop execution and place the computer in the monitor or immediate mode, similar to a STOP statement.

Statement

The BREAK statement can be used to cause any line number (or line numbers) to stop program execution by placing each line number (separated by a comma) after the BREAK statement.

For example, **1∅ BREAK 5∅,7∅,1∅∅** stops the computer before executing lines 5∅, 7∅, and 1∅∅. Program execution is continued after each BREAK by typing **CO**ntinue.

BREAK also accepts a range of line numbers by placing a dash between the first and last line number in the range.

For example, **1∅ BREAK 5∅-1∅∅** stops program execution at the end of each line from 5∅ to 1∅∅.

Execution can be stopped before each program line by using the BREAK ALL statement. This allows the user to "step through" the program one line at a time, typing the CO command after each break.

Unlike the END statement which (in most computers) causes all variables to be reset to zero, values stored in variables are retained when the BREAK statement is executed.

TEST PROGRAM

```
1∅ REM 'BREAK' TEST PROGRAM
2∅ BREAK 3∅,5∅,7∅-9∅
3∅ PRINT "THE COMPUTER SHOULD STOP EXECUTION AT LINE 3∅"
4∅ REM TYPE THE COMMAND 'CO' TO CONTINUE
5∅ PRINT "LINE 5∅"
6∅ REM THIS LINE NOT INCLUDED IN THE BREAK STATEMENT
7∅ PRINT "LINE 7∅"
8∅ PRINT "LINE 8∅"
9∅ PRINT "AND LINE 9∅"
99 END
```

SAMPLE RUN

```
THE COMPUTER SHOULD STOP EXECUTION AT LINE 3∅
LINE 5∅
LINE 7∅
LINE 8∅
AND LINE 9∅
```

BREAK

VARIATIONS IN USAGE

Some terminals have a BREAK key to allow keyboard interruption of the computer's operation.

ALSO SEE

STOP, CO, CON, CONT, END

C. is used in the TRS-80 Level I as an abbreviation for the CONT (continue) statement.

For more information see CONT.

Command

TEST PROGRAM

```
10 REM 'C. (CONT)' TEST PROGRAM
20 PRINT "ENTER THE 'C.' COMMAND"
30 STOP
40 PRINT "THE C. COMMAND PASSED THE TEST"
99 END
```

SAMPLE RUN

```
ENTER THE 'C.' COMMAND
BREAK AT 30
C.
THE C. COMMAND PASSED THE TEST
```

VARIATIONS IN USAGE

None known.

ALSO SEE

CONT, CON, STOP

CDBL is used to change numbers or numeric variables from regular "single precision" to "double precision". Variables used in the CDBL function return to their original single precision status if they are used again without the CDBL.

Double precision variables are capable of storing numbers containing 17 digits (only 16 digits are printed). Single precision variables are accurate to 6 digits.

Function

TEST PROGRAM

```
1Ø REM 'CDBL' TEST PROGRAM
2Ø X=2
3Ø Y=3
4Ø PRINT "CDBL CHANGES X/Y FROM";X/Y;"TO";CDBL(X)/CDBL(Y)
5Ø PRINT "AND BACK TO THE VALUE OF";X/Y;"WHEN REMOVED"
99 END
```

SAMPLE RUN

```
CDBL CHANGES X/Y FROM .666667 TO .6666666666666667
AND BACK TO THE VALUE OF .666667 WHEN REMOVED
```

VARIATIONS IN USAGE

None known.

ALSO SEE

DEFDBL, DEFSNG, DEFINT, CSNG, #, !, %

CHAIN is used to load a new program into the computer's memory from an external device (such as tape or disc) and execute that program without additional RUN commands. Each program may also CHAIN to other programs, including back to the starting one.

CHAIN

Statement

The main advantage of CHAINing is that it permits consecutive execution of related programs without needing to keep more than one of them actually in the computer at a given time. This is especially useful where there is a common file of DATA stored externally which can be accessed and manipulated by all the programs in the CHAIN. CHAIN finds its best application in systems large enough to have disc storage with reasonably fast access times.

The new program's name must be included after the CHAIN statement (a few computers require quotes around the name). Some computers specify the new program's starting line number with a number following the program's name. If the starting line is omitted, the computer automatically starts at the new program's beginning.

For example, 1∅ **CHAIN TEST,3∅** tells the computer to erase the program presently in memory and load a program called "TEST" from an external device, then start execution at its line 3∅. The external storage device can be specified in some computers (e.g. the DEC 1∅ BASIC) by placing the device name after CHAIN, followed by a colon.

For example, 1∅ **CHAIN PTR:TEST,1∅** This tells the computer to load a program named "TEST" from the Paper Tape Reader and start execution at its line 1∅.

TEST PROGRAM

Save this program on disc or tape under the name "TEST".

```
1∅ REM * TEST * PROGRAM
2∅ PRINT "THE 'TEST' PROGRAM IS NOW RUNNING"
3∅ FOR X=1 TO 9
4∅ PRINT X;
5∅ NEXT X
6∅ PRINT "THIS PROGRAM WILL NOW CHAIN BACK TO THE MAIN PROGRAM"
7∅ CHAIN MAIN,4∅
99 END
```

Now, enter the following program into the computer, and save it on disc or tape under the name "MAIN".

```
10 REM *MAIN * PROGRAM
20 PRINT "THIS PROGRAM SHOULD LOAD AND RUN THE 'TEST' PROGRAM"
30 CHAIN TEST
40 PRINT "CHAIN PASSED THE TEST IF THE 'TEST' PROGRAM"
50 PRINT "PRINTED A SERIES OF NUMBERS"
99 END
```

Prepare your disc or tape(s) to be read on command, then RUN.

SAMPLE RUN

```
THIS PROGRAM SHOULD LOAD AND RUN THE 'TEST' PROGRAM
THE 'TEST PROGRAM IS NOW RUNNING
   1   2   3   4   5   6   7   8   9
THIS PROGRAM SHOULD NOW CHAIN BACK TO THE MAIN PROGRAM
CHAIN PASSED THE TEST IF THE 'TEST' PROGRAM
PRINTED A SERIES OF NUMBERS
```

VARIATIONS IN USAGE

None other known.

ALSO SEE

CLOAD, CSAVE

CHAR(n1,n2) is used in some computers with MAX-BASIC to retrieve the character represented by the ASCII decimal code number (n1). The value (n2) specifies the number of characters (n1) to be included in the string. If the value (n2) is omitted, the computer automatically assumes its value to be 5.

Function

TEST PROGRAM

```
10 REM 'CHAR' TEST PROGRAM
20 PRINT "THE CHAR FUNCTION PASSED THE ";
30 FOR X=1 TO 4
40 READ A
50 PRINT CHAR(A,1)
60 NEXT X
70 DATA 84,69,83,84
99 END
```

SAMPLE RUN

```
THE CHAR FUNCTION PASSED THE TEST
```

IF YOUR COMPUTER DOESN'T HAVE IT

If your computer failed the TEST PROGRAM, try the TEST PROGRAMs in CHAR$, CHR$ and CHR.

VARIATIONS IN USAGE

None known.

ALSO SEE

CHAR$, CHR$, CHR, and the ASCII code appendix.

CHAR$(n) is used in some computers (e.g. those using COMPUMAX BASIC) to retrieve the single character represented by a decimal ASCII code (n).

For example, **PRINT CHAR$(75)** prints the letter K.

For more information see CHR$.

Function

TEST PROGRAM

```
10 REM 'CHAR$' TEST PROGRAM
20 PRINT "THE CHAR$ FUNCTION PASSED THE ";
30 FOR X=1 TO 4
40 READ A
50 PRINT CHAR$(A);
60 NEXT X
70 DATA 84,69,83,84
99 END
```

SAMPLE RUN

```
THE CHAR$ FUNCTION PASSED THE TEST"
```

IF YOUR COMPUTER DOESN'T HAVE IT

If your computer failed the TEST PROGRAM, try the TEST PROGRAMs in CHR$ and CHR.

VARIATIONS IN USAGE

None known.

ALSO SEE

CHR$, CHR, and the ASCII code appendix.

The CHR function is used to retrieve the single character represented by the ASCII decimal code number enclosed in parenthesis. Its use (e.g. SWTP 4K) is rare compared to CHR$.

Function

For example, **PRINT CHR(75)** prints the letter K.

For more information see CHR$

TEST PROGRAM

```
1Ø REM 'CHR' TEST PROGRAM
2Ø PRINT "THE CHR FUNCTION PASSED THE ";
3Ø FOR X=1 TO 4
4Ø READ A
5Ø PRINT CHR(A);
6Ø NEXT X
7Ø DATA 84,69,83,84
99 END
```

SAMPLE RUN

```
THE CHR FUNCTION PASSED THE TEST
```

VARIATIONS IN USAGE

None known.

ALSO SEE

CHR$, CHR, CHAR$ and the ASCII Appendix.

The CHR$ function is used to retrieve the single character represented by the decimal ASCII number code enclosed in parenthesis. For example: **PRINT CHR$(75)** prints the letter K.

Function

The ASCII code can be represented by a number or variable within the ASCII code range (typically 0—127). Some computers have an extended ASCII code (up to 255) which includes special capabilities and graphics characters. Many computers set aside certain ASCII numbers for special "non-standard" purposes (typically, control a line printer, erase the screen, "put out the cat," etc.).

This program lets you test any ASCII code number and examine the ASCII character created (or use for some other purpose).

TEST PROGRAM

```
10 REM 'CHR$' TEST PROGRAM
20 PRINT "ENTER THE LOWEST ASCII CODE NUMBER";
30 INPUT L
40 PRINT "ENTER THE HIGHEST ASCII CODE NUMBER";
50 INPUT H
60 FOR X=L TO H
70 PRINT "ASCII CODE";X;"= ";
80 PRINT CHR$(X)
90 FOR Y=1 TO 150
100 NEXT Y
110 NEXT X
999 END
```

SAMPLE RUN *(checking only 4 numbers)*

```
ENTER THE LOWEST ASCII CODE NUMBER? 65
ENTER THE HIGHEST ASCII CODE NUMBER? 68
ASCII CODE 65 = A
ASCII CODE 66 = B
ASCII CODE 67 = C
ASCII CODE 68 = D
```

Try this program using your computer's full range of ASCII codes.

VARIATIONS IN USAGE
None known.

ALSO SEE

CHR, ASC, Appendix

CINT is used to convert individual numbers or numeric variables to their integer value. Unlike the INT function, variables used in the CINT function return to their original precision if they are used again without the CINT function.

Function

Numbers are always rounded down — that is, the whole number remains the same regardless of the value of numbers removed to the right of the decimal point. When a negative number is integered, the resultant number will be rounded off to the next smaller whole number.

For example, **PRINT CINT(-4.65)** will print the number -5.

Most computers do not allow numbers assigned to the CINT function to be smaller than -32767 or larger than +32767.

TEST PROGRAM

```
10 REM 'CINT' TEST PROGRAM
20 DEFDBL X
30 X=12345.6789
40 PRINT "CINT CHANGES THE VALUE OF X FROM";X;"TO" ;CINT(X)
50 PRINT "AND BACK TO THE VALUE OF";X;"WHEN REMOVED"
99 END
```

SAMPLE RUN

```
CINT CHANGES THE VALUE OF X FROM 12345.6789 TO 12345
AND BACK TO THE VALUE OF 12345.6789 WHEN REMOVED
```

VARIATIONS IN USAGE

None known.

ALSO SEE

DEFINT, INT, DEFDBL, DEFSNG, CDBL, CSNG, !, #, %

CLEAR is used to set all numeric variables to zero and clear all data that may be held by string variables.

CLEAR can be used as either a command or program statement.

Command Statement

TEST PROGRAM

```
1Ø REM 'CLEAR' TEST PROGRAM
2Ø A=3ØØ
3Ø A$="TEST STRING"
4Ø PRINT "BEFORE THE 'CLEAR' COMMAND A=";A
5Ø PRINT "AND STRING VARIABLE A$ = ";A$
6Ø CLEAR
7Ø PRINT "AFTER THE 'CLEAR' COMMAND A=";A
8Ø PRINT "AND STRING VARIABLE A$=";A$
99 END
```

SAMPLE RUN

```
BEFORE THE 'CLEAR' COMMAND A=3ØØ
AND STRING VARIABLE A$=TEST STRING
AFTER THE 'CLEAR' COMMAND A=Ø
AND STRING VARIABLE A$=
```

CLEAR is used by some computers to specify the number of bytes to reserve in memory for strings. This feature lets the programmer conserve memory by specifying the actual amount of space needed for string storage.

For example, CLEAR 1ØØ sets 1ØØ bytes of memory aside for string storage.

It is common for interpreters with CLEAR capability to automatically reserve 5Ø bytes in memory for strings. Others reserve up to 2ØØ bytes for this purpose.

The amount of space remaining in memory for string storage can be checked by interpreters with the FRE(A$) function when used in a PRINT statement.

TEST PROGRAM

```
1Ø REM 'CLEAR X' TEST PROGRAM
2Ø CLEAR 5
3Ø PRINT "ENTER FROM 1 TO 5 CHARACTERS";
4Ø INPUT A$
5Ø PRINT "STRING "A$;" USED ALL BUT";FRE(A$);"BYTES"
6Ø PRINT "OF STRING SPACE."
7Ø GOTO 2Ø
99 END
```

CLEAR

SAMPLE RUN *(using T and TEST)*

```
ENTER FROM 1 TO 5 CHARACTERS? T
STRING T USED ALL BUT 4 BYTES
OF STRING SPACE.
ENTER FROM 1 TO 5 CHARACTERS? TEST
STRING TEST USED ALL BUT 1 BYTES
OF STRING SPACE.
ENTER FROM 1 TO 5 CHARACTERS?
```

Some computers with CLEAR capability allow the CLEAR value to be specified by a variable. To test this feature, make these changes to the second Test Program;

```
20 A=5
25 CLEAR A
```

If the interpreter accepted this program change, the sample run should not change.

VARIATIONS IN USAGE

Some computers use CLEAR as a special statement to clear terminal input or output buffers.

ALSO SEE

CLR, FRE(A$)

The CLG(n) function is used by the Honeywell Series 60 BASIC to compute the value of the common (base 1Ø) logarithm of any number (n) whose value is greater than Ø.

Function

TEST PROGRAM

```
1Ø REM 'CLG' TEST PROGRAM
2Ø PRINT "ENTER A POSITIVE NUMBER"
3Ø INPUT N
4Ø X=CLG(N)
5Ø PRINT "THE COMMON LOG OF";N;"IS";X
3Ø999 END
```

SAMPLE RUN *(using 1ØØ)*

```
ENTER A POSITIVE NUMBER? 1ØØ
THE COMMON LOG OF 1ØØ IS 2
```

IF YOUR COMPUTER DOESN'T HAVE IT

If your computer failed the TEST PROGRAM, try the TEST PROGRAMs in LOG1Ø, CLOG, LOG and LGT. If they also fail, substitute the subroutine found under LOG (saves space not to duplicate it here). To make it compute the common logarithm (instead of the natural logarithm), make the following subroutine changes:

```
3Ø17Ø REM * COMMON LOGARITHM SUBROUTINE * INPUT X, OUTPUT X
3Ø2ØØ GOTO 3Ø223
3Ø223 X=L*.4342945
```

To use this subroutine in this TEST PROGRAM, make these TEST PROGRAM changes:

```
35 X=N
4Ø GOSUB 3Ø17Ø
```

CONVERSION FACTORS

To convert a common log to a natural log, multiply the common log value times 2.3Ø26.

For example, X=CLG(N)*2.3Ø26

To convert a natural log to a common log, multiply the natural log value times .434295.

VARIATIONS IN USAGE

None known.

ALSO SEE

LOG1Ø, CLOG, LGT, LOG, LOGE, LN

CLK(n) is used in the Sperry Univac System/9 BASIC to indicate the time of day in hours, minutes, and seconds (hhmmss). A number or numeric variable (enclosed in parenthesis) following CLK is required, although it has no effect on the TIM function.

Function

TEST PROGRAM

```
1Ø REM 'CLK' TEST PROGRAM
2Ø PRINT "THE CURRENT TIME IS ";CLK(N)
3Ø PRINT "THE CLK FUNCTION PASSED THE TEST"
4Ø PRINT "IF A SIX DIGIT NUMBER IS PRINTED"
99 END
```

SAMPLE RUN *(using Ø82515)*

```
THE CURRENT TIME IS Ø82515
THE CLK FUNCTION PASSED THE TEST
IF A SIX DIGIT NUMBER IS PRINTED
```

VARIATIONS IN USAGE

None known.

ALSO SEE

CLK$, TIME, TIME$, TIM, TI, TI$

CLK$ is used with PRINT statements in the DEC BASIC-PLUS-2 and the Texas Instruments 990 BASIC to indicate the time of day in hours (∅ to 24), minutes, and seconds (hh:mm:ss). The computer automatically inserts a colon after the hour and minute values and prints the time as a string.

For example, **PRINT CLK$** will print a time similar to 22:19:15, indicating the current time is 10:19 p.m. plus 15 seconds.

Function

TEST PROGRAM

```
1∅ REM 'CLK$' TEST PROGRAM
2∅ PRINT "THE CURRENT TIME IS ";
3∅ PRINT CLK$
4∅ PRINT "'CLK$' PASSED THE TEST IF A SIX DIGIT NUMBER IS PRINTED"
99 END
```

SAMPLE RUN *(typical)*

```
THE CURRENT TIME IS 10:28:45
'CLK$' PASSED THE TEST IF A SIX DIGIT NUMBER IS PRINTED
```

VARIATIONS IN USAGE

None known.

ALSO SEE

CLK, TIME, TIME$, TI, TI$,

CLOAD is a special command used by some interpreters (e.g. those with Microsoft BASIC) to load a program into the computer from a cassette tape.

CLOAD

**Command
Statement**

TEST PROGRAM

Enter this program into the computer from the keyboard, then store the program on cassette tape. (See CSAVE for details.)

```
1Ø REM 'CLOAD' TEST PROGRAM
2Ø PRINT "THIS PROGRAM TESTS THE CLOAD FEATURE"
99 END
```

Once the program is recorded on cassette tape, erase the computer memory with NEW, SCRATCH, or whatever is appropriate.

Rewind the tape, then set the recorder to the Play mode and type the CLOAD command.

The cassette recorder's motor is controlled by the computer which turns it on and off before and after the "load" cycle. The cassette should "play back" the program, LOADing it into the computer.

List the program to verify that the program held in the computer's memory is identical to that originally entered (see LIST). If all looks well, RUN the program.

SAMPLE RUN

THIS PROGRAM TESTS THE CLOAD FEATURE

CLOAD "program name" is used by some CLOAD-equipped computers to load only that program on the cassette that has a matching program name. A program name used to identify a specific program may contain more than one letter or number, but the computer *may* recognize only the first character.

Record the TEST PROGRAM onto the cassette using CSAVE"A" (see CSAVE), erase the computer memory, then load "A" back into the computer using CLOAD"A". List the program to check for possible errors.

CLOAD? "program name" is used by some CLOAD-equipped computers to compare a program stored in the computer's memory with a program stored on cassette under the program name indicated. The computer does a bit-by-bit comparison of the two and prints an error message if any difference is encountered. This allows you to compare the tape with the memory contents to verify that you executed a successful CSAVE, or CLOAD, before erasing either.

Check the TEST PROGRAM on cassette tape (stored with the program name "A") against the computer using the CLOAD?"A" command. If an error message is not printed, the two programs matched.

CLOAD

Add this line to the test program stored in the computer.

30 REM EXTRA LINE

Again check the "A" program on cassette tape using the command CLOAD?"A". An error message should be printed, indicating the computer found a difference between the program stored in the computer and the program stored on tape.

CLOAD* (array name) is used by a few CLOAD-using computers as a command to load an array stored on cassette tape (under the same array name). Example: CLOAD*A means "load array A".

CLOAD*(array name) can also be used as a program statement so array data can be loaded as a program is being executed.

VARIATIONS IN USAGE

None other known.

ALSO SEE

CSAVE, LIST, CHAIN

The CLOG(n) function computes the value of the common logarithm of any number (n) whose value is greater than $\emptyset$.

Function

TEST PROGRAM

```
1Ø REM 'CLOG' TEST PROGRAM
2Ø PRINT "ENTER A POSITIVE NUMBER";
3Ø INPUT N
4Ø X=CLOG(N)
5Ø PRINT "THE COMMON LOG OF";N;"IS";X
999 END
```

SAMPLE RUN

```
ENTER A POSITIVE NUMBER? 1ØØ
THE COMMON LOG OF 1ØØ IS 2
```

If your computer failed the test program, see LOG1Ø for a substitute subroutine and other conversion tips.

VARIATIONS IN USAGE

None known.

ALSO SEE

LOG1Ø, LGT, LOG, LOGE, LN

CLR is used in a few computers (e.g. the APPLE II BASIC and the Commodore PET) as an abbreviation for the CLEAR command which sets all numeric variables to zero and clears all data that may be held by string variables.

For more information see CLEAR.

Command Statement

TEST PROGRAM

```
10 REM 'CLR' TEST PROGRAM
20 A=300
30 A$="TEST STRING"
40 PRINT "BEFORE THE 'CLR' STATEMENT A = ";A
50 PRINT "AND STRING VARIABLE A$ = ";A$
60 CLR
70 PRINT "AFTER THE 'CLR' STATEMENT A = ";A
80 PRINT "AND STRING VARIABLE A$ = ";A$
99 END
```

SAMPLE RUN

```
BEFORE THE 'CLR' STATEMENT A = 300
AND STRING VARIABLE A$ = TEST STRING
AFTER THE 'CLR' STATEMENT A = 0
AND STRING VARIABLE A$ =
```

IF YOUR COMPUTER DOESN'T HAVE IT

Stopping the program and restarting it with RUN almost always resets the variables to zero. This is often inconvenient or not practical. The other way to reset them is to write them into the program.

```
60 A=0
61 A$ =" "
```

VARIATIONS IN USAGE

None known.

ALSO SEE

CLEAR, NEW

The CLS (clear screen) command is used to perform the same function as the CLEAR key on many keyboards. It erases the entire screen instantly without disturbing the program. CLS can also be used as a program statement to clear the screen before starting a graphics display or a new "page" of printed information.

CLS

**Command
Statement**

TEST PROGRAM

```
10 REM 'CLS' TEST PROGRAM
20 FOR X=1 TO 15
30 PRINT "THIS LINE SHOULD DISAPPEAR"
40 NEXT X
50 CLS
60 PRINT "IF THIS IS ALL THAT'S ON THE SCREEN"
70 PRINT "THE CLS STATEMENT PASSED THE TEST"
99 END
```

SAMPLE RUN

```
IF THIS IS ALL THAT'S ON THE SCREEN
THE CLS STATEMENT PASSED THE TEST
```

IF YOUR COMPUTER DOESN'T HAVE IT

Many video screens can be cleared or "erased" by using an ASCII character. Try this change to the test program:

```
50 PRINT CHR$(24)
```

IF CHR$(24) fails (due to nonconformity of some manufacturer's use of ASCII numbers), try this program to search for an ASCII screen-clear:

TEST PROGRAM

```
10 REM ASCII CLEAR SCREEN SEARCH
20 FOR X=0 TO 128
30 PRINT "ASCII CODE";X;
40 PRINT CHR$(X)
50 FOR Y=1 TO 200
60 NEXT Y
70 NEXT X
99 END
```

VARIATIONS IN USAGE

None other than the use of the CLEAR key. It obviously is of no value with a printer terminal. Note that CLS and CLEAR statements are completely different.

ALSO SEE

ASCII, CHR$(X)

CO is used (by Processor Technology, Harris BASIC-V, etc.) as an abbreviation for the CONTinue command, which restarts program execution after it was "broken" due to a STOP statement, or use of a keyboard "BREAK" key. Unlike the RUN command, which causes execution to start at the program's beginning, CO resumes execution at the line following the break.

CO has no application as a program **statement** since it is only used when the program has stopped.

Command

TEST PROGRAM

```
10 REM 'CO' TEST PROGRAM
20 PRINT "ENTER THE 'CO' COMMAND"
30 STOP
40 PRINT "THE CO COMMAND PASSED THE TEST"
99 END
```

SAMPLE RUN *(typical)*

```
ENTER THE 'CO' COMMAND
BREAK AT LINE 30
CO
THE CO COMMAND PASSED THE TEST
```

VARIATIONS IN USAGE

The Harris BASIC-V allows the CO command to specify a program line to resume program execution.

For example, **CO 20** when used with the TEST PROGRAM should resume program execution at line 20 (not line 40). This of course is a common feature with the RUN command. However, unlike RUN, CO does not reset all variables back to zero before resuming execution.

ALSO SEE

CONT, CON, STOP, BREAK, RUN, END

COLOR is used in the APPLE II BASIC as a special feature to specify a color to be displayed on the screen by the graphics statements PLOT, HLIN-AT and VLIN-AT. The same color is displayed each time a graphics statement is executed. To change colors, a new color must be specified by the COLOR statement.

Command Statement

The computer displays 16 different colors, and each is assigned a number (from Ø to 15). They are:

Ø BLACK	8 BROWN
1 MAGENTA	9 ORANGE
2 DARK BLUE	1Ø GRAY
3 PURPLE	11 PINK
4 DARK GREEN	12 GREEN
5 GREY	13 YELLOW
6 MEDIUM BLUE	14 AQUA
7 LIGHT BLUE	15 WHITE

An equal sign (=) must be placed between COLOR and the COLOR value. This value may be a number or a numeric variable.

For example, **COLOR = 13** selects the color yellow for the next graphics statement. COLOR can be used as both a command and a program statement.

TEST PROGRAM

```
1Ø REM 'COLOR' TEST PROGRAM
2Ø GR
3Ø FOR X=Ø TO 15
4Ø COLOR = X
5Ø Y=X*2
6Ø HLIN Ø,39 AT Y
7Ø NEXT X
99 END
```

SAMPLE RUN

If your computer accepted the TEST PROGRAM, each of the 16 colors should be displayed as a horizontal line across the screen.

VARIATIONS IN USAGE

None known.

ALSO SEE

GR, PLOT, HLIN-AT, VLIN-AT

CON is used in the APPLE II BASIC as an abbreviation for the CONTinue command. It restarts program execution after it was stopped by pressing the CTRL/C keys.

For more information see CONT.

Command

TEST PROGRAM

```
1Ø REM 'CON' TEST PROGRAM
2Ø PRINT "PRESS CTRL/C TO STOP THE COMPUTER"
3Ø GOTO 3Ø
99 END
```

SAMPLE RUN

PRESS CTRL/C TO STOP THE COMPUTER

Once the computer is stopped with CTRL/C, type "CON". The computer should CONtinue program execution.

VARIATIONS IN USAGE

CON is used in computers with MAX BASIC to set the value of each element in array variables to 1.

For example, A=CON sets the value of each element in the A array to 1.

ALSO SEE

CONT, STOP, END, RUN

The CONTinue command restarts program execution after it was "broken" due to a STOP statement, or use of a keyboard "BREAK" key. Unlike the RUN command, which causes execution to start at the program's beginning, CONT resumes execution at the line following the break.

Command

CONT has no application as a program **statement** since it is only used when the program has STOPped.

TEST PROGRAM

```
1Ø REM 'CONT' TEST PROGRAM
2Ø PRINT "ENTER THE 'CONT' COMMAND"
3Ø STOP
4Ø PRINT "THE CONT COMMAND PASSED THE TEST"
99 END
```

SAMPLE RUN

```
ENTER THE 'CONT' COMMAND
BREAK AT 3Ø
CONT
THE CONT COMMAND PASSED THE TEST
```

VARIATIONS IN USAGE

None known.

ALSO SEE

CON, STOP, END, RUN

The COS(A) function computes the COSINE of the angle A, when that value is expressed **in Radians (not in degrees)**. One radian = approximately 57 degrees.

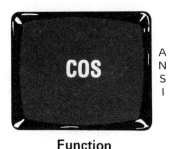

Function

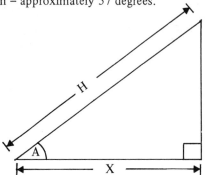

Cosine (COS) is defined as the ratio of the length of the side adjacent to the angle being investigated to the length of the hypotenuse, in a right triangle.

COS(A)=X/H

The opposite of COS is ARCCOS. ARCCOS (abbreviated ACS) finds the value of the angle when its COS, or ratio of sides (X/H) is known.

TEST PROGRAM

```
1Ø REM 'COS' TEST PROGRAM
2Ø PRINT "ENTER AN ANGLE (EXPRESSED IN RADIANS)";
3Ø INPUT R
4Ø Y=COS(R)
5Ø PRINT "THE COSINE OF A";R;"RADIAN ANGLE IS";Y
3Ø999 END
```

SAMPLE RUN *(for input of 1)*

```
ENTER AN ANGLE (EXPRESSED IN RADIANS)? 1
THE COSINE OF A 1 RADIAN ANGLE IS .54Ø3Ø2
```

To convert values from degrees to radians, multiply the angle in degrees times .Ø174533.

For example: R=COS(A*.Ø174533)

To convert values from radians to degrees, multiply radians times 57.29578

IF YOUR COMPUTER DOESN'T HAVE IT

If your interpreter does not have the COSine capability, the following subroutine can be substituted.

The subroutine program you'll find under SIN **must** be added to this one   ake it work (saves space not to duplicate it here).

```
30000 GOTO 30999
30350 REM * COSINE SUBROUTINE * INPUT X IN RADIANS, OUTPUT Y
30352 REM ALSO USES W AND Z INTERNALLY
30354 X=X*57.29578
30356 W=ABS(X)/X
30358 X=X+90
30359 GOSUB 30376
30360 IF Z=-1 THEN 30362
30361 GOTO 30365
30362 IF W=1 THEN 30364
30363 GOTO 30365
30364 Y=-Y
30365 RETURN
```

To use the subroutines with the TEST PROGRAM to find the COSine   n angle (expressed in Radians), make the following TEST PROGRAM changes:

```
35 X=R
40 GOSUB 30350
```

To find the COSine of an angle (expressed in Degrees), either delete line 30354   change line 40 to:

```
40 GOSUB 30356
```

VARIATIONS IN USAGE

Some (rare) interpreters convert everything to degrees automatically.

ALSO SEE

SIN, ASN, ATN, ATAN, TAN

CSAVE is used by some computers (e.g. those with the Microsoft interpreter) to record programs from computer memory onto cassette tape.

TEST PROGRAM

Command

```
10 REM 'CSAVE' TEST PROGRAM
20 PRINT "THIS PROGRAM TESTS THE CSAVE FEATURE"
99 END
```

Set up the cassette recorder for Recording and type the command CSAVE. The computer should control the operation of the cassette recorder by turning the motor on and off at the beginning and end of the record cycle.

Once the program is recorded on cassette tape, type NEW (or whatever is required) to clear the program from memory. Load the program from tape back into the computer (see CLOAD). List the program to verify that the program held in the computer's memory is identical to that originally entered (see LIST).

SAMPLE RUN

THIS PROGRAM TESTS THE CSAVE FEATURE

CSAVE (program name) is used by some computers using CSAVE to assign a specific name to the program being recorded on cassette tape. The file name may contain one or more letters, numbers, or other selected ASCII symbols, but only the first character *may* be recognized by the computer. The program name identifies the program for later retrieval via the CLOAD (program name) command.

Record the TEST PROGRAM on cassette tape using the command CSAVE"A", erase the memory, then load the program back into the computer using the CLOAD"A" command.

List the program to check for possible errors.

VARIATIONS IN USAGE

None known.

ALSO SEE

CLOAD, LIST

CSNG is used to change numbers or numeric variables which are previously defined as being of "double-precision" back to regular "single-precision". Variables listed in the CSNG function return to their original double-precision status if they are used again without the CSNG function.

Function

Single-precision variables are capable of storing numbers containing no more than 7 digits (only 6 digits are printed). Double-precision means being accurate to 17 digits. If CSNG is used with a double-precision number containing more than 6 digits, that number is "rounded-off" to six significant places.

TEST PROGRAM

```
10 REM 'CSNG' TEST PROGRAM
20 DEFDBL X
30 X=12345678901234 56
40 PRINT "CSNG CHANGES THE VALUE OF X FROM";X;"TO";CSNG(X)
50 PRINT "AND BACK TO THE VALUE OF";X;"WHEN REMOVED"
99 END
```

SAMPLE RUN

```
CSNG CHANGES THE VALUE OF X FROM 123456789 TO 1.23457E+08
AND BACK TO THE VALUE OF 123456789 WHEN REMOVED
```

VARIATIONS IN USAGE

None known.

ALSO SEE

DEFSNG, DEFDBL, DEFINT, CDBL, !, #, %

D is used to indicate "double precision" in numbers expressed in "exponential" or "standard scientific notation".

Operator

For example, `1.23456789D+2Ø`. Numbers expressed in single precision are written in exponential notation using the letter "E".

For example, `1.234E+2Ø`

TEST PROGRAM

```
1Ø REM 'D' DOUBLE PRECISION EXPONENT TEST PROGRAM
2Ø A#=123456789Ø123456789
3Ø PRINT "EXPONENTIAL NOTATION 'D' PASSED THE TEST IF"
4Ø PRINT A#; "CONTAINS THE LETTER 'D'"
99 END
```

SAMPLE RUN

```
EXPONENTIAL NOTATION 'D' PASSED THE TEST IF
1.234567890123457D+16 CONTAINS THE LETTER 'D'
```

VARIATIONS IN USAGE

The letter "D", like all other letters of the alphabet, is used by all computers to indicate a numeric variable.

ALSO SEE

E, #, !, DEFDBL, DEFSNG

D. is used in the TRS-80 Level I as an abbreviation for the DATA statement.

For more details see DATA.

Statement

TEST PROGRAM

```
10 REM 'D.' TEST PROGRAM
20 D. 20
30 READ A
40 PRINT "'D.' PASSED THE TEST IN LINE";A
99 END
```

SAMPLE RUN

```
'D.' PASSED THE TEST IN LINE 20
```

VARIATIONS IN USAGE

None known.

ALSO SEE

DATA, DAT, READ

DAT is used in the PDP-8E as an abbreviation for the DATA statement.

For more details see DATA.

Statement

TEST PROGRAM

```
10 REM 'DAT' TEST PROGRAM
20 DAT 20
30 READ A
40 PRINT "'DAT' PASSED THE TEST IN LINE";A
99 END
```

SAMPLE RUN

```
'DAT' PASSED THE TEST IN LINE 20
```

VARIATIONS IN USAGE

None known.

ALSO SEE

DATA, D., READ

A DATA statement contains data to be read by a READ statement. The items in the DATA statement must be separated by commas and may include both positive and negative numbers.

Statement

TEST PROGRAM

```
1Ø REM 'DATA' TEST PROGRAM
2Ø DATA 2Ø,-1Ø,.5
3Ø READ A,B,C
4Ø D=A+B+C
5Ø PRINT "D =";D
6Ø PRINT "DATA PASSED THE TEST IF D = 1Ø.5"
99 END
```

SAMPLE RUN

```
D = 1Ø.5
DATA PASSED THE TEST IF D = 1Ø.5
```

Most computers allow strings in a DATA statement. Some require that the strings always be enclosed in quotes, while others require quotes only when the string is preceded by, encloses, or is followed by a blank, comma or colon.

TEST PROGRAM

```
1Ø REM 'DATA' TEST PROGRAM USING STRINGS
2Ø DATA "LINE NUMBER",2Ø,"PASSED"
3Ø READ A$,A,B$
4Ø PRINT "DATA STATEMENT IN ";A$;A;B$;" THE TEST"
99 END
```

SAMPLE RUN

```
DATA STATEMENT IN LINE NUMBER 2Ø PASSED THE TEST
```

Remove the quotation marks from the String Variables in line 2Ø and run again to see if they are needed in your interpreter.

DATA statements may be placed at any location in a program.

VARIATIONS IN USAGE

None known.

ALSO SEE

DAT, D.,R., REA, READ

The DEF statement allows the user to DEFine (create) new functions (most computers have some built in functions) which can then be used the same as any intrinsic (built in) function.

Statement

For example, **DEF FNA(R)) = R*R*3.14159** The expression R*R*3.14159 (the formula to find the area of a circle, normally written πr^2) is DEFined in this example as the function FNA. FN (an abbreviation for the word FUNCTION) is used in DEF statements followed by any legal numeric variable. "A" is used in this example to identify function FNA as the Area of a circle, but any variable could have been used. Once a function is defined, normally it cannot be redefined in the same program.

The variable enclosed in parenthesis [(R) above] must match the variable used in the statement to the right of the equal sign. These are commonly referred to as "dummy" variables.

The operation stored in the FN (variable) function by the DEF statement can be used to manipulate any number or numeric variable.

For example,

```
1Ø X=2
2Ø DEF FNA(N)=3*N-1
3Ø PRINT FNA(X)
```

The FN function in this example is named "A" (FNA), and is assigned the equation 3*N-1 in line 2Ø. The numeric variable (X) following FNA is substituted for the "dummy variable" (N) in the DEF statement each time FNA is executed.

TEST PROGRAM #1

```
1Ø REM 'DEF' TEST PROGRAM
2Ø PRINT "ENTER THE RADIUS OF A CIRCLE (IN INCHES)";
3Ø INPUT R
4Ø DEF FNC(X)=3*1.4159*X
5Ø PRINT "THE CIRCUMFERENCE OF A CIRCLE"
6Ø PRINT "WITH A RADIUS OF";R;"INCHES IS";FNC(R);"INCHES"
99 END
```

SAMPLE RUN *(using 4)*

```
ENTER THE RADIUS OF A CIRCLE (IN INCHES)? 4
THE CIRCUMFERENCE OF A CIRCLE
WITH A RADIUS OF 4 INCHES IS 25.1327 INCHES
```

DEF

Some computers allow more than one variable in the DEFined expression. Each of these variables must be listed after the FN(variable) function.

TEST PROGRAM #2

```
10 REM 'DEF' MULTIPLE VARIABLE TEST PROGRAM
20 DEF FN(X,Y)=(X+Y)/2
30 PRINT "ENTER ANY TWO NUMBERS";
40 INPUT X,Y
50 A=DEF(X,Y)
60 PRINT "THE AVERAGE OF";X;"AND";Y;"IS";A
999 END
```

SAMPLE RUN *(using 2∅ and 4∅)*

```
ENTER ANY TWO NUMBERS? 20,40
THE AVERAGE OF 20 AND 40 IS 30
```

Some computers allow the same function to be DEFined in more than one line. In the following TEST PROGRAM the function FNA is DEFined as X∗2 if the value of variable X is less than 1∅, or as X/2 if the value of X is greater than or equal to 1∅.

TEST PROGRAM #3

```
10 REM 'DEF' REQUIRING MORE THAN ONE LINE
20 PRINT "ENTER A VALUE FOR X THAT IS GREATER OR LESS THAN 10";
30 INPUT X
40 DEF FNA(X)
50 FNA=X∗2
60 IF X < 10 THEN 80
70 FNA=X/2
80 FNEND
90 PRINT "THE NEW VALUE FOR X IS";FNA(X)
999 END
```

SAMPLE RUN *(using 12)*

```
ENTER A VALUE FOR X THAT IS GREATER OR LESS THAN 10? 12
THE NEW VALUE FOR X IS 6
```

The FNEND statement in the last TEST PROGRAM tells the computer to stop defining function FNA. Multiple line DEF statements must always end with the FNEND statement, and the computer does not allow branching into or out of multiple line DEF statements. For more information see FNEND.

DEF

IF YOUR COMPUTER DOESN'T HAVE IT

If your computer does not have the DEF capability, substitute FN with a subroutine containing the same equation.

For example, The DEF statement in TEST PROGRAM #2 can be replaced with the following subroutine:

```
100 A=(X+Y)/2
110 RETURN
```

and these TEST PROGRAM CHANGES:

Delete line 20 and add
```
50 GOSUB 100
70 GOTO 999
```

VARIATIONS IN USAGE

None other known.

ALSO SEE

FN, FNEND, GOSUB

DEFDBL is used to define (declare) a variable or variables as being accurate to "double-precision". Double-precision variables are capable of storing numbers accurate to 17 digits (only 16 digits are printed). Single-precision variables are typically accurate to 6 digits.

Statement

Caution: DEFDBL should only be used where single-precision accuracy is not adequate since double-precision variables require more memory space and their manipulation requires more time. In most computers the DEFDBL line must be executed before the variable listed in the DEFDBL statement is assigned a numeric value.

TEST PROGRAM

```
10 REM 'DEFDBL' TEST PROGRAM
20 A=1.2345678901234 56
30 PRINT "DEFDBL IN LINE 50 CHANGED THE VALUE OF VARIABLE 'A'"
40 PRINT "FROM";A;"TO" ;
50 DEFDBL A
60 A=1.2345678901234 56
70 PRINT A
99 END
```

SAMPLE RUN

```
DEFDBL IN LINE 40 CHANGED THE VALUE OF VARIABLE 'A'
FROM 1.23457 TO 1.2345678901234 56
```

Most computers with DEFDBL capability also allow designation of more than one variable as "double-precision" by a single DEFDBL statement. For example, **DEFDBL A,F,M** defines the variables A, F and M as having double-precision, and **DEFDBL A-M** defines all variables A **thru** M as being of double-precision.

TEST PROGRAM

```
10 REM 'DEFDBL' (WITH MULTIPLE VARIABLES) TEST PROGRAM
20 DEFDBL A,G,L-N
30 A=1/3
40 G=2/3
50 L=1/9
60 M=1.23456789012345 67D+38
70 N=-1.23456789012345 67D+38
80 PRINT "DEFDBL PASSED THE TEST IF THE FOLLOWING"
90 PRINT "NUMBERS CONTAIN MORE THAN 7 DIGITS:"
100 PRINT A;G;L;M;N
999 END
```

SAMPLE RUN

```
DEFDBL PASSED THE TEST IF THE FOLLOWING
NUMBERS CONTAIN MORE THAN 7 DIGITS:
     .3333333333333333    .6666666666666667   .1111111111111111
   1.2345678901234567D+38    1.2345678901234567D+38
```

The "D" before "+38" is the same as an "E" in exponential notation, but signifies that the number is "double-precision accurate".

Some computers may not print the first three values as shown in the SAMPLE RUN due to pecularities in the interpreter's bit manipulation. This problem can be eliminated in computers that have a Double Precision Declarative sign (e.g. the # sign). Place the sign after each fraction in lines 3Ø,4Ø and 5Ø as follows to produce the correct results.

```
3Ø A 1/3 #
4Ø G 2/3 #
5Ø L 1/9 #
```

VARIATIONS IN USAGE

None known.

ALSO SEE

DEFSNG, DEFINT, #

DEFINT is used to define (declare) that the variables listed by the DEFINT statement are integers. Variables defined as integers store the integer (whole number) value of assigned numbers. This is especially useful in large programs since less memory is required to store integer values than non-integers.

Statement

A potential disadvantage of using the DEFINT statement is the inability of many interpreters to process numeric values larger than that allowed by the interpreter's INT function (typically −32767 to +32767).

The DEFINT line must be executed by the computer before a variable listed in the DEFINT statement is assigned a numeric value.

TEST PROGRAM

```
10 REM 'DEFINT' TEST PROGRAM
20 DEFINT A
30 A=12.68
40 B=12.68
50 IF A=12 THEN 70
60 GOTO 80
70 IF B=12.68 THEN 100
80 PRINT "DEFINT FAILED THE TEST LINE 20"
90 GOTO 999
100 PRINT "THE DEFINT STATEMENT PASSED THE TEST IN LINE 20 BY"
110 PRINT "CHANGING THE VALUE OF VARIABLE A FROM";B;"TO";A
999 END
```

SAMPLE RUN

```
THE DEFINT STATEMENT PASSED THE TEST IN LINE 20 BY
CHANGING THE VALUE OF VARIABLE A FROM 12.68 TO 12
```

Most computers with DEFINT capability also allow assignment of multiple variables (separated by comma) in a single DEFINT statement. For example, **DEFINT A,F,M** defines the variables A,F and M as integers. **DEFINT A-M** defines variables A **thru** M as integers.

TEST PROGRAM

```
10 REM 'DEFINT' (WITH MULTIPLE VARIABLES) TEST PROGRAM
20 DEFINT A,G,L-N
30 A=6.25
40 B=21.42
```

DEFINT

```
5Ø G=-6.19
6Ø L=4.ØØ1
7Ø M=32ØØØ.999
8Ø N=14.8
9Ø PRINT "IF THE NUMBERS";A;G;L;M;N;"ARE INTEGERS,"
1ØØ PRINT "AND THE NUMBER";B;"IS A DECIMAL, THEN DEFINT"
11Ø PRINT "PASSED THE MULTIPLE VARIABLE TEST IN LINE 2Ø."
999 END
```

SAMPLE RUN

```
IF THE NUMBERS 6 -7 4 32ØØØ 14 ARE INTEGERS,
AND THE NUMBER 21.42 IS A DECIMAL, THEN DEFINT
PASSED THE MULTIPLE VARIABLE TEST IN LINE 2Ø.
```

If the interpreter has a double-precision declarative character (e.g. the # sign in the Microsoft BASIC), and this character is assigned to a variable that is listed in the DEFINT statement, the variable is treated as double precision because Double Precision Declarative Characters over-ride the DEFINT statement.

TEST PROGRAM

```
1Ø REM 'DEFINT' TEST PROGRAM
2Ø REM USES DOUBLE-PRECISION TYPE DECLARATION CHARACTER'#'
3Ø DEFINT A,B
4Ø A=9.123456789Ø12345
5Ø B#=9.123456789Ø12345
6Ø IF A=B# THEN 11Ø
7Ø PRINT "A =";A
8Ø PRINT "B# =";B#
9Ø PRINT "THE TEST PASSED, SHOWING # OVER-RIDING DEFINT"
1ØØ GOTO 999
11Ø PRINT "THE # CHARACTER OVER-RIDE FEATURE FAILED THE TEST"
999 END
```

SAMPLE RUN

```
A = 9
B# = 9.123456789Ø12345
THE TEST PASSED, SHOWING # OVER-RIDING DEFINT
```

VARIATIONS IN USAGE

None known.

ALSO SEE

INT, # , DEFSNG, DEFDBL

DEFSNG is used to define (declare) specified variables as being of "single precision". Single precision variables are capable of storing numbers containing no more than 7 digits (only 6 digits are printed). Double precision means having 16-digit precision.

DEFSNG

Since most interpreters automatically treat variables as having single precision, the DEFSNG statement is used in programs to redefine variables as having only single precision after one or more were defined as double precision by a previous DEFDBL statement or # operator.

Statement

In most computers the DEFSNG line must be executed before the variable listed in the DEFSNG statement is assigned a numeric value. Line 2∅ below declares both X and Y to be maintained with double precision.

TEST PROGRAM

```
1∅ REM 'DEFSNG' TEST PROGRAM
2∅ DEFDBL X,Y
3∅ X=1.234567890123456
4∅ Y=X
5∅ PRINT "DOUBLE PRECISION VALUE OF Y=";Y
6∅ DEFSNG Y
7∅ Y=X
8∅ PRINT "SINGLE PRECISION VALUE OF Y=";Y
99 END
```

SAMPLE RUN

```
DOUBLE PRECISION VALUE OF Y = 1.234567890123456
SINGLE PRECISION VALUE OF Y = 1.23457
```

Most computers with DEFSNG capability also allow assignment of multiple variables (separated by comma) in a single DEFSNG statement. For example, **DEFSNG A,F,M** defines the variables A, F and M as single precision, and **DEFSNG A-M** defines all variables **A thru** M as single precision.

TEST PROGRAM

```
1∅ REM 'DEFSNG' (WITH MULTIPLE VARIABLES) TEST PROGRAM
2∅ DEFDBL A,G,L-N
3∅ GOSUB 2∅∅
4∅ PRINT "THE DOUBLE PRECISION VALUES OF A,G,L,M AND N ARE"
5∅ PRINT A;G;L;M;N
6∅ DEFSNG A,G,L-N
7∅ GOSUB 2∅∅
8∅ PRINT "THE SINGLE PRECISION VALUES OF A,G,L,M AND N ARE"
```

DEFSNG

```
9Ø PRINT A;G;L;M;N
1ØØ GOTO 999
2ØØ REM SUBROUTINE
21Ø A=1234.567890
22Ø G=A/1Ø
23Ø L=G/1Ø
24Ø M=L/1Ø
25Ø N=M/1Ø
26Ø RETURN
999 END
```

SAMPLE RUN

```
THE DOUBLE PRECISION VALUES OF A,G,L,M AND N ARE
 1234.56789   123.456789   12.3456789   1.23456789   .123456789
THE SINGLE PRECISION VALUES OF A,G,L,M AND N ARE
 1234.57   123.457   12.3457   1.23457   .123457
```

An Over-Riding Operator

If the interpreter provides for a double precision declarative character (e.g. the # in the MICROSOFT Basic), and this character is shown with a variable that is listed in the DEFSNG statement, the double precision character over-rides the action of the DEFSNG statement and declares the variable to be double precision. See line 5Ø below.

TEST PROGRAM

```
1Ø REM 'DEFSNG' TEST PROGRAM
2Ø REM USES DOUBLE PRECISION DECLARATION CHARACTER '#'
3Ø DEFSNG A,B
4Ø A=1.234567890123456
5Ø B#=1.234567890123456
6Ø IF A=B# THEN 11Ø
7Ø PRINT "A=";A
8Ø PRINT "B#=";B#
9Ø PRINT "THE TEST PASSED WITH # OVER-RIDING DEFSNG"
1ØØ GOTO 999
11Ø PRINT "THE # CHARACTER OVER-RIDE FEATURE FAILED THE TEST"
999 END
```

SAMPLE RUN

```
A = 1.23457
B# = 1.234567890123456
THE TEST PASSED WITH # OVER-RIDING DEFSNG
```

VARIATIONS IN USAGE

None known.

ALSO SEE

DEFINT, #, DEFDBL, !, CSNG, CDBL, CINT

The DEFSTR statement is used to specify designated variables as string variables. A variable listed in the DEFSTR statement is treated the same as if it was defined as a string variable by the $ (string) sign.

It is important in large programs to specify only those variables that need string storage, since string variables require more memory space than numeric variables.

The DEFSTR line must be executed before the defined variable is assigned a string notation.

DEFSTR

Statement

TEST PROGRAM

```
1Ø REM 'DEFSTR' TEST PROGRAM
2Ø A=25
3Ø PRINT "NUMERIC STRING A =";A
4Ø DEFSTR A
5Ø A="TEST STRING"
6Ø PRINT "STRING VARIABLE A = ";A
99 END
```

SAMPLE RUN

```
NUMERIC STRING A = 25
STRING VARIABLE A = TEST STRING
```

Most computers with DEFSTR capability also allow assignment of multiple variables (separated by comma) by a single DEFSTR statement. For example, **DEFSTR A,F,M** defines the variables A, F, and M as string variables. **DEFSTR A-M** defines all variables A **thru** M as string variables.

TEST PROGRAM

```
1Ø REM DEFSTR (WITH MULTIPLE VARIABLES) TEST PROGRAM
2Ø DEFSTR A,G,L-N
3Ø A="DEFSTR "
4Ø G="PASSED THE "
5Ø L="MULTIPLE VARIABLE "
6Ø M="TEST "
7Ø N="IN LINE 2Ø."
8Ø PRINT A;G;L;M;N
99 END
```

SAMPLE RUN

```
DEFSTR PASSED THE MULTIPLE VARIABLE TEST IN LINE 2Ø.
```

DEFSTR

Some interpreters require that space be reserved in memory for the assigned strings using the DIM or CLEAR statements.

Interpreters with declarative characters (e.g. D, E, %, #, or !) take precedence over the DEFSTR function when added to variables listed in the DEFSTR statement. This feature can be tested by making these changes to the second TEST PROGRAM.

```
7Ø N="IN LINE"
8Ø PRINT A;G;L;M;N;
85 A!=2Ø
9Ø PRINT A!
```

The single-precision declarative character (!) added to lines 85 and 9Ø should over-ride the DEFSTR statement in line 2Ø and print the sample run.

VARIATIONS IN USAGE

None known.

ALSO SEE

DEFDBL, DEFINT, DEFSNG, DIM, CLEAR, $, D (exponential notation), E (exponential notation), % (integer operator), # (double precision) and ! (single precision).

DEG is used by a few computers (e.g. the Cromemco 16K Extended BASIC) as a command which causes the computer to execute trigonometric functions in **degrees** (rather than in radians). One degree = approximately .Ø2 radians.

**Command
Function**

TEST PROGRAM

```
1Ø REM 'DEG COMMAND' TEST PROGRAM
2Ø A=SIN(1.4)
3Ø PRINT "THE SINE OF 1.4 RADIANS IS";A
99 END
```

SAMPLE RUN

As shown above, the computer will execute the program and compute the sine of an angle of 1.4 radians.

```
THE SINE OF 1.4 RADIANS IS .98545
```

Type the command DEG and then RUN. The computer will compute the sine of the angle 1.4 converted to DEGrees.

```
THE SINE OF 1.4 RADIANS IS .Ø24432
```

To change the computer back to the radian mode, type RAD or SCR. (SCR will also SCRatch the entire program.)

IF YOUR COMPUTER DOESN'T HAVE IT

If your computer does not have the DEG **command**, it can be simulated in the program instead by multiplying radian values times .Ø174533. To use this conversion in the first TEST PROGRAM, make this program change:

```
2Ø A=SIN(1.4*.Ø174533)
```

VARIATIONS IN USAGE

A few computers (e.g. those using MAX BASIC) have DEG(n) as an intrinsic function to convert a value (n) expressed in **radians** to **degrees**.

DEG

TEST PROGRAM

```
10 REM 'DEG FUNCTION' TEST PROGRAM
20 PRINT "ENTER AN ANGLE (EXPRESSED IN RADIANS)";
30 INPUT A
40 B=DEG(A)
50 PRINT "THE RADIAN ANGLE OF";A;"IS EQUAL TO";B;"DEGREES"
99 END
```

SAMPLE RUN *(using 1.4)*

```
ENTER AN ANGLE (EXPRESSED IN RADIANS)? 1.4
THE RADIAN ANGLE OF 1.4 IS EQUAL TO 80.2141 DEGREES
```

IF YOUR COMPUTER DOESN'T HAVE IT

If your computer does not have the DEG **function**, it can be simulated by multiplying the radian values times 57.29578. To use this conversion in the second TEST PROGRAM, make this program change:

```
40 B=A*57.29578
```

ALSO SEE

SIN, SINE, COS, TAN, ATN

DEL is used as an abbreviation for the DELETE command to "erase" specified program lines from the computer's memory.

For more information see DELETE.

Command

TEST PROGRAM

```
1Ø REM 'DEL' TEST PROGRAM
2Ø PRINT "LINE 2Ø"
3Ø PRINT "LINE 3Ø"
99 END
```

Run the program to ensure that all lines are properly entered.

SAMPLE RUN

```
LINE 2Ø
LINE 3Ø
```

Type the command DEL 2Ø and run the program. This command should have eliminated the printing of "LINE 2Ø". Check by LISTing and RUNning.

VARIATIONS IN USAGE

None known.

ALSO SEE

DELETE, LIST

The DELETE command is used to "erase" specified program lines from the computer's memory.

TEST PROGRAM

```
1Ø REM 'DELETE' TEST PROGRAM
2Ø PRINT "LINE 2Ø"
3Ø PRINT "LINE 3Ø"
4Ø PRINT "LINE 4Ø"
5Ø PRINT "LINE 5Ø"
6Ø PRINT "LINE 6Ø"
7Ø PRINT "LINE 7Ø - END OF DELETE TEST"
99 END
```

Command

RUN the program to ensure that all lines are properly entered.

SAMPLE RUN

```
LINE 2Ø
LINE 3Ø
LINE 4Ø
LINE 5Ø
LINE 6Ø
LINE 7Ø - END OF DELETE TEST
```

A single program line can be eliminated from the computer's memory using the command DELETE(line number). To test this feature, try the command **DELETE5Ø** and run the program. This command should have eliminated the printing of "LINE 5Ø". Check by LISTing and RUNning.

More than one program line can be eliminated from memory by some computers using the command DELETE(line #-line #). All line numbers within the range specified by this command are eliminated. To test this feature, try the command **DELETE3Ø-4Ø**, then RUN the program. Lines 3Ø and 4Ø should be gone.

DELETE-(line number) is used by some computers to eliminate all line numbers from the first line number in the program to the line number specified in the DELETE command. To test this feature, try the command **DELETE-6Ø** and run the program. All lines should be eliminated except line 7Ø and 99.

Some computers with the DELETE feature allow eliminating of groups of line numbers plus individual line numbers by use of commas.

For example, **DELETE 2Ø,4Ø-5Ø,9Ø** eliminates lines 2Ø, 4Ø, 5Ø and 9Ø from the program. To test for this feature, re-enter the test program and try the command **DELETE 2Ø, 4Ø-6Ø**. LIST the program to verify that all lines except 1Ø, 3Ø, 7Ø and 99 have been eliminated.

DELETE

A few computers use DELETE(line number)- to eliminate all line numbers starting from the line number specified in the DELETE command to the end. To test for this feature, try the command **DELETE 3Ø-**. LIST the program to verify that only line 1Ø remains.

IF YOUR COMPUTER DOESN'T HAVE IT

If your computer does not have the DELETE command, the same thing can be accomplished by typing each line number individually, followed by pressing the ENTER or RETURN key. To eliminate all line numbers in one operation, use the NEW or SCRATCH command.

ALSO SEE

NEW, LIST

The DIMension statement is used to establish the number of elements allowed in a numeric or string array.

Statement

An array DIMension is established by placing the array variable after the DIM statement, followed by the array size enclosed in parenthesis.

For example, **DIM A(2Ø)** allows array variable A to use the 21 array elements from A(Ø) to A(2Ø). [Some computers start with array element A(1), while a few computers (e.g. those conforming to ANSI BASIC and MAX BASIC) can define the lowest array element as either Ø or 1 by using the BASE statement. For more information see BASE.]

When the DIM statement is executed, the computer sets the values stored in each designated array element to zero.

TEST PROGRAM

```
1Ø REM 'DIM' NUMERIC ARRAY TEST PROGRAM
2Ø DIM A(1Ø)
3Ø PRINT "THESE NUMBERS ARE STORED IN AND PRINTED"
4Ø PRINT "FROM A SINGLE DIMENSION NUMERIC ARRAY."
5Ø FOR X=1 TO 1Ø
6Ø A(X)=X
7Ø PRINT A(X);
8Ø NEXT X
99 END
```

SAMPLE RUN

```
THESE NUMBERS ARE STORED IN AND PRINTED
FROM A SINGLE DIMENSION NUMERIC ARRAY.
 1   2   3   4   5   6   7   8   9   1Ø
```

To check your interpreter's ability to use array elements starting at Ø, make this change in the TEST PROGRAM:

```
5Ø FOR X=Ø TO 1Ø
```

If your interpreter accepted the array element A(Ø), a SAMPLE RUN should print numbers from Ø to 1Ø.

Most computers allow each array to use elements from Ø (or 1) to 1Ø without the need for DIMensioning. Delete line 2Ø from the TEST PROGRAM to test for this capability.

If it works, make this change in line 5Ø:

```
5Ø FOR X=1 TO 15
```

and RUN. Since a few computers (e.g. TRS-80 Level I) do not require **any** dimensioning, their array size is automatically limited only by the amount of unused memory. TRS-80 Level I only allows arrays named A(n) and B(n). Most computers allow the full range of Alphabetic variables, and many allow arrays to have Alpha/Numeric array names [e.g. A3(n)].

Assuming that line 5Ø change above caused a crash, make this change to line 2Ø:

```
2Ø DIM A(15)
```

and RUN

SAMPLE RUN

```
THESE NUMBERS ARE STORED IN AND PRINTED
FROM A SINGLE DIMENSION NUMERIC ARRAY.
 1   2   3   4   5   6   7   8   9   1Ø   11   12   13   14   15
```

This next program tests the computer's ability to DIMension **string** arrays. Some computers (e.g. Hewlett-Packard) require dimensioning of all strings, including string arrays, with no string space set aside without DIM.

TEST PROGRAM

```
1Ø REM 'DIM' STRING ARRAY TEST PROGRAM
2Ø DIM A$(4)
3Ø FOR X=1 TO 4
4Ø READ A$(X)
5Ø NEXT X
6Ø PRINT "THE 'DIM' STATEMENT PASSED THE ";
7Ø FOR X=1 TO 4
8Ø PRINT A$(X);
9Ø NEXT X
1ØØ DATA T,E,S,T
999 END
```

SAMPLE RUN

```
THE 'DIM' STATEMENT PASSED THE TEST
```

DIM is also used in some computers to set the maximum element size for numeric and string arrays which contain two dimensions (or more).

For example, `DIM A(2Ø,25)` establishes the maximum size of the first dimension at 2Ø, and the second at 25.

DIM

Most computers with two and three dimension array capability automatically reserve space for 1Ø elements in each dimension. Many smaller computers (e.g. Microsoft interpreter variations) reserve element space for only the first and second dimension.

TEST PROGRAM

```
1Ø REM 'DIM' TWO DIMENSION ARRAY TEST PROGRAM
2Ø DIM A(3,4)
3Ø PRINT "THESE NUMBERS ARE STORED IN AND PRINTED"
4Ø PRINT "FROM A TWO DIMENSION NUMERIC ARRAY."
5Ø FOR I=1 TO 3
6Ø FOR J=1 TO 4
7Ø A(I,J)=I
8Ø NEXT J
9Ø NEXT I
1ØØ FOR I=1 TO 3
11Ø FOR J=1 TO 4
12Ø PRINT A(I,J),
13Ø NEXT J
14Ø PRINT
15Ø NEXT I
999 END
```

SAMPLE RUN

```
THESE NUMBERS ARE STORED IN AND PRINTED
FROM A TWO DIMENSION NUMERIC ARRAY.
 1                 1                 1                 1
 2                 2                 2                 2
 3                 3                 3                 3
```

TEST PROGRAM

This program tests the computer's ability to DIMension three dimension numeric array variables.

```
1Ø REM 'DIM' THREE DIMENSION ARRAY TEST PROGRAM
2Ø DIM A(3,4,2)
3Ø PRINT "THESE NUMBERS ARE STORED IN AND PRINTED"
4Ø PRINT "FROM A THREE DIMENSION NUMERIC ARRAY."
5Ø FOR K=1 TO 2
6Ø FOR I=1 TO 3
7Ø FOR J=1 TO 4
8Ø A(I,J,K)=I
9Ø NEXT J
1ØØ NEXT I
11Ø NEXT K
```

```
120 FOR K=1 TO 2
130 FOR I=1 TO 3
140 FOR J=1 TO 4
150 PRINT A(I,J,K),
160 NEXT J
170 NEXT I
180 PRINT
190 NEXT K
999 END
```

SAMPLE RUN

THESE NUMBERS ARE STORED IN AND PRINTED
FROM A THREE DIMENSION NUMERIC ARRAY.

1	1	1	1
2	2	2	2
3	3	3	3
1	1	1	1
2	2	2	2
3	3	3	3

VARIATIONS IN USAGE

None other known.

ALSO SEE

CLEAR, MAT INPUT, MAT PRINT, MAT READ

DSP is used in the APPLE II BASIC as an analytical tool to display a specific variable and its value each time the variable is assigned a value. The variable's associated line number is also displayed preceded by a # sign. More than one DSP statement is allowed in a program.

For example:

Statement

```
1Ø DSP X
2Ø DSP Y
```

instructs the computer to display (print) variables X and Y, and their values, along with the line numbers each time they are assigned or reassigned a value.

TEST PROGRAM

```
1Ø REM 'DSP' TEST PROGRAM
2Ø DSP A
3Ø DSP B
4Ø A=5
5Ø B=1Ø
6Ø C=A*B
7Ø A=A+C
8Ø PRINT "THE DSP STATEMENT PASSED THE TEST"
99 END
```

SAMPLE RUN

```
#4Ø A=5
#5Ø B=1Ø
#7Ø A=55
THE DSP STATEMENT PASSED THE TEST
```

IF YOUR COMPUTER DOESN'T HAVE IT

This very handy troubleshooting feature can be duplicated by adding a temporary test line at each point where the variable being traced is changed. For example,

```
1Ø REM DSP SIMULATION
4Ø A=5
41 PRINT "#4Ø A=";A
5Ø B=1Ø
```

```
51 PRINT "#5Ø B=";B
6Ø C=A*B
7Ø A=A+C
71 PRINT "#7Ø A=";A
8Ø PRINT "END OF THE DSP SIMULATION"
99 END
```

VARIATIONS IN USAGE

None known.

ALSO SEE

TRON, TRACE

E is used to indicate "exponential notation", or "standard scientific notation".

For example, `1.23E+12` means 1.23 followed by 12 zeros.

Numbers expressed in double precision are written in exponential notation using the letter "D".

For example, `1.23456789D+2Ø`

Operator

TEXT PROGRAM

```
1Ø REM 'E' SINGLE PRECISION EXPONENT TEST PROGRAM
2Ø A=123456789
3Ø PRINT "EXPONENTIAL NOTATION'E' PASSED THE TEST IF"
4Ø PRINT A;"CONTAINS THE LETTER 'E'"
99 END
```

SAMPLE RUN

```
EXPONENTIAL NOTATION 'E' PASSED THE TEST IF
1.23457E+Ø8 CONTAINS THE LETTER 'E'
```

VARIATIONS IN USAGE

The letter "E", like all other letters of the alphabet, is used by all computers to indicate a numeric variable.

ALSO SEE

D, !, #, DEFSNG, DEFDBL

E. is used in the TRS-80 Level I as an abbreviation for the END statement.

For more information see END.

Statement

TEST PROGRAM

```
1Ø REM 'E. (END)' TEST PROGRAM
2Ø PRINT "THE COMPUTER SHOULD ONLY PRINT THIS LINE"
3Ø E.
4Ø PRINT "IF THIS LINE IS PRINTED THE TEST FAILED"
99 END
```

SAMPLE RUN

```
THE COMPUTER SHOULD ONLY PRINT THIS LINE
```

VARIATIONS IN USAGE

None known.

ALSO SEE

END

EDIT is a special command used by some computers (e.g. those using Microsoft BASIC) which allows editing of the program line specified by the EDIT command. (It is similar to the RUN and LIST commands in that if no number follows it, the first program line is automatically implied.)

Command

TEST PROGRAM

```
1Ø REM 'EDIT' TEST PROGRAM
2Ø PRINT "CAN THIS PROGRAM BE MODIFIED"
3Ø PRINT "BY THE EDIT COMMAND?"
99 END
```

After loading this program, type **EDIT 2Ø** to determine if the computer has the EDIT feature. The computer should print the number 2Ø followed possibly by a cursor. This indicates the computer is in the EDIT mode and is ready to modify line 2Ø.

VARIATIONS IN USAGE

There are many versions of text, character and line editors. They each speak their own "language," and it is not BASIC. This Handbook will therefore not cover Editor languages.

The EDIT command may call up your editor, but you'll have to check the machine's manual to see how to perform the editing and get back into BASIC. Sometimes it's as easy as hitting the carriage return. Other times (especially on large multi-language time-sharing machines) it takes a whole series of commands to get in and out of the "editor".

ELSE is used to execute an alternate statement when the condition of an IF-THEN statement is not met. For example, IF X=3 THEN 1ØØ ELSE STOP instructs the computer to branch to line 100 if X equals 3, but STOP if X does not equal 3.

Statement

TEST PROGRAM

```
1Ø REM 'ELSE' TEST PROGRAM
2Ø X=1
3Ø IF X < 5 THEN 6Ø ELSE GOTO 9Ø
4Ø PRINT "ELSE FAILED THE TEST"
5Ø GOTO 99
6Ø PRINT X;
7Ø X=X+1
8Ø GOTO 3Ø
9Ø PRINT "'ELSE' PASSED THE TEST"
99 END
```

SAMPLE RUN

```
1  2  3  4  'ELSE' PASSED THE TEST
```

IF YOUR COMPUTER DOESN'T HAVE IT

If your computer does not have the ELSE statement, it can be simulated in the test program by changing line 3Ø to 3Ø IF X < 5 THEN 6Ø and adding the following new line.
35 GOTO 9Ø

VARIATIONS IN USAGE

None known.

ALSO SEE

IF-THEN, GOTO

The END statement is used to terminate execution of the program. Many computers require it to be placed at the highest line number in the program, while others accept it at any point.

The END statement is optional with many computers (mostly micros).

Statement

TEST PROGRAM

```
10 REM 'END' TEST PROGRAM
20 PRINT "THE FIRST END STATEMENT FOLLOWS"
30 END
40 PRINT "THE SECOND END STATEMENT FOLLOWS"
99 END
```

SAMPLE RUN

```
THE FIRST END STATEMENT FOLLOWS
```

If your computer does not pass this test and will not allow an END statement at line 30, then delete line 30 and run the program again.

Then delete line 99 to see if your computer accepts END as an **optional** statement.

ALSO SEE

STOP (for the many problems encountered when using END and STOP in the same program).

EQ is used in a few computers (e.g. the T.I. 99∅) as an optional word for the equal sign (=).

For more information see =.

Operator

TEST PROGRAM

```
1∅ REM 'EQ (EQUAL)' TEST PROGRAM
2∅ A EQ 1∅
3∅ IF A EQ 1∅ THEN 6∅
4∅ PRINT "THE EQ OPERATOR FAILED THE TEST"
5∅ GOTO 99
6∅ PRINT "THE EQ OPERATOR PASSED THE TEST"
99 END
```

SAMPLE RUN

```
THE EQ OPERATOR PASSED THE TEST
```

VARIATIONS IN USAGE

None known.

ALSO SEE

=, < >, IF-THEN

The ERL function is used with the ON-ERROR statement to identify the last line number in which an error has occurred.

Function

The ERL function initializes at the numeric line number value of 65535 (the maximum two-byte value). When an error occurs, ERL changes to the line number in which the error occurred. The line number contained in the ERL function changes each time an error occurs in a different line.

By using ERL in "error-trapping" routines, it is possible to identify the "errored" line and take appropriate action.

TEST PROGRAM

```
1Ø REM 'ERL' TEST PROGRAM
2Ø ON ERROR GOTO 1ØØ
3Ø PRINT "ENTER THE NUMBER 1Ø, 2Ø, THEN 3Ø";
4Ø INPUT N
5Ø A=1Ø/(N-1Ø)
6Ø A=1Ø/(N-2Ø)
7ØA=1Ø/(N-3Ø)
8Ø PRINT "THE NUMBER ";N;"DID NOT CAUSE AN ERROR"
9Ø GOTO 3Ø
1ØØ PRINT "AN ERROR HAS JUST OCCURRED IN LINE"; ERL
11Ø RESUME 3Ø
999 END
```

SAMPLE RUN

```
ENTER THE NUMBER 1Ø, 2Ø, THEN 3Ø? 1Ø
AN ERROR HAS JUST OCCURRED IN LINE 5Ø
ENTER THE NUMBER 1Ø, 2Ø, THEN 3Ø? 2Ø
AN ERROR HAS JUST OCCURRED IN LINE 6Ø
ENTER THE NUMBER 1Ø, 2Ø, THEN 3Ø? 3Ø
AN ERROR HAS JUST OCCURRED IN LINE 7Ø
ENTER THE NUMBER 1Ø, 2Ø, THEN 3Ø?
```

VARIATIONS IN USAGE

None known.

ALSO SEE

ERROR, ON-ERROR-GOTO, RESUME

ERR is used in some computers (e.g. those with Microsoft BASIC) to identify the error code of the last error which occurred in a program. The error code contained in the ERR function changes each time a different error occurs. By using ERR in "error-trapping" routines, it is possible to identify the type of error which occurred and take appropriate action. Refer to the computer's manual for a listing of its particular error codes.

Function

TEST PROGRAM

```
10 REM 'ERR' TEST PROGRAM
20 DIM A(5)
30 CLEAR
40 ON ERROR GOTO 100
50 PRINT "ENTER A SAMPLE NUMBER";
60 INPUT N
70 A(N)=10/N
80 PRINT "THE NUMBER";N;"DID NOT CAUSE AN ERROR"
90 GOTO 50
100 IF ERR = 9 THEN 130
110 IF ERR = 11 THEN 160
120 GOTO 180
130 PRINT "THE NUMBER";N;"IS TOO LARGE"
140 PRINT "USE A NUMBER BETWEEN 1 AND 5"
150 RESUME 30
160 PRINT "THE SMALLEST NUMBER ALLOWED IS 1"
170 RESUME 0
180 PRINT "THE NUMBER";N;"CAUSED AN ERROR CODE OF";ERR
999 END
```

SAMPLE RUN *(Typical)*

```
ENTER A SAMPLE NUMBER? 12
THE NUMBER 12 IS TOO LARGE
USE A NUMBER BETWEEN 1 AND 5
ENTER A SAMPLE NUMBER? 0
THE SMALLEST NUMBER ALLOWED IS 1
THE NUMBER 1 DID NOT CAUSE AN ERROR
ENTER A SAMPLE NUMBER?
```

VARIATIONS IN USAGE

The TRS-80 Level II BASIC stores a value in the ERR function that does not equal the actual error code. To convert the value stored in the ERR function to the actual error code, divide the ERR value by 2 and add 1.

ERR

For example, **PRINT ERR** /2+1

ALSO SEE

ERL, ON-ERROR, RESUME, DIM, CLEAR

ERROR is used to intentionally cause the computer to ERROR. The type of error is specified by an error code in the ERROR statement. The ERROR statement is commonly used in programs to execute error trapping routines, or to print a specified error message.

Command Statement

TEST PROGRAM #1 *(for a Microsoft Interpreter)*

```
1Ø INPUT N
2Ø IF N > 32ØØØ THEN ERROR 7
99 END
```

When a value greater than 32ØØØ is assigned to variable N, the condition of the IF-THEN statement in line 2Ø is met and the computer generates the ERROR message.

```
OM ERROR IN 2Ø
```

(out of memory in line 2Ø), even though the computer is not actually out of memory.

Variables cannot be used as ERROR codes. Each code must be specified by an actual integer error code number. If the specified error code is not recognized by the computer's interpreter, then ERROR message "UNPRINTABLE ERROR" is printed by most computers.

ERROR can also be entered as a command to test specific error codes. See your computer's manual for a listing of its error messages.

TEST PROGRAM #2

```
1Ø REM 'ERROR' TEST PROGRAM
2Ø PRINT 'ERROR PASSED THE TEST IF ERROR MESSAGE 'OS' OR''
3Ø PRINT "'OUT OF STRING SPACE' IS PRINTED."
4Ø ERROR 14
99 END
```

SAMPLE RUN *(typical)*

```
ERROR PASSED THE TEST IF ERROR MESSAGE 'OS'''
OR 'OUT OF STRING SPACE' IS PRINTED.
?OS ERROR IN 4Ø
```

VARIATIONS IN USAGE

None known.

ALSO SEE

ON-ERROR-GOTO, RESUME, ERR, ERL

EXAM(n) is used by some computers (e.g. the Digital Group MAXI-BASIC, the North Star BASIC, and the Processor Technology 8K BASIC) to read the contents of specified addresses in the computer's memory.

Function

For example, X=**EXAM(2ØØ)** assigns the value stored in memory address 2ØØ to variable X.

The EXAM function gives us the contents of that memory address as a decimal number between Ø and 255 (the range of values that can be held in an 8 bit memory byte). EXAM can be used with the FILL statement to read what FILL has stored in memory. (Some computers use POKE or STUFF.) The highest number address that can be EXAMined depends of course on the computer's memory size.

Check your computer's manual before executing this TEST PROGRAM to determine that memory addresses 18368 to 1838Ø are reserved as "free" memory. This avoids FILLing data into memory addresses reserved for other computer operations. If addresses 18368 to 1838Ø are not reserved as free memory in your computer, select a group of 12 adjacent memory addresses and change lines 2Ø and 6Ø in the TEST PROGRAM accordingly.

TEST PROGRAM

```
1Ø REM 'EXAM' TEST PROGRAM
2Ø FOR X=18368 TO 1838Ø
3Ø READ Y
4Ø FILL X,Y
5Ø NEXT X
6Ø FOR X=18368 TO 1838Ø
7Ø Y=EXAM(X)
8Ø PRINT CHR$(Y);
9Ø NEXT X
1ØØ DATA 84,69,83,84,128,67,79,77,8Ø,76,69,84,69
999 END
```

SAMPLE RUN

TEST COMPLETE

VARIATIONS IN USAGE

None known.

ALSO SEE

FILL, POKE, PEEK, USR, SYSTEM

The EXP(n) function computes the natural logarithm's base value e (2.71828. . .) raised to the power of (n).

This is just the opposite of what happens when the LOG function is used.

For example, **A=EXP(3)** is the same as A=2.71828 * 2.71828 * 2.71828.

Function

The value (n) can be written as a number or a numeric variable.

TEST PROGRAM

```
10 REM 'EXP' TEST PROGRAM
20 N=4.60517
30 E=EXP(N)
40 PRINT "IF THE NATURAL EXPONENTIAL OF";N;"IS";E
50 PRINT "THEN THE EXP FUNCTION PASSED THE TEST."
99 END
```

SAMPLE RUN

```
IF THE NATURAL EXPONENTIAL OF 4.60517 IS 100
THEN THE EXP FUNCTION PASSED THE TEST.
```

IF YOUR COMPUTER DOESN'T HAVE IT

If your interpreter did not accept the EXP function, then substitute the following sub-routine for EXP:

```
30000 GOTO 30999
30240 REM * EXPONENTIAL SUBROUTINE * INPUT X, OUTPUT E
30242 REM ALSO USES L AND A INTERNALLY
30244 L=INT(1.4427*X)+1
30246 IF L<127 THEN 30258
30248 IF X<=0 THEN 30254
30250 PRINT X;"IS OUT OF RANGE"
30252 STOP
30254 E=0
30256 RETURN
30258 E=.693147*L-X
30260 A=1.32988E-3-1.41316E-4*E
30262 A=((A*E-8.30136E-3)*E+4.16574E-2)*E
30264 E=(((A-.166665)*E+.5)*E-1)*E+1
30266 A=2
30268 IF L>0 THEN 30276
30270 A=.5
```

```
30272 L=-L
30274 IF L=0 THEN 30282
30276 FOR X=1 TO L
30278 E=A*E
30280 NEXT X
30282 RETURN
```

To use this subroutine with the TEST PROGRAM, make the following program changes:

```
35 X=N
40 GOSUB 30244
```

ALSO SEE

LOG, LOGE, LOG10, CLOG

F. is used in the TRS-80 Level I and other variations of Palo Alto Tiny BASIC as an abbreviation for the FOR statement.

For more information see FOR.

Statement

TEST PROGRAM

```
1Ø REM 'F. (FOR)' TEST PROGRAM
2Ø F. X=1 TO 5
3Ø PRINT X;
4Ø NEXT X
5Ø PRINT "'F.' PASSED THE TEST"
99 END
```

SAMPLE RUN

```
1   2   3   4   5   'F.' PASSED THE TEST
```

VARIATIONS IN USAGE

None known.

ALSO SEE

FOR, FOR-NEXT

FETCH(n) is used in the Digital Group Opus 1 and Opus 2 BASIC to read the contents of addresses in the computer's memory.

FETCH

Function

For example, X=FETCH(3ØØØ) assigns the decimal value stored in memory address 3ØØØ to the variable X.

That value will be a number between Ø and 255 (the range of values that can be held in an 8 bit memory byte). The highest number that can be FETCHed depends of course on the computer's memory size.

FETCH can be used with the STUFF statement to check what STUFF has stored in memory. (Some computers use POKE or FILL instead).

Check your computer's manual before executing this TEST PROGRAM to determine that memory addresses 18368 to 18377 are reserved as free memory. This avoids STUFFing data into memory used for special purposes. If addresses 18368 to 18377 are not reserved as free memory in your computer, then select a group of 1Ø free consecutive memory addresses and change lines 3Ø and 7Ø in the TEST PROGRAM accordingly.

TEST PROGRAM

```
1Ø REM 'FETCH' TEST PROGRAM
2Ø Y=1
3Ø FOR X=18368 TO 18377
4Ø STUFF X,Y
5Ø Y=Y+1
6Ø NEXT X
7Ø FOR X=18368 TO 18377
8Ø Y=FETCH(X)
9Ø PRINT Y;
1ØØ NEXT X
11Ø PRINT
12Ø PRINT "'FETCH' PASSED THE TEST IF #1 THRU #1Ø ARE PRINTED"
999 END
```

SAMPLE RUN

```
1   2   3   4   5   6   7   8   9   1Ø
'FETCH' PASSED THE TEST IF #1 THRU #1Ø ARE PRINTED
```

VARIATIONS IN USAGE

None known.

ALSO SEE

STUFF, POKE, PEEK, FILL, USR, SYSTEM

FILL is used by a few interpreters (e.g. the NORTH STAR BASIC and the Digital Group MAXI-BASIC) to fill a specified byte in the computer's memory with an integer value between Ø and 255 (the maximum 8 bit value).

FILL

Statement

For example, FILL 3ØØØ,15 fills memory address 3ØØØ with the decimal number 15.

The EXAM function can be used with FILL to inspect what FILL has stored into memory. (Some computers use PEEK or FETCH instead).

Computers vary in the amount of available memory and memory addresses that can be FILLed without erasing memory dedicated to other purposes. Check your computer's manual before running this TEST PROGRAM to determine that memory addresses 18368 to 1838Ø are noncritical memory locations.

TEST PROGRAM

```
1Ø REM 'FILL' TEST PROGRAM
2Ø FOR X=18368 TO 1838Ø
3Ø READ Y
4Ø FILL X,Y
5Ø NEXT X
6Ø FOR X=18368 TO 1838Ø
7Ø Y=EXAM(X)
8Ø PRINT CHR$(Y);
9Ø NEXT X
1ØØ DATA 84,69,83,84,128,67,79,77,8Ø,76,69,84,69
999 END
```

SAMPLE RUN

```
TEST COMPLETE
```

VARIATIONS IN USAGE

None known.

ALSO SEE

POKE, STUFF, EXAM, PEEK

The FIX function is used to remove all numbers to the right of the decimal point. Its operation is similar to the INT function except FIX does not round negative numbers down.

FIX

Function

Example: 1Ø PRINT FIX(3.6)
         2Ø PRINT FIX(-3.6)

prints the numbers 3 and -3. While

         1Ø PRINT INT(3.6)
         2Ø PRINT INT(-3.6)

prints the numbers 3 and -4.

FIX is capable of handling any number, large or small, within the limitations of the computer's interpreter.

TEST PROGRAM

```
1Ø REM 'FIX' TEST PROGRAM
2Ø N=-12.3456
3Ø A=FIX(N)
4Ø PRINT "FIX PASSED THE TEST IF ";N;"IS CHANGED TO ";A
99 END
```

SAMPLE RUN

```
FIX PASSED THE TEST IF -12.3456 IS CHANGED TO -12
```

IF YOUR COMPUTER DOESN'T HAVE IT

If your interpreter does not have the FIX function capability, but has the ABS, INT and SGN functions, then line 3Ø in the TEST PROGRAM can be replaced with:

```
3Ø A=SGN(N)*INT(ABS(N))
```

VARIATIONS IN USAGE

None known.

ALSO SEE

INT, ABS, SGN

The FN function is used with the DEF statement to specify variables as "user defined". The FN function is not executed when preceded by DEF. For more information see DEFine.

Function

The FN function can be manipulated like any built-in function.

For example,

```
10 DEF FNA(X)=1/X
20 PRINT FNA(N)
```

The FN function in this example is named "A" (FNA), and is assigned the equation 1/X in line 10. FNA is used here to compute the reciprocal of **any** numeric variable.

The numeric variable (N) following FNA is substituted for the "dummy variable" (X in this example) in the DEF statement each time FNA is executed.

TEST PROGRAM

```
10 REM 'FN' TEST PROGRAM
20 DEF FNX(A)=(A-32)*5/9
30 PRINT "ENTER A TEMPERATURE IN FAHRENHEIT";
40 INPUT F
50 C=FNX(F)
60 PRINT F;"DEGREES FAHRENHEIT =";C;"DEGREES CELSIUS."
99 END
```

SAMPLE RUN *(using 70)*

```
ENTER A TEMPERATURE IN FAHRENHEIT? 70
70 DEGREES FAHRENHEIT = 21.1111 DEGREES CELSIUS.
```

VARIATIONS IN USAGE

None known.

ALSO SEE

DEF, FNEND

The FNEND statement is used in computers which have the capability of DEFining and reDEFining a function at different points throughout a program. It ENDs the function's DEFining process.

FNEND

Statement

Each DEF statement which is spread out over more than one line must end with a FNEND statement, and the computer cannot branch out of or into these DEF statements before the FNEND statement is executed.

TEST PROGRAM

```
10 REM 'FNEND' TEST PROGRAM
20 PRINT "ENTER A VALUE FOR X THAT IS GREATER OR LESS THAN 10";
30 INPUT X
40 DEF FNA(X)
50 FNA=X*2
60 IF X < 10 THEN 80
70 FNA=X/2
80 FNEND
90 PRINT "THE NEW VALUE FOR X IS";FNA(X)
999 END
```

SAMPLE RUN *(using 6)*

```
ENTER A VALUE FOR X THAT IS GREATER OR LESS THAN 10? 6
THE NEW VALUE FOR X IS 12
```

VARIATIONS IN USAGE

None known.

ALSO SEE

DEF, FN

The FOR statement is part of a FOR-TO-NEXT statement and is used to assign numbers to numeric variables within the range specified by FOR-TO.

The first number immediately following the FOR is incremented by 1 each time its corresponding NEXT statement is executed. When the number following TO is exceeded, program execution continues at the line following the corresponding NEXT statement.

A
N
S
I

Statement

TEST PROGRAM

```
10 REM 'FOR' TEST PROGRAM
20 FOR X=1 TO 5
30 PRINT X;
40 NEXT X
50 PRINT "THE 'FOR' STATEMENT PASSED THE TEST"
99 END
```

SAMPLE RUN

```
1   2   3   4   5 THE 'FOR' STATEMENT PASSED THE TEST
```

Some computers use the STEP statement to increment FOR-TO-NEXT by a value other than one, and to allow decrementing (changing numbers in descending order).

For more information see STEP.

VARIATIONS IN USAGE

Some computers (e.g. DEC BASIC-PLUS-2), under specific conditions allow a FOR-TO with the NEXT only implied, not actually written.

ALSO SEE

NEXT, FOR-NEXT, STEP, F.

The FRE(string) function is used to report the number of bytes of total string space allocated but unused in the computer's memory. Any character (enclosed in quotes) or string variable can be used with the FRE function. The B$ in line 5Ø below is completely arbitrary.

Function

Most computers with FRE capability automatically reserve 50 bytes of string space when the computer is turned on.

TEST PROGRAM

```
1Ø REM 'FRE(STRING)' TEST PROGRAM
2Ø PRINT "ENTER ANY COMBINATION OF LETTERS AND NUMBERS";
3Ø INPUT A$
4Ø PRINT "THE AMOUNT OF UNUSED STRING SPACE =";
5Ø PRINT FRE(B$)
99 END
```

SAMPLE RUN *(Typical, using computer)*

```
ENTER ANY COMBINATION OF LETTERS AND NUMBERS? COMPUTER
THE AMOUNT OF UNUSED STRING SPACE = 42
```

Try various combinations of letters and numbers in the test program to demonstrate the action of the FRE function.

Some computers use numbers or numeric variables in the FRE function to report the **total** amount of memory remaining (not just that part reserved for strings), similar to the MEM statement.

VARIATIONS IN USAGE

None known.

ALSO SEE

MEM, CLEAR, $

FREE(∅) is used by some computers (e.g. the NORTH STAR BASIC, Processor Technology Extended BASIC, and Digital Group MAXI-BASIC) to report the **total** amount of remaining memory (i.e. similar to the MEM statement).

Function

TEST PROGRAM

```
1∅ REM 'FREE(∅)' TEST PROGRAM
2∅ PRINT FREE(∅);"BYTES OF MEMORY ARE REMAINING"
99 END
```

SAMPLE RUN *(typical)*

```
135∅4 BYTES OF MEMORY ARE REMAINING
```

The amount of memory remaining will of course depend on your computer.

VARIATIONS IN USAGE

None known.

ALSO SEE

MEM, FRE

G. is used in the TRS-80 Level I and other variations of Palo Alto Tiny BASIC as an abbreviation for the GOTO statement.

For more information see GOTO.

Statement

TEST PROGRAM

```
1Ø REM 'G.' TEST PROGRAM
2Ø PRINT "THE G. STATEMENT";
3Ø G. 6Ø
4Ø PRINT "FAILED"
5Ø STOP
6Ø PRINT "HAS PASSED THE TEST."
99 END
```

SAMPLE RUN

```
THE G. STATEMENT HAS PASSED THE TEST.
```

VARIATIONS IN USAGE

None known.

ALSO SEE

GOTO, GOT

GE is used in some computers (e.g. the TI 990) as an abbreviation for the "greater than or equal to" sign (> =).

For more information see > =.

Operator

TEST PROGRAM

```
1Ø REM 'GE' (GREATER THAN OR EQUAL TO) TEST PROGRAM
2Ø IF 2Ø GE 1Ø THEN 5Ø
3Ø PRINT "THE GE OPERATOR FAILED THE TEST IN LINE 2Ø"
4Ø GOTO 99
5Ø IF 2Ø GE 2Ø THEN 8Ø
6Ø PRINT "THE GE OPERATOR FAILED THE TEST IN LINE 5Ø"
7Ø GOTO 99
8Ø PRINT "THE GE OPERATOR PASSED THE TEST"
99 END
```

SAMPLE RUN

```
THE GE OPERATOR PASSED THE TEST
```

VARIATIONS IN USAGE

None known.

ALSO SEE

> =, = > , IF-THEN

GO is used as part of GO TO and GO SUB statements. The BASIC language does not recognize the word GO by itself. Most computers don't care if there is a space after the GO, converting automatically to GOTO or GOSUB. Others (e.g. TRS-80 Level I) do not allow the space.

Statement

This program uses GO in the GO TO statement. For more information see GOTO.

TEST PROGRAM

```
10 REM 'GO' TEST PROGRAM
20 PRINT "THE GO STATEMENT ";
30 GO TO 60
40 PRINT "FAILED THE TEST"
50 GOTO 99
60 PRINT "PASSED THE TEST."
99 END
```

SAMPLE RUN

```
THE GO STATEMENT PASSED THE TEST.
```

This program uses GO in the GO SUB statement. For more information see GOSUB.

TEST PROGRAM

```
10 REM 'GO' (USED WITH SUB) TEST PROGRAM
20 GO SUB 100
30 PRINT "PASSED THE TEST WHEN USED WITH SUB."
40 GO TO 999
100 REM SUBROUTINE
110 PRINT "THE GO STATEMENT ";
120 RETURN
999 END
```

SAMPLE RUN

```
THE GO STATEMENT PASSED THE TEST WHEN USED WITH SUB.
```

VARIATIONS IN USAGE

None known.

ALSO SEE

GOTO, GOT, G., GOSUB, GOS.

GOS. is used in the TRS-80 Level I and other variations of Palo Alto Tiny BASIC as an abbreviation for the GOSUB statement.

For more information see GOSUB.

Statement

TEST PROGRAM

```
1Ø REM 'GOS.' TEST PROGRAM
2Ø GOS. 1ØØ
3Ø PRINT "PASSED THE TEST AT LINE 2Ø"
4Ø GOTO 999
1ØØ REM SUBROUTINE
11Ø PRINT "THE GOS. STATEMENT ";
12Ø RETURN
999 END
```

SAMPLE RUN

```
THE GOS. STATEMENT PASSED THE TEST AT LINE 2Ø
```

VARIATIONS IN USAGE

None known.

ALSO SEE

GOSUB, ON-GOSUB, IF-GOSUB, RETURN

GOSUB is used to branch out of a program's "main-stream" to a Subroutine. The GOSUB statement must be followed by a line number to indicate the first line of the subroutine to be executed.

A RETURN statement must be used at the end of a subroutine execution to return control from the subroutine to the main program.

GOSUB

A N S I

Statement

TEST PROGRAM

```
1Ø REM 'GOSUB' TEST PROGRAM
2Ø GOSUB 1ØØ
3Ø PRINT "PASSED THE TEST AT LINE 2Ø"
4Ø GOTO 999
1ØØ REM SUBROUTINE
11Ø PRINT "THE GOSUB STATEMENT ";
12Ø RETURN
999 END
```

SAMPLE RUN

```
THE GOSUB STATEMENT PASSED THE TEST AT LINE 2Ø
```

VARIATIONS IN USAGE

None known.

ALSO SEE

RETURN, ON-GOSUB, IF-GOSUB, GOS.

GOT is used in the PDP-8E as an abbreviation for the GOTO statement.

For more details see GOTO.

Statement

TEST PROGRAM

```
10 REM 'GOT' TEST PROGRAM
20 PRINT "THE GOT STATEMENT ";
30 GOT 60
40 PRINT "FAILED"
50 GOTO 99
60 PRINT "HAS PASSED THE TEST."
99 END
```

SAMPLE RUN

THE GOT STATEMENT HAS PASSED THE TEST.

VARIATIONS IN USAGE

None known.

ALSO SEE

GOTO, G.

The GOTO statement is used to "jump" program execution to a specified line number. Many computers also accept this statement as two words; GO TO.

GOTO

A
N
S
I

Statement

TEST PROGRAM

```
1∅ REM 'GOTO' STATEMENT TEST PROGRAM
2∅ PRINT "THE GOTO STATEMENT ";
3∅ GOTO 6∅
4∅ PRINT "FAILED"
5∅ STOP
6∅ PRINT "HAS PASSED THE TEST."
99 END
```

SAMPLE RUN

```
THE GOTO STATEMENT HAS PASSED THE TEST.
```

VARIATIONS IN USAGE

GOTO is often used in conjunction with other expressions.

ALSO SEE

GOT, G., IF-GOTO, ON-GOTO, GOTO-OF, etc.

GOTO-OF is used by some computers (e.g. the Hewlett Packard 3000 and the Tektronix 4051) as a multiple branching tool which incorporates a number of IF-THEN tests into a single statement.

GOTO-OF

Statement

For example, **GOTO X OF 1ØØ,2ØØ,3ØØ** instructs the computer to branch to lines 1ØØ, 2ØØ or 3ØØ if the integer value of X is 1, 2 or 3 respectively. If INT X is less than 1 or more than 3, the tests in this example all fail and execution defaults to the next program line. The INT value of X cannot exceed the number of possible branches in the statement.

TEST PROGRAM

```
1Ø REM 'GOTO-OF' TEST PROGRAM
2Ø X=2
3Ø GOTO X OF 4Ø,6Ø
4Ø PRINT "'GOTO-OF' FAILED THE TEST"
5Ø GOTO 99
6Ø PRINT "'GOTO-OF' PASSED THE TEST"
99 END
```

SAMPLE RUN

```
'GOTO-OF' PASSED THE TEST
```

VARIATIONS IN USAGE

None known.

ALSO SEE

GO-TO-OF, ON-GOTO, ON-GOT, ON-GOSUB, IF-THEN and INT

GO-TO-OF is used in a few computers (e.g. the VARIAN 620 BASIC) as a multiple branching scheme which incorporates a number of IF-THEN tests into a single statement.

GO-TO-OF

Statement

For example, **GO TO X OF 1ØØ,2ØØ,3ØØ** instructs the computer to branch to lines 1ØØ, 2ØØ, or 3ØØ if the value of X is 1, 2, or 3 respectively. If INT of X is less than 1 or more than 3 the tests in this GO-TO-OF example all fail and execution defaults to the next program line. The value of X cannot exceed the number of possible branches in the statement.

Most computers accept both GO TO (two words) or GOTO (one word) while a few (e.g. VARIAN 620 BASIC) accept only the two words GO TO.

TEST PROGRAM

```
1Ø REM 'GO-TO-OF' TEST PROGRAM
2Ø X=2
3Ø GO TO X OF 4Ø,6Ø
4Ø PRINT "'GO-TO-OF' FAILED THE TEST"
5Ø GOTO 99
6Ø PRINT "'GO-TO-OF' PASSED THE TEST"
99 END
```

SAMPLE RUN

```
'GO-TO-OF' PASSED THE TEST
```

VARIATIONS IN USAGE

See ON-GOTO for various multiple branching schemes.

ALSO SEE

GOTO-OF, ON-GOTO, ON-GOT, GOSUB-OF, ON-GOSUB, IF-THEN

GR is used in the APPLE II BASIC as both a command and a program statement to change the computer's operation from the TEXT mode to the GRaphics mode. GR must be executed before using the special graphics statements PLOT, HLIN-AT and VLIN-AT.

GR can also be used to clear the screen before starting a new graphics display. Each time GR is executed, the computer erases the entire screen.

**Command
Statement**

TEST PROGRAM

```
1Ø REM 'GR' TEST PROGRAM
2Ø GR
3Ø COLOR=6
4Ø HLIN Ø,39 AT 2Ø
5Ø END
```

SAMPLE RUN

If the computer accepted the GR statement, a blue horizontal line should appear across the screen.

VARIATIONS IN USAGE

None known.

ALSO SEE

TEXT, COLOR, HLIN-AT, VLIN-AT, PLOT

GT is used in some computers (e.g. the TI 990) as an alternate word for the "greater-than" sign (>).

For more information see > .

Operator

TEST PROGRAM

```
1Ø REM 'GT (GREATER THAN)' TEST PROGRAM
2Ø IF 1Ø GT 5 THEN 5Ø
3Ø PRINT "THE GT OPERATOR FAILED THE TEST"
4Ø GOTO 99
5Ø PRINT "THE GT OPERATOR PASSED THE TEST"
99 END
```

SAMPLE RUN

```
THE GT OPERATOR PASSED THE TEST
```

VARIATIONS IN USAGE

None known.

ALSO SEE

> , IF-THEN

HLIN-AT is used in the APPLE II BASIC as a special feature to display a Horizontal LINe AT a specified row on the screen.

The horizontal line length is determined by two numbers following the HLIN statement. These numbers indicate the bounds between which the line will extend. The line may extend any length between columns ∅ to 39.

The number following AT represents the row number which the line must occupy. This number may range from ∅ to 39.

For example, **HLIN 1∅,3∅ AT 2∅** tells the computer to draw a horizontal line from column 1∅ to column 3∅ AT row 2∅.

The **GR**aphics statement must be executed before the computer can accept the HLIN-AT statement (see GR). The line's color is determined by the COLOR statement (see COLOR).

TEST PROGRAM

```
1∅ REM 'HLIN-AT' TEST PROGRAM
2∅ GR
3∅ Y=∅
4∅ FOR X=∅ TO 39
5∅ COLOR = Y
6∅ HLIN ∅,39 AT X
7∅ Y=Y+1
8∅ IF Y < 16 THEN 1∅∅
9∅ Y=∅
1∅∅ NEXT X
999 END
```

SAMPLE RUN

If the computer accepted the HLIN-AT statement, the screen should be filled with 39 horizontal lines of various colors.

VARIATIONS IN USAGE

None known.

ALSO SEE

GR, COLOR, PLOT, VLIN-AT, TEXT

I. is used in the TRS-80 Level I and other variations of Palo Alto Tiny BASIC as an abbreviation for the INT function.

For more information see INT.

Function Statement

TEST PROGRAM

```
1Ø REM 'I. (INT)' TEST PROGRAM
2Ø X=2.864
3Ø PRINT "THE INTEGER VALUE OF";X;
4Ø X=I.(X)
5Ø PRINT "IS";X
99 END
```

SAMPLE RUN *(using 1Ø)*

```
THE INTEGER VALUE OF 2.864 IS 2
```

VARIATIONS IN USAGE

I. can also be used in the TRS-80 Level I BASIC as an abbreviation for the INPUT statement when I. is not followed by a value enclosed in parenthesis.

TEST PROGRAM

```
1Ø REM 'I. (INPUT)' TEST PROGRAM
2Ø PRINT "ASSIGN A VALUE TO THE VARIABLE X";
3Ø I.X
4Ø PRINT "THE VALUE OF X IS";X
99 END
```

SAMPLE RUN *(using 1Ø)*

```
ASSIGN A VALUE TO THE VARIABLE X?1Ø
THE VALUE OF X IS 1Ø
```

ALSO SEE

INPUT, INPUTL, IN., INP

The IF statement is part of the conditional branching statements IF-THEN, IF-GOTO, IF-GOSUB, IF-LET, etc., and is used to indicate the variable to be tested by one of the relational operators (see =, < , > , < =, > =, < >).

Statement

For example, IF X=3 THEN 1ØØ the computer branches or "jumps" to line 1ØØ **IF** X equals 3. If the condition is not met (i.e. X≠3), the test "falls through" and program execution continues on the next line.

These conditional IF-THEN tests must be used last in multiple statement lines because the computer either branches to the indicated line number (if the test is true), or falls through to the next **numbered** line (if the test is false).

For example, 3Ø IF X=3 THEN 1ØØ:PRINT "X=3" The PRINT statement can never be executed.

TEST PROGRAM

```
1Ø REM 'IF' TEST PROGRAM
2Ø X=1Ø
3Ø IF X=1Ø THEN 6Ø
4Ø PRINT "'IF' FAILED THE TEST"
5Ø GOTO 99
6Ø PRINT "'IF' PASSED THE TEST"
99 END
```

SAMPLE RUN

```
'IF' PASSED THE TEST
```

To further check the computer's IF capability, see the TEST PROGRAMS under IF-GOTO, IF-GOSUB and IF-LET.

VARIATIONS IN USAGE

None known.

ALSO SEE

IF-THEN, IF-GOTO, IF-GOSUB, IF-LET, IF-G., IF-GOS., IF-GOT, IF-T., IF-THE

IF-G. is used in the TRS-80 Level I and other variations of Palo Alto Tiny BASIC as an abbreviation for the IF-GOTO statement.

For more information see IF-GOTO.

Statement

TEST PROGRAM

```
10 REM 'IF-G. (IF-GOTO)' TEST PROGRAM
20 X=30
30 IF X=30 G.60
40 PRINT "THE IF-G. STATEMENT FAILED THE TEST"
50 GOTO 99
60 PRINT "THE IF-G. STATEMENT PASSED THE TEST"
99 END
```

SAMPLE RUN

```
THE IF-G. STATEMENT PASSED THE TEST
```

VARIATIONS IN USAGE

None known.

ALSO SEE

IF-GOTO, IF-GOT, IF-THEN, GOTO

IF-GOS. is used in the TRS-80 Level I and other variations of Palo Alto Tiny BASIC as an abbreviation for the IF-GOSUB statement.

Statement

For more information see IF-GOSUB.

TEST PROGRAM

```
1Ø REM 'IF-GOS.' TEST PROGRAM
2Ø X=3
3Ø IF X=3 GOS. 1ØØ
4Ø PRINT "PASSED THE TEST AT LINE 3Ø."
5Ø GOTO 999
1ØØ REM SUBROUTINE
11Ø PRINT "THE IF-GOS. STATEMENT ";
12Ø RETURN
999 END
```

SAMPLE RUN

THE IF-GOS. STATEMENT PASSED THE TEST AT LINE 3Ø.

VARIATIONS IN USAGE

None known.

ALSO SEE

IF-GOSUB, GOSUB, RETURN, IF-THEN, ELSE

The IF-GOSUB statement is a conditional subroutine branching statement using one of the relational operators (see =,<,>,<=,>=,<>).

IF-GOSUB

When the condition of the IF-GOSUB statement is met, the computer executes the GOSUB statement.

Statement

For example, IF X=3 GOSUB 100 tells the computer to branch or "jump" to the subroutine starting at line 100 if X equals 3. If the condition is not met (i.e. X≠3), the test "falls through" and program execution continues on the next line.

TEST PROGRAM

```
10 REM 'IF-GOSUB' TEST PROGRAM
20 X=3
30 IF X=3 GOSUB 100
40 PRINT "PASSED THE TEST AT LINE 30"
50 GOTO 999
100 REM SUBROUTINE
110 PRINT "THE IF-GOSUB STATEMENT ";
120 RETURN
999 END
```

SAMPLE RUN

```
THE IF-GOSUB STATEMENT PASSED THE TEST AT LINE 30
```

VARIATIONS IN USAGE

None known.

ALSO SEE

GOSUB, IF-GOS., RETURN, IF-THEN, ELSE

IF-GOT is used in the PDP-8E as an abbreviation for the IF-GOTO statement.

For more details see IF-GOTO.

Statement

TEST PROGRAM

```
1Ø REM 'IF-GOT' TEST PROGRAM
2Ø X=1Ø
3Ø IF X=1Ø GOT 6Ø
4Ø PRINT "'IF-GOT' FAILED THE TEST"
5Ø GOTO 99
6Ø PRINT "'IF-GOT' PASSED THE TEST"
99 END
```

SAMPLE RUN

```
'IF-GOT' PASSED THE TEST
```

VARIATIONS IN USAGE

None known.

ALSO SEE

IF-GOTO, IF-G.

IF-GOTO is a conditional branching statement using one of the relational operators (see =, < ,> , <=,> =,< >).

When the condition of the IF-GOTO statement is met, the computer executes the branching statement GOTO.

For example, IF X=3 GOTO 1∅∅ tells the computer to branch or "jump" to line 1∅∅ if X equals 3. If the condition is not met (i.e. X≠3), the test "falls through" and the program execution continues on the next line.

IF-GOTO

Statement

TEST PROGRAM

```
1∅ REM 'IF-GOTO' TEST PROGRAM
2∅ X=3∅
3∅ IF X=3∅ GOTO 6∅
4∅ PRINT "THE IF-GOTO STATEMENT FAILED THE TEST"
5∅ GOTO 99
6∅ PRINT "THE IF-GOTO STATEMENT PASSED THE TEST"
99 END
```

SAMPLE RUN

```
THE IF-GOTO STATEMENT PASSED THE TEST
```

VARIATIONS IN USAGE

Some interpreters allow the statement THEN to be used in place of GOTO. See IF-THEN.

ALSO SEE

GOTO, GOSUB, ELSE, IF-THEN

The IF-LET statement is a conditional LET statement using one of the relational operators (see =,<,>,<=,>=,< >).

When the condition of the IF-LET statement is met, the computer assigns a value to the variable following LET.

IF-LET

Statement

TEST PROGRAM

```
10 REM 'IF-LET' TEST PROGRAM
20 X=30
30 IF X>20 LET X=10
40 PRINT "X =";X
50 PRINT "'IF-LET' PASSED THE TEST IF THE VALUE OF X IS 10"
99 END
```

SAMPLE RUN

```
X = 10
'IF-LET' PASSED THE TEST IF THE VALUE OF X IS 10
```

VARIATIONS IN USAGE

Computers are not uniform in their use of the LET statement. Many allow LET to be omitted while others allow the THEN statement in place of LET.

ALSO SEE

IF-THEN, LET

IF-T. is used in the TRS-80 Level I as an abbreviation for the IF-THEN statement.

For more information see IF-THEN.

Statement

TEST PROGRAM

```
10 REM 'IF-T.' TEST PROGRAM
20 X=10
30 IF X=10 T.60
40 PRINT "'IF-T.' FAILED THE TEST"
50 GOTO 99
60 PRINT "'IF-T.' PASSED THE TEST"
99 END
```

SAMPLE RUN

```
'IF-T.' PASSED THE TEST
```

VARIATIONS IN USAGE

None known.

ALSO SEE

IF-THEN, IF-THE

IF-THE is used in the PDP-8E as an abbreviation for the IF-THEN statement.

For more information see IF-THEN.

IF-THE

Statement

TEST PROGRAM

```
1Ø REM 'IF-THE' TEST PROGRAM
2Ø X=1Ø
3Ø IF X=1Ø THE 6Ø
4Ø PRINT "'IF-THE' FAILED THE TEST"
5Ø GOTO 99
6Ø PRINT "'IF-THE' PASSED THE TEST"
99 END
```

SAMPLE RUN

```
'IF-THE' PASSED THE TEST
```

VARIATIONS IN USAGE

None known.

ALSO SEE

IF-THEN, IF-T.

The IF-THEN statement is a conditional branching statement using one of the relational operators (see=, < , >, < =, > =, < >).

IF-THEN

Statement

A
N
S
I

When the condition of the IF-THEN statement is met, the computer executes the branching statement number following THEN. For example, IF X=3 THEN 1ØØ tells the computer to branch or "jump" to line 1ØØ if X equals 3. If the condition is not met (i.e. X≠3), the test "falls through" and program execution continues on the next line.

TEST PROGRAM

```
1Ø REM 'IF-THEN' TEST PROGRAM
2Ø X=3Ø
3Ø IF X=3Ø THEN 6Ø
4Ø PRINT "THE IF-THEN STATEMENT FAILED THE TEST"
5Ø GOTO 99
6Ø PRINT "THE IF-THEN STATEMENT PASSED THE TEST IN LINE 3Ø"
99 END
```

SAMPLE RUN

```
THE IF-THEN STATEMENT PASSED THE TEST IN LINE 3Ø
```

Some computers allow math operations to be performed when the IF-THEN statement is satisfied. For example, IF A=3 THEN X=2∗(A + 6)/3 calculates for the value of X if the variable A is equal to 3. If not, the test fails and execution proceeds to the next line.

To test this feature in your computer, add the following program lines:

```
7Ø IF X=3Ø THEN X=X+9Ø
8Ø PRINT "X=";X
9Ø PRINT"IF-THEN PASSED THE TEST IN LINE 7Ø IF X=12Ø"
```

SAMPLE RUN

```
THE IF-THEN STATEMENT PASSED THE TEST IN LINE 3Ø
X=12Ø
IF-THEN PASSED THE TEST IN LINE 7Ø IF X=12Ø
```

Some interpreters allow any of the operating statements to be performed when the IF-THEN condition is met. For example, IF X=3 THEN END will stop program execution when the value of X equals 3.

IF-THEN

Add the following line to the test program to check this capability:

```
100 IF X=120 THEN PRINT "IF-THEN PASSED THE TEST IN LINE 100"
```

SAMPLE RUN

```
THE IF-THEN STATEMENT PASSED THE TEST IN LINE 30
X=120
IF-THEN PASSED THE TEST IN LINE 70 IF X=120
IF-THEN PASSED THE TEST IN LINE 100
```

Computers are not uniform in their use of the THEN statement. Many allow THEN to be omitted when IF is followed directly by a math operator, operating statement, or branching statement.

TEST PROGRAM

This program tests for three variations which imply (but do not use) THEN.

```
10 REM TEST PROGRAM WITH IMPLIED 'THEN' IN LINES 30, 60 AND 999
20 X=30
30 IF X=30 GOTO 60
40 PRINT "LINE 30 FAILED THE TEST"
50 GOTO 999
60 IF X=30 GOSUB 100
70 GOTO 999
100 REM SUBROUTINE
110 PRINT "LINES 30 AND 60 PASSED THE TEST. DOES LINE 999?"
120 RETURN
999 IF X=30 END
```

SAMPLE RUN

```
LINES 30 AND 60 PASSED THE TEST. DOES LINE 999?
```

Great caution must be used with interpreters which allow use of multiple statement lines. The "falling thru" of an IF-THEN test is to the **next line**, not the next statement on the same line. For this reason, IF-THEN tests are usually not followed by other statements on the same line.

For example: IF X=5 THEN X=X+Y:PRINT X. The PRINT statement is not executed if the value of X does not equal 5.

ALSO SEE

ELSE, GOTO, GOSUB, STOP, END, PRINT and other IF . . . statement BASIC words which allow use of THEN by implication.

IN. is used in the TRS-80 Level I and other variations of Palo Alto Tiny BASIC as an abbreviation for the statement INPUT.

For more information see INPUT.

Statement

TEST PROGRAM

```
10 REM 'IN.' TEST PROGRAM
20 PRINT "ASSIGN A VALUE TO THE VARIABLE X";
30 IN. X
40 PRINT "THE VALUE OF X IS";X
99 END
```

SAMPLE RUN *(using 1Ø)*

```
ASSIGN A VALUE TO THE VARIABLE X? 1Ø
THE VALUE OF X IS 1Ø
```

VARIATIONS IN USAGE

None known.

ALSO SEE

INPUT, INPUTL, INKEY$, INP, I.

The INKEY$ function is used in the TRS-80 Level II BASIC to read a character from the keyboard each time INKEY$ is executed. Unlike the INPUT statement, INKEY$ does not halt execution waiting for the ENTER key to be pressed. The computer just keeps "circling" until it receives a message from the keyboard. Until a key on the keyboard is pressed, INKEY$ simply reads an "empty" string (ASCII code of ∅).

Function

Since INKEY$ doesn't wait for you to enter a character from the keyboard and "ENTER", it usually is placed in a program loop to repeatedly scan the keyboard looking for a pressed key.

For example:

```
1∅ IF INKEY$="X" GOTO 1∅∅
2∅ GOTO 1∅
1∅∅ PRINT "YOU HIT 'X' DIDN'T YOU!"
```

The INKEY$ function repeatedly looks for the letter X at the keyboard to meet the condition of the IF-THEN statement. When the letter X is entered, the condition of the IF-THEN statement is met and the computer branches to line 1∅∅.

TEST PROGRAM

```
1∅ REM 'INKEY$' TEST PROGRAM
2∅ CLS
3∅ PRINT "PRESS ANY KEY ON THE KEYBOARD"
4∅ A$=INKEY$
5∅ IF A$="" GOTO 4∅
6∅ PRINT "YOU HAVE JUST PRESSED THE ";A$;" KEY"
7∅ PRINT: PRINT "PRESS THE ";A$;" KEY AGAIN TO START OVER"
8∅ IF INKEY$=A$ GOTO 2∅
9∅ GOTO 8∅
99 END
```

SAMPLE RUN *(using R)*

```
PRESS ANY KEY ON THE KEYBOARD
YOU HAVE JUST PRESSED THE R KEY

PRESS THE R KEY AGAIN TO START OVER
```

VARIATIONS IN USAGE

None known.

ALSO SEE

INPUT, IF-THEN

INP stands for "Input from a port".

The INP statement is used to read the decimal value of a byte of information at a specified computer port. The byte value can be any positive integer from Ø to 255.

For example, **PRINT INP(X)** prints the decimal value of the byte at port X.

Statement

INP is a useful tool to monitor ports for a specific condition, such as an input request from a remote peripheral device. Other applications might include reading temperatures from remote sensors on a solar hot water heating system, etc.

TEST PROGRAM

```
1Ø REM 'INP' TEST PROGRAM
2Ø FOR X=Ø TO 255
3Ø PRINT "THE DECIMAL VALUE OF THE BYTE AT PORT#";X;"IS";INP(X)
4Ø NEXT X
99 END
```

SAMPLE RUN *(typical)*

```
THE DECIMAL VALUE OF THE BYTE AT PORT# Ø IS 255



THE DECIMAL VALUE OF THE BYTE AT PORT# 255 IS 127
```

INP is also used in versions of the PDP-8 as an abbreviation for the INPUT statement.

For more information see INPUT.

TEST PROGRAM

```
1Ø REM 'INP (INPUT)' TEST PROGRAM
2Ø PRINT "ASSIGN A VALUE TO THE VARIABLE X"
3Ø INP X
4Ø PRINT "THE VALUE OF X IS";X
99 END
```

SAMPLE RUN *(using 1Ø)*

```
ASSIGN A VALUE TO THE VARIABLE X
? 1Ø
THE VALUE OF X IS 1Ø
```

VARIATIONS IN USAGE

None other known.

ALSO SEE

OUT, PEEK, POKE, INPUT, I., IN.

The INPUT statement allows the user to assign data to variables from the keyboard. When the computer executes an INPUT statement, it prints a question mark indicating it is waiting for you to assign a value to a variable. It will continue to wait until the ENTER (or RETURN) key is pressed.

INPUT

A N S I

Statement

TEST PROGRAM

```
10 REM 'INPUT' STATEMENT TEST PROGRAM
20 PRINT "ASSIGN A VALUE TO THE VARIABLE X"
30 INPUT X
40 PRINT "THE VALUE OF X IS";X
99 END
```

SAMPLE RUN *(using 10)*

```
ASSIGN A VALUE TO THE VARIABLE X
? 10
THE VALUE OF X IS 10
```

VARIATIONS IN USAGE

An increasingly common variation found in microcomputer interpreters allows INPUT to serve in both PRINT and INPUT capacities (thus conserving space).

TEST PROGRAM

```
10 REM 'INPUT/PRINT' STATEMENT TEST PROGRAM
20 INPUT "ASSIGN A VALUE TO THE VARIABLE 'X'"
30 PRINT "THE VALUE OF X IS";X
99 END
```

SAMPLE RUN *(using 10)*

```
ASSIGN A VALUE TO THE VARIABLE 'X'
? 10
THE VALUE OF X IS 10
```

Note that no PRINT statement preceded the INPUT statement. Both functions were combined in line 20.

ALSO SEE

INPUTL, INKEY$, INP, IN., I.

The INPUTL statement is used by a few computers (e.g. the Digital Group Maxi-BASIC) in a manner similar to the INPUT statement, but INPUTL stops the carriage return after the INPUT data has been assigned to a variable.

For more information see INPUT.

Statement

TEST PROGRAM

```
10 REM 'INPUTL' TEST PROGRAM
20 PRINT "ASSIGN A VALUE TO THE VARIABLE X"
30 INPUT X
40 PRINT "VARIABLE X=";X
50 PRINT "INPUTL PASSED THE TEST IF THE WORDS VARIABLE X =";X
60 PRINT "ARE PRINTED ON THE SAME LINE AS THE ? SIGN"
99 END
```

SAMPLE RUN *(using 10)*

```
ASSIGN A VALUE TO THE VARIABLE X
? 10 VARIABLE X = 10
INPUTL PASSED THE TEST IF THE WORDS VARIABLE = 10
ARE PRINTED ON THE SAME LINE AS THE ? SIGN
```

VARIATIONS IN USAGE

None known.

ALSO SEE

INPUT, INP, IN. I.

The INTeger function is used to round numbers off to their integer (whole number) value. In BASIC *numbers are always rounded down*. The whole number remains the same regardless of the value of the numbers removed from the right of the decimal point; except, when a negative number is integered, the resultant number is rounded off to the next smaller whole number. For example, INT (−4.65) returns a value of 5.

Function

There are limits to the size of the number that some computers will process with the INT function. Some microcomputers will not accept a number smaller than −32767 or larger than +32767 within the parenthesis.

TEST PROGRAM

```
1∅ REM 'INT' TEST PROGRAM
2∅ READ X
3∅ PRINT "THE INTEGER VALUE OF"; X;
4∅ X = INT(X)
5∅ PRINT "IS"; X
6∅ IF X=999 THEN 999
7∅ GOTO 2∅
8∅ DATA 3.33,2.864,.35,-3.15,32766.853,-32766.853,999.99
999 END
```

SAMPLE RUN

```
THE INTEGER VALUE OF 3.33 IS 3
THE INTEGER VALUE OF 2.864 IS 2
THE INTEGER VALUE OF .35 IS ∅
THE INTEGER VALUE OF -3.15 IS -4
THE INTEGER VALUE OF 32766.853 IS 32766
THE INTEGER VALUE OF -32766.853 IS -32767
THE INTEGER VALUE OF 999.99 IS 999
```

VARIATIONS IN USAGE

None, other than the limitation indicated.

ALSO SEE

CINT, %

L. is used in the TRS-80 Level I and other variations of Palo Alto Tiny BASIC as an abbreviation of the LIST command.

For more information see LIST.

Command

TEST PROGRAM

```
1Ø REM 'L. (LIST)' TEST PROGRAM
2Ø REM THIS COMMAND
3Ø REM WILL DISPLAY EACH LINE
4Ø REM AS HELD BY THE COMPUTER
5Ø PRINT "'L.' TEST COMPLETE"
99 END
```

SAMPLE RUN

After entering the L. command, the computer should LIST the entire program. With longer programs, it will list only enough of it to fill the screen; to see more, press the ↑ key.

VARIATIONS IN USAGE

None known.

ALSO SEE

LIST, LI, LIS

LE is used in some computers (e.g. the TI 990) as an alternate word for the "less than or equal to" sign (< =).

For more information see < =.

Operator

TEST PROGRAM

```
1Ø REM 'LE (LESS THAN OR EQUAL TO) TEST PROGRAM
2Ø IF 1Ø LE 2Ø THEN 5Ø
3Ø PRINT "THE LE OPERATOR FAILED THE TEST IN LINE 2Ø"
4Ø GOTO 99
5Ø IF 2Ø LE 2Ø THEN 8Ø
6Ø PRINT "THE LE OPERATOR FAILED THE TEST IN LINE 5Ø"
7Ø GOTO 99
8Ø PRINT "THE LE OPERATOR PASSED THE TEST"
99 END
```

SAMPLE RUN

```
THE LE OPERATOR PASSED THE TEST
```

VARIATIONS IN USAGE

None known.

ALSO SEE

< =, = < , IF-THEN

The LEFT(string,n) function is used in some computers (e.g. those using MAX BASIC) to isolate a specific number (n) of string characters, starting from the left-most character in the string.

For example, **PRINT LEFT("RUNNING",3)** prints the letters RUN, which are the left 3 characters in RUNNING, which is a string.

For more information see LEFT$.

Function

TEST PROGRAM

```
10 REM 'LEFT' TEST PROGRAM
20 A$="TESTING"
30 B$=LEFT(A$,4)
40 PRINT "THE 'LEFT' FUNCTION PASSED THE ";B$
99 END
```

SAMPLE RUN

```
THE 'LEFT' FUNCTION PASSED THE TEST
```

VARIATIONS IN USAGE

None known.

ALSO SEE

LEFT$

The LEFT$(string,n) function is used to isolate a specific number (n) of string characters starting from the left-most character in the string.

Function

For example, **PRINT LEFT$("RUNNING",3)** prints the letters RUN, which are the left 3 characters in the string RUNNING.

The string must be enclosed in quotes or listed as a string variable. The number of characters (n) can be expressed as a variable, number or arithmetic operation. A comma must separate the string from the number.

If the value of (n) is a decimal, the computer automatically finds its integer value.

TEST PROGRAM

```
10 REM 'LEFT$' TEST PROGRAM
20 A$="TESTING"
30 B$=LEFT$(A$,4)
40 PRINT LEFT$("THEATER",3);" 'LEFT$' FUNCTION PASSED THE " ;B$
99 END
```

SAMPLE RUN

```
THE 'LEFT$' FUNCTION PASSED THE TEST
```

VARIATIONS IN USAGE

None known.

ALSO SEE

PRINT, RIGHT$, MID$, CHR$, SPACE$, STR$, STRING$, INKEY$

The LEN function is used to measure the LENgth of strings by counting the number of characters enclosed in quotes or assigned to string variables.

For example, 1∅ **PRINT LEN("TEST")** should print 4, the number of letters in the word "TEST".

Function

TEST PROGRAM

```
1∅ REM 'LEN' TEST PROGRAM
2∅ PRINT "TYPE ANY COMBINATION OF LETTERS AND NUMBERS"
3∅ INPUT A$
4∅ PRINT "YOU ENTERED ";A$" WHICH CONTAINS";
5∅ PRINT LEN(A$); "CHARACTERS";
99 END
```

SAMPLE RUN *(using ABC123)*

```
TYPE ANY COMBINATION OF LETTERS AND NUMBERS
? ABC123
YOU ENTERED ABC123 WHICH CONTAINS 6 CHARACTERS
```

VARIATIONS IN USAGE

None known.

ALSO SEE

ASC, FRE, LEFT$, MID$, RIGHT$, STR$, VAL

The LET statement is used to assign values to variables (e.g. **LET X=2Ø**). LET is required by a few computers, but is optional on most. When not required, it is sometimes used as a method of "flagging" variables that are being assigned new values or where special identification is desired.

A
N
S
I

Statement

TEST PROGRAM

```
1Ø REM 'LET' TEST PROGRAM
2Ø LET X=2Ø
3Ø PRINT "THE LET STATEMENT PASSED THE TEST IN LINE";X
99 END
```

SAMPLE RUN

THE LET STATEMENT PASSED THE TEST IN LINE 2Ø

To determine if LET is required by your computer, delete LET from line 2Ø and try again.

VARIATIONS IN USAGE

None known.

The LGT(n) function computes the value of the common logarithm of any number (n) whose value is greater than ∅. It is used in the Tektronix 4051 BASIC and MAX BASIC.

Function

TEST PROGRAM

```
1∅ REM 'LGT' TEST PROGRAM
2∅ PRINT "ENTER A POSITIVE NUMBER";
3∅ INPUT N
4∅ X=LGT(N)
5∅ PRINT "THE COMMON LOG OF";N;"IS";X
3∅999 END
```

SAMPLE RUN *(using 1∅∅)*

```
ENTER A POSITIVE NUMBER? 1∅∅
THE COMMON LOG OF 1∅∅ IS 2
```

If your computer failed the test program, see LOG1∅ for a substitute subroutine and other conversion tips.

VARIATIONS IN USAGE

None known.

ALSO SEE

LOG1∅, CLOG, LOG, LOGE, LN

LI is used by some computers (e.g. the T.I. 990) as an abbreviation for the LIST command.

For more information see LIST.

Command

TEST PROGRAM

```
1Ø REM 'LI (LIST)' TEST PROGRAM
2Ø REM THIS COMMAND
3Ø REM WILL DISPLAY EACH LINE
4Ø REM AS HELD BY THE COMPUTER
5Ø PRINT "'LI' TEST COMPLETE"
99 END
```

SAMPLE RUN

After typing LI as a command, the computer should LIST the entire program.

VARIATIONS IN USAGE

None known.

ALSO SEE

LIST, LIS, L.

The LIN(n) statement (used in the Hewlett-Packard 2000 BASIC and the Digital Group Opus 1 and Opus 2 BASIC) causes the computer to skip a specified number (n) of lines on a printer or CRT before printing the next line.

LIN

Statement

TEST PROGRAM

```
1Ø REM 'LIN' TEST PROGRAM
2Ø PRINT "THE LIN STATEMENT PASSED THE TEST"
3Ø LIN(5)
4Ø PRINT "IF 5 LINES ARE SKIPPED BEFORE THIS LINE IS PRINTED"
99 END
```

SAMPLE RUN

```
THE LIN STATEMENT PASSED THE TEST




IF 5 LINES ARE SKIPPED BEFORE THIS LINE IS PRINTED
```

IF YOUR COMPUTER DOESN'T HAVE IT

If your computer does not have LN(n), it can be easily simulated by substituting (n) number of PRINT statements for LIN(n).

For example, substitute the following line for line 3Ø in the TEST PROGRAM:

```
3Ø PRINT:PRINT:PRINT:PRINT:PRINT
```

Since each PRINT statement triggers a line-feed, the above line will cause the computer to perform the same operation as LIN(5).

VARIATIONS IN USAGE

None known.

ALSO SEE

PRINT

LIS is used in the PDP-8E as an abbreviation for the LIST command.

For more information see LIST.

Command

TEST PROGRAM

```
1Ø REM 'LIS' TEST PROGRAM
2Ø REM THIS COMMAND
3Ø REM WILL DISPLAY EACH LINE
4Ø REM AS HELD BY THE COMPUTER
5Ø PRINT "'LIS' TEST COMPLETE"
99 END
```

SAMPLE RUN

After entering LIS the computer should LIST the entire program.

VARIATIONS IN USAGE

None known.

ALSO SEE

LIST, LIS, L.

The LIST command is used to display each program line in the numerical order in which it appears in the program. Some computers (or terminals) will scroll through the entire program list unless stopped by a specified key function. (Control C, Control S, etc.) Others will stop after displaying the first 12, 16, 24 or more lines, then advance one additional line each time the up-arrow, down-arrow or other appropriate key is pressed.

Command Statement

The LIST command can also be used in conjunction with a line number to specify a starting point other than at the beginning. Many computers will also accept a start and finish line number. For example, **LIST1Ø-2Ø** or **LIST 1Ø-2Ø** will list only those program lines with numbers from 1Ø to 2Ø.

TEST PROGRAM

```
1Ø REM 'LIST' COMMAND TEST PROGRAM
2Ø REM THIS COMMAND
3Ø REM WILL DISPLAY EACH LINE
4Ø REM AS HELD BY THE COMPUTER
5Ø PRINT "LIST TEST COMPLETE"
99 END
```

SAMPLE RUN

Type in **LIST2Ø-3Ø** and your computer should print:

```
2Ø REM THIS COMMAND
3Ø REM WILL DISPLAY EACH LINE
```

If your computer will not accept the line number limitations, then try entering LIST2Ø. If this test fails, try entering LIST without line numbers.

VARIATIONS IN USAGE

Enter a longer program and try the following LIST commands: **LIST- LIST1ØØ- LIST-1ØØ LIST—1ØØ**

If your computer accepted these LIST commands, LIST- should have listed the entire program, LIST1ØØ- the program starting at line 1ØØ, and LIST-1ØØ the program starting with the first line and ending with line 1ØØ.

The LIST command is accepted by some computers as part of a program statement. To test this on your computer, add the following line to the Test Program: **6Ø LIST**

LIST

If LIST is accepted as a program statement then it will print:

```
LIST TEST COMPLETE
10 REM 'LIST' COMMAND TEST PROGRAM
20 REM THIS COMMAND
30 REM WILL DISPLAY EACH LINE
40 REM AS HELD BY THE COMPUTER
50 PRINT "LIST TEST COMPLETE"
60 LIST
99 END
```

ALSO SEE

L., LIS, LI

The LN(n) function (used by COMPAL Micropolis BASIC and DEC-17D BASIC) computes the value of the natural logarithm of any number (n) whose value is greater than $\emptyset$. It is a "shorthand" for the more common LOG(n)

Function

TEST PROGRAM

```
1Ø REM 'LN' TEST PROGRAM
2Ø PRINT "ENTER A POSITIVE NUMBER";
3Ø INPUT N
4Ø L=LN(N)
5Ø PRINT "THE NATURAL LOG OF";N;"IS";L
3Ø999 END
```

SAMPLE RUN *(using 1ØØ)*

```
ENTER A POSITIVE NUMBER? 1ØØ
THE NATURAL LOG OF 1ØØ IS 4.6Ø517
```

If your computer failed the test program, see LOG for a substitute subroutine and other conversion tips.

VARIATIONS IN USAGE

None known.

ALSO SEE

LOG, LOGE, LN, LOG1Ø, LGT

The LOAD command is used to load a program into the computer from cassette tape.

Command

TEST PROGRAM

Enter this program into the computer from the keyboard, then store it on cassette tape. (See SAVE for details.)

```
10 REM 'LOAD' TEST PROGRAM
20 PRINT "THIS PROGRAM TESTS THE LOAD FEATURE"
99 END
```

Once the program is recorded on cassette tape, erase the computer memory with NEW, SCRATCH or whatever is appropriate.

Rewind the tape, then set the recorder to the PLAY mode and type the LOAD command.

The cassette recorder's motor is controlled by the computer which turns it on and off before and after the LOAD cycle. The cassette should "play back" the program, LOADing it into the computer.

List the program to verify that the program held in the computer's memory is identical to that originally entered (see LIST). If all looks well, RUN the program.

SAMPLE RUN

```
THIS PROGRAM TESTS THE LOAD FEATURE
```

VARIATIONS IN USAGE

None known.

ALSO SEE

CLOAD, SAVE, CSAVE, LIST, NEW

The LOG(n) function computes the **natural** logarithm of any number (n) whose value is greater than Ø. For common logs see LOG1Ø, CLOG, CLG or LGT.

LOG

A
N
S
I

Function

TEST PROGRAM

```
1Ø  REM 'LOG' TEST PROGRAM
2Ø PRINT "ENTER A POSITIVE NUMBER";
3Ø INPUT N
4Ø L=LOG(N)
5Ø PRINT "THE NATURAL LOG OF";N;"IS";L
3Ø999 END
```

SAMPLE RUN *(using 1ØØ)*

```
ENTER A POSITIVE NUMBER? 1ØØ
THE NATURAL LOG OF 1ØØ IS 4.6Ø517
```

DIFFERENT WORDS FOR NATURAL LOG

See LOGE and LN.

IF YOUR COMPUTER HAS NONE OF THEM

If they all fail, substitute the following subroutine:

```
3ØØØØ GOTO 3Ø999
3Ø17Ø REM * NATURAL LOGARITHM SUBROUTINE * INPUT X, OUTPUT L
3Ø172 REM USES A,B,C AND L INTERNALLY
3Ø174 IF X > Ø THEN 3Ø18Ø
3Ø176 PRINT "LOG UNDEFINED AT";X
3Ø178 STOP
3Ø18Ø A=1
3Ø182 B=2
3Ø184 C=.5
3Ø186 E=Ø
3Ø188 IF X  >=A THEN 3Ø2Ø2
3Ø19Ø IF X < C THEN 3Ø2Ø8
3Ø192 X=(X-.7Ø71Ø7)/(X+.7Ø71Ø7)
3Ø194 L=X*X
3Ø196 L=(((.598979*L+.961471)*L+2.88539)*X+E-.5)*.693147
```

```
30198 IF ABS(L) < 1E-6 THEN 30220
30200 RETURN
30202 X=C*X
30204 E=E+A
30206 GOTO 30188
30208 X=B*X
30210 E=E-A
30215 GOTO 30190
30220 L=0
30225 RETURN
```

To use this subroutine in the TEST PROGRAM, make these program additions:

```
35 X=N
40 GOSUB 30170
```

CONVERSION FACTORS

To convert natural log to common log, multiply the natural log times .434295. For example, **X=LOG(N)*.434295**. To convert common log to natural log, multiply the common log times 2.3026.

VARIATIONS IN USAGE

A few computers (e.g. IMSAI 4K) use LOG to compute the COMMON LOG, **not** the NATURAL LOG (but this is the exception).

ALSO SEE

LN, LOGE, LOG 10, CLOG, CLG and LGT.

The LOGE(n) function computes the value of the natural logarithm of any number (n) whose value is greater than ∅. For common logs see CLG, LOG1∅, CLOG or LGT.

Function

TEST PROGRAM

```
1∅ REM 'LOGE' TEST PROGRAM
2∅ PRINT "ENTER A POSITIVE NUMBER";
3∅ INPUT N
4∅ L=LOGE(N)
5∅ PRINT "THE NATURAL LOG OF";N;"IS";L
3∅999 END
```

SAMPLE RUN *(for 1∅∅)*

```
ENTER A POSITIVE NUMBER? 1∅∅
THE NATURAL LOG OF 1∅∅ IS 4.6∅517
```

If your computer failed the TEST PROGRAM, try the TEST PROGRAMS in LOG and LN. If they also fail, substitute the subroutine found under LOG (saves space not to duplicate it here).

To use that subroutine with this TEST PROGRAM, make these TEST PROGRAM changes:

```
35 X=N
4∅ GOSUB 3∅17∅
```

CONVERSION FACTORS

To convert a natural log to a common log, multiply the natural log value times .434295.

For example: `X=LOGE(N)*.434295`

To convert a common log to a natural log, multiply the common log value times 2.3∅26.

ALSO SEE

LOG, LN, CLG, CLOG, LOG1∅, LGT

The LOG1Ø(n) function computes the value of the common (base 1Ø) logarithm of any number (n) whose value is greater than Ø.

Function

TEST PROGRAM

```
1Ø REM 'LOG1Ø' TEST PROGRAM
2Ø PRINT "ENTER A POSITIVE NUMBER";
3Ø INPUT N
4Ø X=LOG1Ø(N)
5Ø PRINT "THE COMMON LOG OF";N;"IS";X
3Ø999 END
```

SAMPLE RUN *(for 1ØØ)*

```
ENTER A POSITIVE NUMBER? 1ØØ
THE COMMON LOG OF 1ØØ IS 2
```

IF YOUR COMPUTER DOESN'T HAVE IT

If your computer failed the TEST PROGRAM, try the TEST PROGRAMS in LOG, CLOG and LGT. If they also fail, substitute the subroutine found under LOG (saves space not to duplicate it here).

To make the subroutine compute the common logarithm (instead of the natural logarithm), make the following subroutine changes:

```
3Ø17Ø REM * COMMON LOGARITHM SUBROUTINE * INPUT X, OUTPUT X
3Ø2ØØ GOTO 3Ø223
3Ø223 X=L* .4342945
```

To use the LOG subroutine with the TEST PROGRAM, make these TEST PROGRAM changes:

```
35 X=N
4Ø GOSUB 3Ø17Ø
```

CONVERSION FACTORS

To convert a common log to a natural log, multiply the common log value times 2.3Ø26.

For example: `X=LOG1Ø(N)*2.3Ø26`

To convert a natural log to a common log, multiply the natural log value times .434295.

ALSO SEE

CLG, CLOG, LGT, LOG, LOGE, LN

LT is used in some computers (e.g. the TI 990) as an alternate word for the "less-than" sign (<).

For more information see < .

Operator

TEST PROGRAM

```
1Ø REM 'LT (LESS-THAN)' TEST PROGRAM
2Ø IF 5 LT 1Ø THEN 5Ø
3Ø PRINT "THE LT OPERATOR FAILED THE TEST"
4Ø GOTO 99
5Ø PRINT "THE LT OPERATOR PASSED THE TEST"
99 END
```

SAMPLE RUN

```
THE LT OPERATOR PASSED THE TEST
```

VARIATIONS IN USAGE

None known.

ALSO SEE

<·, IF-THEN

M. is used in the TRS-80 Level I as an abbreviation for the MEM (memory) function.
For more information see MEM.

TEST PROGRAM

```
10 REM 'M. (MEM)' TEST PROGRAM
20 PRINT M.; "BYTES OF MEMORY REMAINING"
99 END
```

SAMPLE RUN *(typical)*

```
3500 BYTES OF MEMORY ARE REMAINING
```

VARIATIONS IN USAGE

None known.

ALSO SEE

MEM, FRE, FREE(∅)

MAN is used in the APPLE II BASIC to allow MANual insertion of program line numbers.

If the computer is in the AUTOmatic line numbering mode, control X must be typed before the computer can accept the MAN command.

MAN

Command

TEST PROCEDURE

To test the computer's MANual feature, place the computer in the AUTOmatic line numbering mode by typing the command AUTO and pressing the RETURN key. If line number 1∅ is printed, the computer successfully went into the AUTOmatic mode. Now type control X and the command MAN. Enter a few test program lines to verify that the computer passed the MANual command test.

VARIATIONS IN USAGE

None known.

ALSO SEE

AUTO

MAT INPUT is used to assign values to each element in an array via the keyboard. The DIM statement establishes the number of array elements that may be assigned values.

For example,

Statement

```
1Ø DIM A(5)
2Ø MAT INPUT A
```

The DIM statement allows variable A to use 5 array elements named A(1) to A(5). They are assigned values by the MAT INPUT statement. (For more information see DIM.)

When the MAT INPUT statement is executed, the computer prints a ? indicating it is ready to receive a value for the first element in the array. If all elements are to be filled in one pass, a comma must be typed after each value before the RETURN or ENTER key is pressed. If each element in the array did not receive a value before the RETURN or ENTER key is pressed, the computer prints a double question mark (??) indicating more values are needed. As with an ordinary INPUT statement, values can be entered one at a time, each followed by the RETURN.

The MAT INPUT statement assigns values to each vertical column in the first row of two-dimensional-array variables before assigning values to the following horizontal row.

For example,

```
1Ø DIM A(2,3)
2Ø MAT INPUT A
```

The computer assigns values to array variable elements A(1,1), A(1,2), and A(1,3) before A(2,1), A(2,2), and A(2,3).

Most MAT INPUT handling computers allow the array size to be established with the MAT INPUT statement if not more than 1Ø array elements are used. [e.g. MAT INPUT A(2,3).] If an array requires more than 1Ø elements, it must be DIMensioned.

For example,

```
1Ø DIM B(2Ø,2Ø)
2Ø MAT INPUT A(3,5)
3Ø MAT INPUT B(15,11)
```

MAT INPUT

TEST PROGRAM

```
10 REM 'MAT INPUT' TEST PROGRAM
20 DIM A(3,4)
30 PRINT "ENTER 12 NUMBERS (TYPE A COMMA BETWEEN EACH NUMBER)"
40 MAT INPUT A
50 FOR I= 1 TO 3
60 FOR J=1 TO 4
70 PRINT A(I,J);
80 NEXT J
90 PRINT
100 NEXT I
110 PRINT "THE MAT INPUT STATEMENT PASSED THE TEST"
120 PRINT "IF THE INPUT VALUES ARE PRINTED"
130 PRINT "IN A MATRIX HAVING THREE ROWS OF FOUR COLUMNS."
999 END
```

SAMPLE RUN *(typical)*

```
ENTER 12 NUMBERS (TYPE A COMMA BETWEEN EACH NUMBER)
?1,2,3,4,5,6,7,8,9,10,11,12
  1     2     3     4
  5     6     7     8
  9    10    11    12
THE MAT INPUT STATEMENT PASSED THE TEST
IF THE INPUT VALUES ARE PRINTED
IN A MATRIX HAVING THREE ROWS OF FOUR COLUMNS.
```

IF YOUR COMPUTER DOESN'T HAVE IT

If your computer does not have the MAT INPUT capability, it can be replaced by FOR-NEXT and INPUT statements. Substitute the following lines in the TEST PROGRAM:

```
33 FOR I=1 TO 3
36 FOR J=1 TO 4
40 INPUT A(I,J)
43 NEXT J
46 NEXT I
```

This substitution differs slightly from the MAT INPUT statement in that it **does** require the RETURN or ENTER key to be pressed after each value is typed.

VARIATIONS IN USAGE

None known.

ALSO SEE

MAT PRINT, MAT READ, FOR-NEXT, INPUT, DIM

MAT PRINT is used to print the values stored in specified array elements. The number of elements printed is determined by the DIMensioned value assigned to the array. For more DIMensioning information see DIM.

MAT PRINT

Statement

For example,

```
1∅ DIM A(3)
2∅ MAT PRINT A
```

prints the three element values assigned to the "A" array.

TEST PROGRAM #1

```
1∅ REM 'MAT PRINT' TEST PROGRAM
2∅ DIM A(5)
3∅ FOR X=1 TO 5
4∅ A(X)=X
5∅ NEXT X
6∅ MAT PRINT A
7∅ PRINT "END OF MAT PRINT TEST"
99 END
```

SAMPLE RUN

```
1
2
3
4
5
END OF MAT PRINT TEST
```

Most computers with MAT PRINT capability allow a comma following the MAT PRINT statement, to print the array values in pre-established horizontal zones. (See Comma.) To test this feature in the TEST PROGRAM, change line 6∅ to:

```
6∅ MAT PRINT A,
```

and RUN.

SAMPLE RUN

```
1              2              3              4              5
END OF MAT PRINT TEST
```

162

MAT PRINT

A semicolon (;) following the MAT PRINT statement may be used to print the array values in a horizontal line with spaces inserted for its + or − sign. (See Semicolon.) To test this feature, change line 6Ø to:

```
6Ø MAT PRINT A;
```

and RUN.

SAMPLE RUN

```
1   2   3   4   5
END OF MAT PRINT TEST
```

The MAT PRINT statement can print the contents of arrays having more than one dimension. The number of elements in the first dimension specifies the number of rows to be printed while the number of elements in the second column determines the number of columns.

For example,

```
DIM A(2,3)
MAT PRINT A
```

The DIM statement establishes the A variable as being capable of storing values in a two dimensioned array which is printed by the MAT PRINT statement as a matrix having 2 rows and 3 columns.

The printing of more than one array can be ordered in one MAT PRINT statement by inserting a comma or semicolon between each array specified. The results are shown by the following TEST PROGRAM.

TEST PROGRAM #2

```
1Ø REM 'MAT PRINT' WITH MULTIPLE ARRAY VARIABLES TEST PROGRAM
2Ø DIM A(3),B(3,5)
3Ø    FOR I=1 TO 3
4Ø      FOR J=1 TO 5
5Ø        B(I,J)=J
6Ø      NEXT J
7Ø    A(I)=I
8Ø    NEXT I
9Ø MAT PRINT A;B,
1ØØ PRINT "END OF MAT PRINT TEST"
999 END
```

MAT PRINT

SAMPLE RUN

```
1    2    3
1              2              3              4              5
1              2              3              4              5
1              2              3              4              5
END OF MAT PRINT TEST
```

IF YOUR COMPUTER DOESN'T HAVE IT

If your computer does not have the MAT PRINT capability, it can be simulated with
FOR-NEXT and PRINT statements. Substitute the following lines in TEST PROGRAM
#2:

```
81    FOR X=1 TO 5
82    PRINT A(X),
84    NEXT X
86 PRINT
88    FOR I=1 TO 3
90      FOR J=1 TO 5
92        PRINT B(I,J);
94      NEXT J
96    NEXT I
98 PRINT
```

ALSO SEE

MAT INPUT, MAT READ, ,(comma), ;(semicolon), FOR-NEXT, PRINT, DIM

MAT READ is used to read values from a DATA statement and assign them to an array. The DIM statement establishes the array size.

For example,

```
10 DIM A(5)
20 MAT READ A
```

Statement

The DIM statement allows variable A to use 5 array elements named A(1) to A(5). For more information see DIM.

The MAT READ statement assigns values to each column in the first row of two-dimensional-array variables before assigning values to the following row.

For example,

```
10 DIM A(2,3)
20 MAT READ A
```

The computer reads six values from the DATA statement and assigns them to array variables elements A(1,1), A(1,2), and A(1,3) before A(2,1), A(2,2), and A(2,3).

TEST PROGRAM

```
10 REM 'MAT READ' TEST PROGRAM
20 DIM A(3,4)
30 MAT READ A
40 FOR I=1 TO 3
50 FOR J=1 TO 4
60 PRINT A(I,J);
70 NEXT J
80 PRINT
90 NEXT I
100 DATA 1,2,3,4,5,6,7,8,9,10,11,12
110 PRINT "THE MAT READ STATEMENT PASSED THE TEST"
120 PRINT "IF A MATRIX IS PRINTED HAVING 3 ROWS OF 4 COLUMNS"
999 END
```

SAMPLE RUN

```
1    2    3    4
5    6    7    8
9    10   11   12
THE MAT READ STATEMENT PASSED THE TEST
IF A MATRIX IS PRINTED HAVING 3 ROWS OF 4 COLUMNS
```

MAT READ

Most MAT READ handling computers allow the array size to be established with the MAT READ statement if not more than 10 array elements are used. If more than 10 elements are required in an array, it must be DIMensioned.

For example,

```
110 DIM B(20,20)
120 MAT READ A(3,5)
130 MAT READ B(15,11)
```

To test this feature in your computer, omit line 20 in the TEST PROGRAM and change line 30 TO:

```
30 MAT READ A(3,4)
```

If your computer accepts this feature, the SAMPLE RUN should not change.

IF YOUR COMPUTER DOESN'T HAVE IT

If your computer does not have the MAT READ capability, it can be replaced by FOR-NEXT and READ statements.

Substitute the following lines in the TEST PROGRAM:

```
23 FOR I=1 TO 3
26 FOR J=1 TO 4
30 READ A(I,J)
33 NEXT J
36 NEXT I
```

VARIATIONS IN USAGE

None known.

ALSO SEE

MAT PRINT, MAT INPUT, READ, DATA, DIM, FOR-NEXT

MEM is used with the Print statement to display the amount of unused bytes of MEMory remaining in the computer. MEM can also be used as a program statement.

**Command
Statement**

TEST PROGRAM

```
10 REM 'MEM' TEST PROGRAM
20 PRINT MEM; "BYTES OF MEMORY ARE REMAINING"
99 END
```

SAMPLE RUN

```
13504 BYTES OF MEMORY REMAINING
```

(The amount of memory available will of course depend on the size of your computer.)

VARIATIONS IN USAGE

None known.

ALSO SEE

FRE, FREE(∅), M.

MID(string,n1,n2) is used in the Harris BASIC-V and the DEC BASIC-PLUS-2 to isolate a specific number (n2) of string characters that are (n1) characters from the left-most character in the string.

For example, **PRINT MID("COMPUTER",4,3)** prints the letters PUT, which are the 3 MIDdle characters starting with the fourth string character from the left.

For more information see MID$.

Function

TEST PROGRAM

```
1Ø REM 'MID' TEST PROGRAM
2Ø A$="CONTESTANT"
3Ø PRINT "'MID' PASSED THE ";
4Ø PRINT MID(A$,4,4)
99 END
```

SAMPLE RUN

```
'MID' PASSED THE TEST
```

VARIATIONS IN USAGE

None known.

ALSO SEE

MID$

The MID$(string,nl,n2) function is used to isolate a specific number (n2) of string characters that are (nl) characters from the left-most character in the string.

For example, **PRINT MID$("COMPUTER",4,3)** prints the letters PUT, which are 3 MIDdle characters starting with the fourth string character from the left.

Function

The string must be enclosed in quotes or assigned to a string variable. The number of characters and the starting position can be expressed as variables, numbers or arithmetic operations. A comma must separate each element in the MID$ function.

If the value of n1 or n2 is a decimal, the computer automatically converts to the integer value.

TEST PROGRAM

```
1Ø REM 'MID$' TEST PROGRAM
2Ø A$="CONTESTANT"
3Ø B$=MID$(A$,4,4)
4Ø PRINT MID$("ATHENA",2,3)" 'MID$' FUNCTION PASSED THE ";B$
99 END
```

SAMPLE RUN

```
THE 'MID$' FUNCTION PASSED THE TEST
```

VARIATIONS IN USAGE

None known.

ALSO SEE

MID, PRINT, RIGHT$, LEFT$, CHR$, SPACE$, STR$, STRING$, INKEY$

X MOD Y is used in some computers (e.g. the H.P. 3000, COMPAL, Harris Computer Systems, and Apple Computer) to compute the arithmetic remainder (MODulo) when the value X is divided by the value Y.

Function

For example, **PRINT 8 MOD 5** prints the number 3, which is the remainder of 8 divided by 5.

A few computers automatically integer the MODule value.

For example, **PRINT 1Ø.5 MOD 4** may print the number 2 (the integer value of the 2.5 remainder).

TEST PROGRAM

```
1Ø REM 'MOD' TEST PROGRAM
2Ø A = 13 MOD 5
3Ø IF A = 3 THEN 6Ø
4Ø PRINT "THE MOD FUNCTION PASSED THE TEST"
5Ø GOTO 99
6Ø PRINT "THE MOD FUNCTION PASSED THE TEST"
99 END
```

SAMPLE RUN

```
THE MOD FUNCTION PASSED THE TEST
```

IF YOUR COMPUTER DOESN'T HAVE IT

MOD is handy but by no means indispensable. Here, step-by-step, is a way around it.

```
2Ø A = 13/5
22 A = A—INT(A)+.ØØ1
24 A = INT(A*5)
```

A more general form of the equation is

```
2Ø A = INT(Y*(X/Y—INT(X/Y))+.ØØ1)
```

Substitute 13 for X and 5 for Y and try it in the TEST PROGRAM.

MOD

VARIATIONS IN USAGE

A few computers (e.g. the Harris BASIC-V) use MOD(X,Y) to compute the X MODulo Y value.

ALSO SEE

INT, FIX

N. is used in the TRS-80 Level I and other variations of Palo Alto Tiny BASIC as an abbreviation for the NEW command and the NEXT statement.

The interpreter recognizes N. as NEW when it is used in the command mode, and as NEXT when it is used as a program statement following the FOR statement.

This program uses N. as the command NEW. For more information see NEW.

**Command
Statement**

TEST PROGRAM

```
1Ø REM 'N. (NEW)' TEST PROGRAM
2Ø PRINT "HELLO THERE"
99 END
```

SAMPLE RUN

LIST the program to ensure it has been entered as shown. Type N. to erase the test program, then type LIST again to be certain the program has been "erased".

This next program uses N. as the statement NEXT. For more information see NEXT.

TEST PROGRAM

```
1Ø REM 'N. (NEXT)' TEST PROGRAM
2Ø FOR X=1 TO 5
3Ø PRINT X;
4Ø N. X
5Ø PRINT " 'N.' PASSED THE TEST"
99 END
```

SAMPLE RUN

```
1  2  3  4  5  'N.' PASSED THE TEST
```

VARIATIONS IN USAGE

None other known.

ALSO SEE

NEW, NEXT, NEX, NE

NE is used in a few computers (e.g. the T.I. 990) as an abbreviation for the NEW command and the "not-equal" (< >) relational operator. It is recognized as NEW when used in the command mode, and as < > when used as a program statement.

Command
Operator

This program uses NE as the command NEW. For more information see NEW.

TEST PROGRAM

```
10 REM 'NE (NEW)' TEST PROGRAM
20 PRINT "HELLO THERE"
99 END
```

SAMPLE RUN

LIST the program to ensure it has been entered as shown. Type NE to erase the TEST PROGRAM, then type LIST again to be certain the program has been "erased".

This next program uses NE as the "not-equal" relational operator. For more information see < >.

TEST PROGRAM

```
10 REM 'NE ( < >)' TEST PROGRAM
20 A=10
30 IF A NE 20 THEN 60
40 PRINT "THE NE OPERATOR FAILED THE TEST"
50 GOTO 99
60 PRINT "THE NE OPERATOR PASSED THE TEST"
99 END
```

SAMPLE RUN

```
THE NE OPERATOR PASSED THE TEST
```

VARIATIONS IN USAGE

None other known.

ALSO SEE

NEW, N., < >, ><

The NEW command erases the BASIC program(s) stored in memory. However, it does not erase the interpreter itself. NEW is normally used when a new program is to be entered into the computer but the existing program is to be deleted.

NEW

Command

TEST PROGRAM

```
1Ø REM 'NEW' COMMAND TEST PROGRAM
2Ø PRINT "HELLO THERE."
99 END
```

SAMPLE RUN

LIST the program to be sure it has been entered as shown. Check the remaining memory space with the PRINT MEMory command (or PRINT FRE(Ø), or other appropriate command).

Type NEW to erase the test program, then test for memory space again. There should be a corresponding increase in available memory.

To be certain the program has been "erased", double-check by typing LIST.

Some computers use the commands SCRATCH or UNSAVE instead.

VARIATIONS IN USAGE

None known.

NEX is used in the PDP-8E as an abbreviation for the NEXT statement.

For more information see NEXT.

Statement

TEST PROGRAM

```
1Ø REM 'NEX' TEST PROGRAM
2Ø FOR X=1 TO 5
3Ø PRINT X;
4Ø NEX X
5Ø PRINT "'NEX' PASSED THE TEST"
99 END
```

SAMPLE RUN

'NEX' PASSED THE TEST

VARIATIONS IN USAGE

None known.

ALSO SEE

NEXT, N.

The NEXT statement is used to return program execution to the preceding FOR statement which uses the same variable. When the range of the FOR statement is exceeded, the computer continues program execution at the line following the NEXT statement.

For example:

Statement

```
1Ø FOR X=1 TO 3
2Ø NEXT X
99 END
```

The fourth time the NEXT statement is executed, the value of X is incremented to 4 which exceeds the FOR statement range of 3 causing the computer to "fall through" to line 99.

TEST PROGRAM

```
1Ø REM 'NEXT' TEST PROGRAM
2Ø FOR X=1 TO 4
3Ø PRINT X,
4Ø NEXT X
5Ø PRINT "THE 'NEXT' STATEMENT PASSED THE TEST."
99 END
```

SAMPLE RUN

```
1               2               3               4
THE 'NEXT' STATEMENT PASSED THE TEST.
```

Because NEXT statements return only to the preceding FOR statement which uses the same variable, it is possible with most computers to use "nested" FOR-NEXT statements. For more information see FOR-NEXT.

TEST PROGRAM

```
1Ø REM TEST PROGRAM WITH NESTED 'NEXT' STATEMENTS
2Ø FOR A=1 TO 3
3Ø FOR B=1 TO 4
4Ø PRINT A;B,
5Ø NEXT B
6Ø NEXT A
7Ø PRINT "THE 'NEXT' STATEMENT PASSED THE TEST WHEN NESTED"
99 END
```

SAMPLE RUN

1 1	1 2	1 3	1 4
2 1	2 2	2 3	2 4
3 1	3 2	3 3	3 4

THE 'NEXT' STATEMENT PASSED THE TEST WHEN NESTED

A few computers allow execution of a NEXT statement which does not contain a variable. In this case, the computer returns to the preceeding FOR statement (regardless of its associated variable) so long as it has not exceeded its stated range.

To test for this feature, run the second TEST PROGRAM after removing the variables A and B from the NEXT statements in line 5∅ and 6∅. The sample run should remain the same.

VARIATIONS IN USAGE

Some computers (e.g. DEC BASIC-PLUS-2) allow NEXT to be implied, *under certain circumstances.* The FOR is written, but not the NEXT.

ALSO SEE

FOR-NEXT, FOR

The NOTRACE command is used by the APPLE II BASIC to disable the trace function (see TRACE). NOTRACE may be used as a program statement to turn the trace off at specified areas in the program.

Command Statement

TEST PROGRAM

```
10 REM 'NOTRACE' TEST PROGRAM
20 TRACE
30 PRINT "EACH LINE SHOULD BE TRACED"
40 NOTRACE
50 PRINT "BY THE 'TRACE' STATEMENT"
60 PRINT "UNTIL TURNED OFF BY THE 'NOTRACE' STATEMENT"
99 END
```

SAMPLE RUN

```
#30 EACH LINE SHOULD BE TRACED
#40 BY THE 'TRACE' STATEMENT
UNTIL TURNED OFF BY THE 'NOTRACE' STATEMENT
```

VARIATIONS IN USAGE

None known.

ALSO SEE

TRACE, TRACE OFF, TROFF, TRACE ON, TRON

The ON ERROR GOTO statement is used to branch to an error subroutine, when a program error is encountered, without stopping program execution. The ON ERROR GOTO statement must appear in the program before an execution error is anticipated. Any error encountered after the ON ERROR GOTO statement causes the computer to execute the line number listed in the ON ERROR GOTO statement.

Statement

TEST PROGRAM

```
10 REM 'ON-ERROR-GOTO' TEST PROGRAM
20 ON ERROR GOTO 100
30 PRINT "ENTER A NUMBER AND IT'S INVERSE WILL BE COMPUTED";
40 INPUT N
50 A=1/N
60 PRINT "THE INVERSE OF";N;"IS";A
70 GOTO 30
100 PRINT "THE INVERSE OF 0 CANNOT BE COMPUTED - TRY AGAIN"
110 RESUME 30
999 END
```

SAMPLE RUN *(using 4 and 0)*

```
ENTER A NUMBER AND ITS INVERSE WILL BE COMPUTED?4
THE INVERSE OF 4 IS .25
ENTER A NUMBER AND ITS INVERSE WILL BE COMPUTED? 0
THE INVERSE OF 0 CANNOT BE COMPUTED - TRY AGAIN
ENTER A NUMBER AND ITS INVERSE WILL BE COMPUTED?
```

(The error here was DIVISION BY ZERO.)

If ON ERROR GOTO 0 is executed during an ON ERROR GOTO subroutine, the error message is printed and program execution stops. Test this feature by adding the follow-in line to the test program:

```
105 ON ERROR GOTO 0
```

A syntax error encountered by some computers causes the line containing the error to be printed by the edit feature after the ON ERROR GOTO statement has been executed and program execution has stopped. The computer is then in the Edit mode. To test this feature change line 50 in the TEST PROGRAM to:

```
50 ILLEGAL LINE
```

The RESUME statement is normally used to return to the main program from an ON ERROR GOTO subroutine.

ON ERROR
GOTO

VARIATIONS IN USAGE

None known.

ALSO SEE

ERROR, RESUME, ERR, ERL

ON-G. is used in the TRS-80 Level I and other variations of Palo Alto Tiny BASIC as an abbreviation for the ON-GOTO statement.

For more information see ON-GOTO.

Statement

TEST PROGRAM

```
10 REM 'ON-G. (ON-GOTO)' TEST PROGRAM
20 X=1
30 ON X G. 60
40 PRINT "'ON-G.' FAILED THE TEST"
50 GOTO 99
60 PRINT "'ON-G.' PASSED THE TEST"
99 END
```

SAMPLE RUN

```
'ON-G.' PASSED THE TEST
```

VARIATIONS IN USAGE

None known.

ALSO SEE

ON-GOTO, ON-GOT

ON-GOSUB is a multiple subroutine branching scheme which incorporates a number of IF-GOSUB tests into a single statement.

For example, **ON X GOSUB 1ØØ,2ØØ,3ØØ** instructs the computer to branch to subroutines starting at lines 1ØØ, 2ØØ or 3ØØ if the integer value of X is 1, 2 or 3 respectively. If INT X is less than 1 or more than 3 the tests in this ON-GOSUB example all fail. In some computers, execution then defaults to the next program line; in other computers, the program "crashes" and an error message is printed.

ON-GOSUB

Statement

TEST PROGRAM

```
1Ø REM 'ON-GOSUB' TEST PROGRAM
2Ø PRINT "ENTER THE NUMBER 1, 2 OR 3";
3Ø INPUT X
4Ø PRINT "THE ON-GOSUB STATEMENT ";
5Ø ON X GOSUB 1ØØ,2ØØ,3ØØ
6Ø GOTO 2Ø
1ØØ REM SUBROUTINE #1
11Ø PRINT "BRANCHED TO SUBROUTINE #1"
12Ø RETURN
2ØØ REM SUBROUTINE #2
21Ø PRINT "BRANCHED TO SUBROUTINE #2"
22Ø RETURN
3ØØ REM SUBROUTINE #3
31Ø PRINT "BRANCHED TO SUBROUTINE #3"
32Ø RETURN
999 END
```

SAMPLE RUN

```
ENTER THE NUMBER 1, 2 OR 3? 1
THE ON-GOSUB STATEMENT BRANCHED TO SUBROUTINE #1
ENTER THE NUMBER 1, 2 OR 3? 2
THE ON-GOSUB STATEMENT BRANCHED TO SUBROUTINE #2
ENTER THE NUMBER 1, 2 OR 3? 3
THE ON-GOSUB STATEMENT BRANCHED TO SUBROUTINE #3
ENTER THE NUMBER 1, 2 OR 3?
```

Use the same TEST PROGRAM and try entering decimal values larger than 1 but smaller than 4.

Try values smaller than 1, then larger than 4.

ON-GOSUB

IF YOUR COMPUTER DOESN'T HAVE IT

If your computer did not pass the ON-GOSUB test, substitute these lines:

```
45 IF X=1 GOSUB 100
50 IF X=2 GOSUB 200
55 IF X=3 GOSUB 300
```

If this subroutine works, the intrinsic INT functions can be duplicated by substituting these lines:

```
45 IF INT(X)=1 GOSUB 100
50 IF INT(X)=2 GOSUB 200
55 IF INT(X)=3 GOSUB 300
```

For other tricks involving the ON-GOSUB statement, see ON-GOTO.

VARIATIONS IN USAGE

None known.

ALSO SEE

ON-GOTO, ON-ERROR-GOTO, ON-GOT, ON-G.

ON-GOT is used in the PDP-8E as an abbreviation for the ON-GOTO statement.

For more information see ON-GOTO.

Statement

TEST PROGRAM

```
1Ø REM 'ON-GOT' TEST PROGRAM
2Ø X=1
3Ø ON X GOT 6Ø
4Ø PRINT "'ON-GOT' FAILED THE TEST"
5Ø GOTO 99
6Ø PRINT "'ON-GOT' PASSED THE TEST"
99 END
```

SAMPLE RUN

```
'ON-GOT' PASSED THE TEST
```

VARIATIONS IN USAGE

None known.

ALSO SEE

ON-GOTO, ON-G.

ON-GOTO is a multiple branching scheme which incorporates a number of IF-THEN tests into a single statement. For example, **ON X GOTO 1ØØ,2ØØ,3ØØ** instructs the computer to branch to lines 1ØØ, 2ØØ, or 3ØØ if the value of X is 1, 2, or 3 respectively. If X is less than 1 or more than 3.999 the tests in this ON-GOTO example all fail and execution defaults to the next program line.

ON-GOTO

A N S I

Statement

The integer value of X cannot exceed the number of possible branches in the statement. If the value of X is a decimal, the computer automatically finds its integer value and selects the appropriate branching line number.

TEST PROGRAM

```
1Ø REM 'ON(X)GOTO' TEST PROGRAM
2Ø PRINT "ENTER THE NUMBER 1, 2 OR 3"
3Ø INPUT X
4Ø PRINT "THE ON-GOTO STATEMENT";
5Ø ON X GOTO 1ØØ,2ØØ,3ØØ
6Ø PRINT "FAILED THE TEST"
7Ø GOTO 999
1ØØ PRINT "BRANCHED TO LINE 1ØØ"
11Ø GOTO 2Ø
2ØØ PRINT "BRANCHED TO LINE 2ØØ"
21Ø GOTO 2Ø
3ØØ PRINT "BRANCHED TO LINE 3ØØ"
31Ø GOTO 2Ø
999 END
```

SAMPLE RUN *(using 1, 2 and then 3)*

```
ENTER THE NUMBER 1, 2 OR 3
? 1
THE ON-GOTO STATEMENT BRANCHED TO LINE 1ØØ
ENTER THE NUMBER 1, 2 OR 3
? 2
THE ON-GOTO STATEMENT BRANCHED TO LINE 2ØØ
? 3
THE ON-GOTO STATEMENT BRANCHED TO LINE 3ØØ
ENTER THE NUMBER 1, 2 OR 3
?
```

Using the same TEST PROGRAM, try values smaller than 1, then larger than 3.999.

ON-GOTO

If the computer did not pass the ON-GOTO test, substitute these lines:

```
45 IF X=1 THEN 100
50 IF X=2 THEN 200
55 IF X=3 THEN 300
```

If this substitution works, the intrinsic INT functions can be duplicated by substituting these lines.

```
45 IF INT(X)=1 THEN 100
50 IF INT(X)=2 THEN 200
55 IF INT(X)=3 THEN 300
```

A TRICK

Errors might occur in prior rounding of the value X producing a value slightly lower than the expected integer value. The ON-GOTO statement can be protected from this shortcoming by slightly increasing the value X. For example:

```
ON X+.1 GOTO 100
```

If the value of X in this case had been rounded down to 1.99 instead of the expected value of 2.0, adding .1 puts X above 2 (2.09), which is then rounded down to the desired 2.0 by the intrinsic integer function. If not, no harm is done.

SHIFTING THE BASE

When the value of X is not 1, 2 or 3, an equation can take its place in order to make ON-GOTO usable. For example:

```
ON X—50 GOTO 100, 200, 300
```

branches to lines 100, 200 or 300 when the value of X is 51, 52 or 53 respectively.

VARIATIONS IN USAGE

Different interpreters may have a limit to the number of branching options (3 were used only for an example).

ALSO SEE

ON-GOSUB, ON-ERROR, ON-GOT, ON-G.

OPTION is used in the Harris BASIC-V with the BASE statement to define the BASE (lowest) variable array element as any integer value from ∅ to 1∅.

A
N
S
I

Statement

For example,

```
1∅ OPTION BASE=5
2∅ DIM A(1∅)
```

The OPTION BASE statement defines this array as having 6 elements [A(5) to A(1∅)].

If the OPTION BASE value is not specified, the computer assumes the BASE value to be ∅.

For more information see BASE.

TEST PROGRAM

```
1∅ REM 'OPTION' TEST PROGRAM
2∅ OPTION BASE=3
3∅ DIM A(5)
4∅ FOR X=3 TO 5
5∅ A(X)=X
6∅ NEXT X
7∅ OPTION BASE=∅
8∅ FOR X=∅ TO 2
9∅ A(X)=X
1∅∅ NEXT X
11∅ FOR X=∅ TO 5
12∅ PRINT A(X);
13∅ NEXT X
14∅ PRINT "THE OPTION STATEMENT DID NOT CRASH"
999 END
```

SAMPLE RUN

```
∅   1   2   3   4   5 THE OPTION STATEMENT DID NOT CRASH
```

VARIATIONS IN USAGE

ANSI BASIC uses OPTION BASE values ∅ and 1, and an equal sign is not required following the word BASE.

The OUT statement is used to send a number (byte value) to a specified computer OUTput port.

OUT

Statement

The OUT statement format is OUT (port,byte).

The byte and port values must be positive integers or variables between Ø and 255. For example: OUT 255,4 sends the binary equivalent of 4 (decimal) to port number 255.

Press a PLAY, REWIND or FAST-FORWARD button on the cassette recorder and try this program.

TEST PROGRAM *(Configured for TRS-80 Level II)*

```
1Ø REM 'OUT' TEST PROGRAM
2Ø PRINT "ENTER '4' TO TURN ON THE CASSETTE RECORDER MOTOR"
3Ø INPUT X
4Ø OUT 255,X
5Ø PRINT "ENTER 'Ø' TO TURN THE MOTOR OFF"
6Ø INPUT X
7Ø OUT 255,X
99 END
```

SAMPLE RUN

```
ENTER '4' TO TURN ON THE CASSETTE RECORDER MOTOR
? 4
ENTER 'Ø' TO TURN THE MOTOR OFF
? Ø
```

If the cassette recorder motor did not turn on, try this program to find which port and byte numbers work for your computer.

TEST PROGRAM

```
1Ø REM 'OUT' SEARCH PROGRAM
2Ø FOR P=Ø TO 255
3Ø FOR B=Ø TO 255
4Ø PRINT "PORT#";P,
5Ø PRINT "BYTE #";B
6Ø OUT P,B
7Ø NEXT B
8Ø NEXT P
99 END
```

VARIATIONS IN USAGE

None known.

ALSO SEE

INP, PIN, PEEK, POKE

P. is used in the TRS-80 Level I and other variations of Palo Alto Tiny BASIC as an abbreviation for the PRINT statement.

For more details see PRINT.

Statement

TEST PROGRAM

```
1Ø REM 'P.' TEST PROGRAM
2Ø P. "'P.' PASSED THE TEST"
99 END
```

SAMPLE RUN

```
'P.' PASSED THE TEST
```

VARIATIONS IN USAGE

None known.

ALSO SEE

PRINT, PRI, ?, #

P.A. is used in the TRS-80 Level I as an abbreviation for the graphics PRINT AT statement.

For more information see PRINT and AT.

P.A.

Statement

TEST PROGRAM

```
1Ø REM 'P.A. (PRINT AT)' TEST PROGRAM
2Ø P.A.128,"2. IF THIS LINE IS PRINTED AFTER LINE 1."
3Ø P.A.Ø,"1.  THE 'P.A.' STATEMENT PASSED THE TEST."
4Ø GOTO 4Ø
99 END
```

SAMPLE RUN

```
1. THE 'P.A.' STATEMENT PASSED THE TEST
2. IF THIS LINE IS PRINTED AFTER LINE 1.
```

VARIATIONS IN USAGE

None known.

ALSO SEE

PRINT AT, PRINT, AT, @, TAB

PDL is a special function used in APPLE II BASIC to indicate the settings of two game control units. The control units are identified as PDL(∅) and PDL(1). (PDL is an abbreviation for Paddle and refer to control game "paddles".)

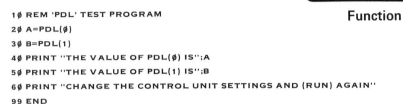

Function

TEST PROGRAM

```
1∅ REM 'PDL' TEST PROGRAM
2∅ A=PDL(∅)
3∅ B=PDL(1)
4∅ PRINT "THE VALUE OF PDL(∅) IS";A
5∅ PRINT "THE VALUE OF PDL(1) IS";B
6∅ PRINT "CHANGE THE CONTROL UNIT SETTINGS AND (RUN) AGAIN"
99 END
```

SAMPLE RUN *(typical)*

```
THE VALUE OF PDL(∅) IS 13
THE VALUE OF PDL(1) IS 146
CHANGE THE CONTROL UNIT SETTINGS AND (RUN) AGAIN
```

VARIATIONS IN USAGE

None known.

ALSO SEE

GR, PLOT, COLOR

PEEK is used to read the contents of a specified address in the computer's memory.

For example, `X=PEEK 18370` assigns the numeric value stored in memory address 18370 to the variable X.

Statement

The PEEK statement reports the contents of a memory address as a number between 0 and 255 (the range of values that can be held in an 8-bit memory cell). PEEK can be used with the POKE statement to read what POKE has POKEd into memory. The highest number address that can be PEEKed of course depends on the computer's memory size.

Check your computer's manual before executing this TEST PROGRAM to determine that memory addresses 18368 to 18380 are reserved as free memory. This avoids POKing data into memory addresses reserved for normal computer operation. If addresses 18368 to 18380 are not reserved as free memory in your computer, then select a group of 12 consecutive free memory addresses and change lines 20 and 60 in the TEST PROGRAM accordingly.

TEST PROGRAM *(Configured for TRS-80 Level II)*

```
10 REM 'PEEK' TEST PROGRAM
20 FOR X=18368 TO 18380
30 READ Y
40 POKE X,Y
50 NEXT X
60 FOR X=18368 TO 18380
70 Y=PEEK(X)
80 PRINT CHR$(Y);
90 NEXT X
100 DATA 84,69,83,84,128,67,79,77,80,76,69,84,69
999 END
```

SAMPLE RUN

TEST COMPLETE

The PEEK and POKE statements are also used with the USR(X) statement to run machine language subroutines.

VARIATIONS IN USAGE

None known.

ALSO SEE

POKE, USR(X), SYSTEM, EXAM, FETCH

PI is used to represent the value of π (3.14159265).

TEST PROGRAM

Function

```
10 REM 'PI' TEST PROGRAM
20 R=6
30 C=2*PI*R
40 PRINT "THE CIRCUMFERENCE OF A CIRCLE"
50 PRINT "WITH A RADIUS OF 6 FEET IS";C;"FEET"
99 END
```

SAMPLE RUN

```
THE CIRCUMFERENCE OF A CIRCLE
WITH A RADIUS OF 6 FEET IS 37.6991 FEET
```

IF YOUR COMPUTER DOESN'T HAVE IT

If your computer does not have the PI capability, substitute the value 3.14159265 for it.

VARIATIONS IN USAGE

None known.

PIN is used by a few interpreters (e.g. Heath Benton Harbor BASIC) to read the decimal value of a byte of information at a specified computer port. The byte value can be any positive integer from ∅ to 255.

For example, **PRINT PIN(X)** prints the decimal value of the byte at port X.

Function

TEST PROGRAM

```
10 REM 'PIN' TEST PROGRAM
20 FOR X=∅ TO 255
30 PRINT "THE DECIMAL VALUE OF THE BYTE AT PORT#";X;IS";INP(X)
40 NEXT X
99 END
```

SAMPLE RUN *(Typical)*

```
THE DECIMAL VALUE OF THE BYTE AT PORT# ∅ IS 255




THE DECIMAL VALUE OF THE BYTE AT PORT# 225 IS 127
```

ANOTHER WORD FOR PIN

See INP

VARIATIONS IN USAGE

None known.

ALSO SEE

INP, OUT, PEEK, USR, INPUT

PLOT (n1, n2) is used in the APPLE II BASIC as a special feature to "turn on" or "light up" a colored graphics block in a predetermined grid on the screen. The graphics block color is determined by the COLOR statement. (See COLOR)

Statement

The grid block to be lit is specified by the two numbers following the PLOT statement. The first number (n1) specifies the column and the second number (n2) specifies the row.

For example, **PLOT 1Ø,25** instructs the computer to color a graphics block located in the 1Øth column and the 25th row (of the graphics grid).

To "turn off" individual graphics blocks, the color Ø (black) must be selected for each block. Executing the GR statement erases the entire screen (See GR).

The column number (n1) may range from Ø to 39 and the row number from Ø to 47, although only the rows Ø to 39 are within the graphics area. The bottom 8 graphics rows on the screen are reserved for TEXT. Each line of text requires 2 rows, making it possible to place 4 lines of text under the graphics display.

TEST PROGRAM

```
1Ø REM 'PLOT' TEST PROGRAM
2Ø GR
3Ø COLOR = 4
4Ø PLOT Ø,Ø
5Ø PLOT 39,Ø
6Ø PLOT 39,39
7Ø PLOT Ø,39
99 END
```

SAMPLE RUN

If the computer accepted the PLOT statement, a green dot should appear at each corner of the screen.

VARIATIONS IN USAGE

None known.

ALSO SEE

GR, COLOR, TEXT, HLIN-AT, VLIN-AT, SET, RESET, POINT

The POINT statement is used with IF-THEN statements by the TRS-80 as a special feature to indicate whether or not a specific graphics block is "turned on".

The graphics block is specified by the X,Y coordinates enclosed in parentheses following the POINT statement. For Level I a value of 1 is reported back when the block is lit (level II gives back -1), and Ø when the block is not lit.

POINT

Statement

TEST PROGRAM

```
1Ø REM 'POINT' TEST PROGRAM
2Ø CLS
3Ø FOR X=2Ø TO 3Ø STEP 2
4Ø SET(X,8)
5Ø NEXT X
6Ø PRINT "POINT PASSED THE TEST IF NUMBERS 1Ø1Ø1Ø1Ø1Ø1 APPEAR"
7Ø FOR X=2Ø TO 3Ø
8Ø A=Ø
9Ø IF POINT (X,8)=1 THEN A=1
1ØØ PRINT A;
11Ø NEXT X
12Ø GOTO 12Ø
999 END
```

SAMPLE RUN *(Level I)*

To obtain the same results for Level II, change line 9Ø to

```
9Ø IF POINT(X,8)=-1 THEN A=1
```

```
POINT PASSED THE TEST IF NUMBERS 1Ø1Ø1Ø1Ø1Ø1 APPEAR
 1  Ø  1  Ø  1  Ø  1  Ø  1  Ø  1  Ø  1
```

VARIATIONS IN USAGE

None known.

ALSO SEE

SET, RESET, CLS

POKE is used to store integer values from $\emptyset$ to 255 (decimal) in specified memory locations. For example, **POKE 65,1536$\emptyset$** places the ASCII number 65 (which is the letter 'A') in memory address 1536$\emptyset$.

Check your computer's manual before running this test program to determine that memory addresses 1536$\emptyset$ to 16383 are in the computer's CRT memory area, and can be POKEd without erasing memory dedicated to another use.

POKE

Statement

TEST PROGRAM

```
1Ø REM 'POKE' TEST PROGRAM
2Ø REM USES CRT MEMORY ADDRESSES 1536Ø TO 16383
3Ø FOR Y=65 TO 9Ø
4Ø FOR X=1536Ø TO 16383
5Ø POKE X,Y
6Ø NEXT X
7Ø NEXT Y
99 END
```

SAMPLE RUN

The computer passed this POKE test if the screen filled with letters from A to Z.

VARIATIONS IN USAGE

None known.

ALSO SEE

PEEK, FILL, STUFF

PRI is used in the PDP-8E as an abbreviation for the PRINT statement.

For more details see PRINT.

Statement

TEST PROGRAM

```
10 REM 'PRI' TEST PROGRAM
20 PRI "'PRI' PASSED THE TEST"
99 END
```

SAMPLE RUN

```
'PRI' PASSED THE TEST
```

VARIATIONS IN USAGE

None known.

ALSO SEE

PRINT, P.

PRINT has a wide range of uses. The most common is in program statements used to display variable values or whatever may be enclosed in quotes. For example, PRINT X prints the numeric value of the variable X, while PRINT "X" prints the letter X.

Command Statement

Most computers use PRINT both as a command (as you would on a standard calculator), and a program statement.

For example, the **command**, PRINT 4*12/(2+6) prints the answer 6.

TEST PROGRAM #1

```
1Ø REM 'PRINT' TEST PROGRAM
2Ø PRINT "THE PRINT STATEMENT WORKS"
99 END
```

SAMPLE RUN

```
THE PRINT STATEMENT WORKS
```

A comma can be used in a PRINT statement to cause individual items to be printed in pre-established horizontal zones of about 16 spaces wide.

For example, PRINT 1,2,3,4 prints in a format similar to;

```
1               2               3               4
```

For more information see ,(comma).

TEST PROGRAM #2

```
1Ø REM 'PRINT' WITH COMMA TEST PROGRAM
2Ø PRINT "THE COMMA WORKED IN THE PRINT STATEMENT"
3Ø PRINT "IF THESE NUMBERS ARE PRINTED IN 4 ZONES"
4Ø PRINT 1,2,3,4
99 END
```

SAMPLE RUN

```
THE COMMA WORKED IN THE PRINT STATEMENT
IF THESE NUMBERS ARE PRINTED IN 4 ZONES
1               2               3               4
```

PRINT

A semicolon works like a comma, but prints the output values tightly together, instead of in pre-established zones.

Change line 4Ø to read

```
4Ø PRINT 1;2;3;4
```

Run the Test Program once more and note the new spacing.

The semicolon (;) is often used in PRINT statements to join together (concatenize) parts of words or sentences on one line.

For example, **PRINT "H";"I"** prints the word "HI".

For more information see ;(semicolon).

TEST PROGRAM #3

```
1Ø REM 'PRINT' WITH SEMICOLON TEST PROGRAM
2Ø PRINT "IS THIS PRINTED ";
3Ø PRINT "ON ONE LINE?"
99 END
```

SAMPLE RUN

```
IS THIS PRINTED ON ONE LINE?
```

TAB(n) is used with the PRINT statement in a manner similar to the tab key on a typewriter. It inserts (n) spaces before the printed statement as specified by the value enclosed in parentheses. For more information see **TAB**.

The AT function is used with PRINT in the TRS-80 Level I BASIC (the @ operator is used by the TRS-80 Level II) to specify the PRINT statement's starting location. For more information see AT and @.

PRINT USING is used by some computers as a special PRINT feature which allows numbers or strings to be printed USING a specified format.

For example, **PRINT USING "**####.##";12.5** prints the number *****12.5Ø**.

For more information see PRINT USING.

MAT PRINT prints the values stored in array variables.

PRINT

For example,

```
10 DIM A(3)
20 MAT PRINT A
```

will print the values assigned to array variables A(1), A(2), and A(3). For more information see MAT PRINT.

PRINT# is used in the TRS-80 Level I BASIC to store data on cassette tape. To store more than one value with one PRINT# statement, the following format is used;

```
PRINT#A;",";B;",";C etc.
```

To test this feature, set the cassette recorder to the Record mode and RUN this program.

TEST PROGRAM #4

```
10 REM 'PRINT#' TEST PROGRAM
20 PRINT "DATA SHOULD BE RECORDING ON CASSETTE TAPE"
30 A$="TEST"
40 PRINT#A$;",";1;",";2;",";3
50 PRINT "PRINT # HAS COMPLETED THE DATA TRANSFER"
99 END
```

SAMPLE RUN

```
DATA SHOULD BE RECORDING ON CASSETTE TAPE
PRINT# HAS COMPLETED THE DATA TRANSFER
```

The TRS-80 Level II BASIC requires -1 following the PRINT# statement for use with a single cassette.

For example, PRINT#-1,A,B,C$ stores on tape the values assigned to variables A, B and C$.

TEST PROGRAM #5

Set the cassette recorder to the Record mode and RUN this program.

```
10 REM 'PRINT#' TEST PROGRAM
20 PRINT "DATA SHOULD BE RECORDING ON CASSETTE TAPE"
30 PRINT#-1,"TEST",1,2,3
40 PRINT "PRINT#-1 HAS COMPLETED THE DATA TRANSFER"
99 END
```

PRINT

SAMPLE RUN

```
DATA SHOULD BE RECORDING ON CASSETTE TAPE
PRINT#-1 HAS COMPLETED THE DATA TRANSFER
```

To verify that the data was stored, rewind the tape, set the recorder to the Play mode and RUN this program.

```
1Ø REM * INPUT DATA FROM CASSETTE *
2Ø PRINT "THE COMPUTER SHOULD BE READING DATA FROM CASSETTE"
3Ø INPUT#-1,A$,A,B,C
4Ø PRINT "THE FOLLOWING DATA WAS READ FROM THE CASSETTE"
5Ø PRINT A$,A,B,C
99 END
```

SAMPLE RUN

```
THE COMPUTER SHOULD BE READING DATA FROM CASSETTE
THE FOLLOWING DATA WAS READ FROM THE CASSETTE
TEST            1              2              3
```

PRINT# is used in mini and maxi computers with file handling capability to store data in "files" on an external device such as cassette or disc. Each data file is identified by a number (file name) which can be listed in the PRINT# statement to specify the file in which the data is to be stored. The data can consist of numeric values or string characters.

For example, PRINT#3;A,B,"TESTING" stores the contents of variables A and B and the word "TESTING" in a file named #3. FILE#, INPUT# and READ# are used to assign file names and space for data storage, and to READ the data back out of file storage.

ALSO SEE

TAB, AT, @, PRINT USING, MAT PRINT, #, ,(comma), ;(semicolon)

PRINT AT is used by the TRS-80 Level I BASIC to indicate a PRINT statement's starting location. The AT function value may be a number, numeric variable, or mathematical operation. A comma or semi-colon must be inserted between the AT value and the string.

PRINT AT

Statement

For example:

```
1Ø PRINT AT 42Ø, "HELLO"
2Ø PRINT AT (42Ø);"HELLO"
```

Both lines print the word "HELLO" AT location 42Ø. The parentheses are optional.

For more information see AT.

TEST PROGRAM

```
1Ø REM 'PRINT AT' TEST PROGRAM
2Ø PRINT AT 128,"2. IF THIS LINE IS PRINTED AFTER LINE 1."
3Ø PRINT AT Ø,"1. THE 'PRINT AT' STATEMENT PASSED THE TEST"
4Ø GOTO 4Ø
99 END
```

SAMPLE RUN

```
1. THE 'PRINT AT' STATEMENT PASSED THE TEST
2. IF THIS LINE IS PRINTED AFTER LINE 1.
```

VARIATIONS IN USAGE

None known.

ALSO SEE

PRINT, AT, @, TAB, P.A.

PRINT USING is used in some computers (e.g. the ADDS BASIC, Sperry/Univac VS/9, H.P. 2000 and those using Microsoft BASIC) as a special PRINT feature which allows numbers or strings to be printed USING a variable format. PRINT USING is by far the most powerful (and complex) PRINT statement available in BASIC, so its many features will be covered here one at a time. Not every feature is part of every computer, but the TEST PROGRAMS will quickly let you identify what yours can do. See your own computer's manual for other possible capabilities.

Statement

The pound sign (#) reserves a position for each digit in a number or numeric variable to the left and right of a decimal point. Zeros are automatically inserted if nothing exists to the right, making it valuable for financial printing. # always prints the decimal point in the same place, making it easier to examine rows of numbers. For more information see #.

TEST PROGRAM #1

```
10 REM 'PRINT USING' TEST PROGRAM
20 PRINT "THE # OPERATOR PASSED THE PRINT USING TEST"
30 PRINT "IF THE FOLLOWING NUMBERS ARE PRINTED"
40 FOR X=1 TO 5
50 READ N
60 PRINT USING "#######.##";N
70 NEXT X
80 DATA 1.2,400,2400000,82450.5,-.25
99 END
```

SAMPLE RUN

```
THE # OPERATOR PASSED THE PRINT USING TEST
IF THE FOLLOWING NUMBERS ARE PRINTED
      1.20
    400.00
2400000.00
  82450.00
     -0.25
```

An asterisk (*) can be printed in all unused spaces to the left of a specified number's decimal point by placing a double asterisk (**) before the #. Its primary purpose is to prevent someone from increasing the size of a check printed by computer.

PRINT USING

For example, **PRINT USING "**#####.##";234.25** will print ****234.25. This feature can be tested by making these changes to the TEST PROGRAM #1.

```
2Ø PRINT "THE ** OPERATOR PASSED THE PRINT USING TEST
6Ø PRINT USING "*********.##";N
```

SAMPLE RUN

```
THE ** OPERATOR PASSED THE PRINT USING TEST
IF THE FOLLOWING NUMBERS ARE PRINTED
*******1.2Ø
*****4ØØ.ØØ
*24ØØØØ.ØØ
***8245Ø.5Ø
******-Ø.25
```

A $ sign can be printed before the number listed in the PRINT USING statement by inserting a double dollar sign ($$) before the # sign.

For example, **PRINT USING "$$###.##";1.25** will print **$1.25**. To test this feature in your computer, make these changes to TEST PROGRAM #1:

```
2Ø PRINT "THE $$ OPERATOR PASSED THE PRINT USING TEST
6Ø PRINT USING "$$######.##";N
```

SAMPLE RUN

```
THE $$ OPERATOR PASSED THE PRINT USING TEST
IF THE FOLLOWING NUMBERS ARE PRINTED
       $1.2Ø
     $4ØØ.ØØ
  $24ØØØØ.ØØ
    $8245Ø.5Ø
      -$Ø.25
```

It is possible to insert a comma between every third number to the left of the decimal point by using a comma between one or more left # signs. The position of the comma in the PRINT USING statement does **not** effect the position of the printed comma.

For example,

```
PRINT USING "#,####.##";12ØØØ
PRINT USING "####,#.##";12ØØØ
PRINT USING "#,##,#,#.##";12ØØØ
```

will each print the number 12,ØØØ.ØØ.

PRINT USING

To test this feature, make these changes to TEST PROGRAM #1.

```
20 PRINT "PRINT USING 'COMMA' PASSED THE TEST"
60 PRINT USING "#,#######.##";N
```

SAMPLE RUN

```
PRINT USING 'COMMA' PASSED THE TEST
IF THE FOLLOWING NUMBERS ARE PRINTED
            1.20
          400.00
    2,400,000.00
        82,450.50
           -0.25
```

A + sign placed to the **left** of the #'s causes a + sign to be printed **before** each positive number and a − sign before each negative number. If a + sign is placed to the **right** of the #'s, the computer prints a − sign to the **right** of all negative numbers, and a space is inserted to the right of all positive numbers.

For example,

```
PRINT USING "+####";123
PRINT USING "####+";-123
```

will print the numbers

```
            +123
and         123-
```

To test this feature, make these changes to TEST PROGRAM #1

```
20 PRINT "THE + OPERATOR PASSED THE PRINT USING TEST"
60 PRINT USING "+#######.##";N
```

SAMPLE RUN

```
THE + OPERATOR PASSED THE PRINT USING TEST
IF THE FOLLOWING NUMBERS ARE PRINTED
           +1.20
         +400.00
     +2400000.00
       +82450.50
           -0.25
```

Four exponentiation signs (∧ ∧ ∧ ∧) can be used following a # to print numbers expressed in exponential or scientific notation. A few computers (e.g. the TRS-80 Level II) use ↑↑↑↑ instead.

PRINT USING

For example, PRINT USING "## ∧ ∧ ∧ ∧ ";1∅∅ prints the number 1E+∅2

TEST PROGRAM #2

```
1∅ REM 'PRINT USING EXPONENTIATION' TEST PROGRAM
2∅ PRINT "PRINT USING ' ∧ ∧ ∧ ∧ ' PASSED THE TEST"
3∅ PRINT "IF THE NUMBER";123456
4∅ PRINT "IS PRINTED USING SCIENTIFIC NOTATION"
5∅ PRINT USING "## ∧ ∧ ∧ ∧ ";123456
99 END
```

SAMPLE RUN

```
PRINT USING ' ∧ ∧ ∧ ∧ ' PASSED THE TEST
IF THE NUMBER 123456
IS PRINTED USING SCIENTIFIC NOTATION
 1E+∅5
```

Some computers (e.g. those with variations of the Microsoft BASIC) use the ! (enclosed in quotes) to print only the left-most character in a string or string variable listed in a PRINT USING statement.

For example, PRINT USING "!";"WORD" prints the letter "W".

TEST PROGRAM #3

```
1∅ REM 'PRINT USING !' TEST PROGRAM
2∅ PRINT "ENTER A SAMPLE WORD";
3∅ INPUT A$
4∅ PRINT "THE PRINT USING STATEMENT AND THE ! OPERATOR"
5∅ PRINT "PASSED THE TEST IF THE FIRST LETTER IN ";A$;" IS ";
6∅ PRINT USING "!";A$
99 END
```

SAMPLE RUN *(using HANDBOOK)*

```
ENTER A SAMPLE WORD? HANDBOOK
THE PRINT USING STATEMENT AND THE ! OPERATOR
PASSED THE TEST IF THE FIRST LETTER IN HANDBOOK IS H
```

Use of \\ (backslash) permits printing only the left-most characters in strings. The number printed is determined by the number of spaces between the two \ signs. The computer also counts the two \ signs as character positions, therefore, no less than two characters can be specified by \\.

For example, PRINT USING "\ \";"COMPUSOFT" prints the first three letters "COM" because one space is included between the two \ signs (1 space + 2 backslashes = 3 letters). The TRS-80 Level II uses the % sign instead of the \ sign.

PRINT USING

TEST PROGRAM #4

```
10 REM 'PRINT USING \' TEST PROGRAM
20 A$ = "TESTIFIED"
30 PRINT "THE PRINT USING STATEMENT ";
40 PRINT "AND THE \ OPERATOR PASSED THE ";
50 PRINT USING "\   \";A$
99 END
```

SAMPLE RUN

THE PRINT USING STATEMENT AND THE \ OPERATOR PASSED THE TEST

Most computers allow the PRINT USING operators, numbers and strings to be specified as variables.

For example,

```
10 A$="!"
20 B$="ABCD"
30 PRINT USING A$;B$
```

will print the letter "A" which is the left-most character assigned to string variable B$.

Test Program #5 shows how 3 different PRINT formats can be linked together by semi-colons.

TEST PROGRAM #5

```
10 REM 'PRINT USING VARIABLES' TEST PROGRAM
20 A$="**$####.##"
30 B$="\       \"
40 C$="TESTIMONIAL"
50 A=14.95
60 PRINT "THE BASIC HANDBOOK PASSED THE ";
70 PRINT USING A$;A;
80 PRINT USING B$;C$
99 END
```

SAMPLE RUN

THE BASIC HANDBOOK PASSED THE ****$14.95 TEST

The same results can be achieved by putting the format on one line, and on another line the variables to be printed. Delete lines 30 and 80 and change

```
20 A$ = "**$####.##\   \"
```

PRINT USING

Or better yet,

```
2Ø A$ = ''%                                        %****$####.##%     %''
7Ø PRINT USING $A;B$,A,C$
```

(Note that commas can be used instead of semicolons after all but the PRINT USING specifier.)

VARIATIONS IN USAGE

Some computers (e.g. the DEC-10, DEC-17D and the Sperry/Univac VS/9) require that when variables are printed in one line, and the PRINT USING format in another line, the format line must be addressed by number and must start with a colon.

For example,

```
6Ø A = 12.34
7Ø B = 14.95
8Ø C$ = ''MAIN FRAME''
9Ø PRINT USING 1ØØ,A,B,C$
1ØØ :###.##   $$$$.##   /CCCCCCC/
```

will print

```
12.34   $14.95   MAIN FRAME
```

TEST PROGRAM #6

```
1Ø REM 'PRINT USING LINE NUMBER' TEST PROGRAM
2Ø PRINT "THE PRINT USING STATEMENT PASSES THE TEST"
3Ø PRINT "IF THE NUMBER";125.5Ø;"IS PRINTED NEXT"
4Ø PRINT USING 5Ø,125.5
5Ø :###.##
99 END
```

SAMPLE RUN

```
THE PRINT USING STATEMENT PASSES THE TEST
IF THE NUMBER 125.5Ø IS PRINTED NEXT
125.5Ø
```

ALSO SEE

PRINT, #, **, $\wedge$, !, $\uparrow$, +, $-$, %

R. is used in the TRS-80 Level I and other variations of Palo Alto Tiny BASIC as an abbreviation for the RUN command, the RND function, and the graphics RESET statement.

Command Function Statement

The interpreter recognizes R. as RUN when used in the command mode, as RND when followed by a value enclosed in parenthesis [e.g. R. (1Ø)], and as RESET when followed by two values enclosed in parenthesis and separated by a comma [e.g. R.(X,Y)].

This first program uses R. as a RUN command. For more information see RUN.

TEST PROGRAM

```
1Ø REM 'R. (RUN)' TEST PROGRAM
2Ø PRINT "THIS LINE PRINTED COURTESY OF THE R. COMMAND."
99 END
```

SAMPLE RUN

After entering the R. command, the computer should print

THIS LINE PRINTED COURTESY OF THE R. COMMAND.

This program uses R. as a RND function. For more information see RND.

TEST PROGRAM

```
1Ø REM 'R. (RND)' TEST PROGRAM
2Ø N=1Ø
3Ø FOR X=1 TO 4
4Ø PRINT R.(N),
5Ø NEXT X
6Ø PRINT "'R.' PASSED THE TEST"
99 END
```

R.

```
1               7              5              6
'R', PASSED THE TEST
```

This last program uses R. as the graphics RESET statement. For more information see RESET.

TEST PROGRAM

```
10 REM 'R. (RESET)' TEST PROGRAM
20 FOR X=0 TO 127
30 SET(X,1)
40 R.(X,1)
50 NEXT X
60 PRINT "'R.' PASSED THE TEST"
99 END
```

SAMPLE RUN

Will produce a blinking dot moving from left to right across the screen.

VARIATIONS IN USAGE

None other known.

ALSO SEE

RUN, RND, RESET, SET

RAN is used in the PDP-8E as an abbreviation for the RANDOMIZE statement.

For more information see RANDOMIZE.

Statement

TEST PROGRAM

```
1Ø REM 'RAN' TEST PROGRAM
2Ø RAN
3Ø FOR X=1 TO 8
4Ø PRINT RND(Ø),
5Ø NEXT X
99 END
```

SAMPLE RUN *(Typical)*

.34Ø512	.6Ø4461	.48Ø241	.1Ø1441
.4Ø7168	.Ø72483	.659667	.517459

VARIATIONS IN USAGE

None known.

ALSO SEE

RANDOMIZE, RANDOM, RAND, RND

RANDOM is used to "shuffle" or "randomize" a set of numbers (held in the computer) in a random order. These numbers are selected by the RND function.

Placing RANDOM in a program before the RND function causes the generation of a new set of random numbers for the RND function each time the program is run.

RANDOM

Statement

TEST PROGRAM

```
1Ø REM 'RANDOM' TEST PROGRAM
2Ø RANDOM
3Ø FOR X=1 TO 8
4Ø PRINT RND(Ø),
5Ø NEXT X
99 END
```

SAMPLE RUN *(Typical)*

.361529	.913284	.289381	.819987
.999239	.4Ø7567	.458299	.684127

Each time the test program is run, a new set of random numbers should be printed. Be sure you have your own version of RND working before trying to include line 2Ø.

VARIATIONS IN USAGE

None known.

ALSO SEE

RANDOMIZE, RAN, RND, RAND

RANDOMIZE is used to "shuffle" or "reseed" a set of numbers (held in the computer) in a random order. These numbers are held in memory for selection by the RND function.

RANDOMIZE

A
N
S
I

Statement

Placing RANDOMIZE in a program before the RND function causes the generation of a new set of random numbers for the RND function each time the program is run.

TEST PROGRAM

```
1Ø REM 'RANDOMIZE' TEST PROGRAM
2Ø RANDOMIZE
3Ø FOR X=1 TO 8
4Ø PRINT RND,
5Ø NEXT X
99 END
```

SAMPLE RUN *(Typical)*

.25Ø186	.9757Ø7	.775985	.544615
.89Ø564	.227299	.4Ø8976	.771341

Each time the test program is run, a new set of random numbers should be printed. Be sure you have your own version of RND working before trying to include line 2Ø.

VARIATIONS IN USAGE

None known.

ALSO SEE

RANDOM, RAN, RND, RAND

REA is used in the PDP-8E as an abbreviation for the READ statement.

For more details see READ.

Statement

TEST PROGRAM

```
1Ø REM 'REA' TEST PROGRAM
2Ø REA A
3Ø PRINT "'REA' PASSED THE TEST IN LINE";A
4Ø DATA 2Ø
99 END
```

SAMPLE RUN

```
'REA' PASSED THE TEST IN LINE 2Ø
```

VARIATIONS IN USAGE

None known.

ALSO SEE

READ, REA.

REA. is used in the TRS-80 Level I as an abbreviation for the READ statement.

For more information see READ.

Statement

TEST PROGRAM

```
10 REM 'REA.' TEST PROGRAM
20 REA.A
30 PRINT "'REA.' PASSED THE TEST IN LINE";A
40 DATA 20
99 END
```

SAMPLE RUN

```
'REA.' PASSED THE TEST IN LINE 20
```

VARIATIONS IN USAGE

None known.

ALSO SEE

READ, REA, DATA

The READ statement is used to read data from a DATA line and assign that data to a variable.

Each time the READ statement is executed, data is read from a DATA line. The pointer then moves to the next item of data in the DATA line(s) and waits for another READ statement. When the last piece of data has been read from all DATA statements, the data pointer must be reset to the beginning of the DATA list before additional READ statements can be executed. (See RESTORE)

A
N
S
I

Statement

TEST PROGRAM

```
10 REM 'READ' STATEMENT TEST PROGRAM
20 READ A
30 PRINT "THE READ STATEMENT WORKED IN LINE";A
40 DATA 20
99 END
```

SAMPLE RUN

```
THE READ STATEMENT WORKED IN LINE 20
```

Since computers will allow more than one variable to be placed in one READ statement, each variable must be separated by a comma and the number of "reads" must not exceed the number of data items.

TEST PROGRAM

```
10 REM 'MULTIPLE READ' STATEMENT TEST PROGRAM
20 READ A,B,C
30 D=A+B+C
40 PRINT "D =";D
50 PRINT "THE READ STATEMENT PASSED THE TEST IF D = 60"
60 DATA 10,20,30
99 END
```

SAMPLE RUN

```
D = 60
THE READ STATEMENT PASSED THE TEST IF D = 60
```

Most computers will also allow strings to be read from DATA statements. Each time a string is to be read from the DATA statement, it must have a corresponding string variable in a READ statement.

READ

TEST PROGRAM

```
1Ø REM 'READ STRINGS' TEST PROGRAM
2Ø READ D$
3Ø PRINT "THE READ STATEMENT PASSED THE ";D$
4Ø DATA TEST
99 END
```

SAMPLE RUN

```
THE READ STATEMENT PASSED THE TEST
```

Many computers allow both numeric and string data to be read by the same READ
statement and be contained in the same DATA line.

TEST PROGRAM

```
1Ø REM 'MULTIPLE READ' STATEMENT TEST PROGRAM
2Ø READ A,B,C,D$
3Ø D=A+B+C
4Ø PRINT "THE READ STATEMENT PASSED THE TEST IN ";D$;D
5Ø DATA 2,8,1Ø,LINE
99 END
```

SAMPLE RUN

```
THE READ STATEMENT PASSED THE TEST IN LINE 2Ø
```

VARIATIONS IN USAGE

None. The only other way to store and call up data is by inputting it through a keyboard
or from off-line storage on tape, disc, etc.

ALSO SEE

DATA, RESTORE, Comma(,)

The REMark statement is used at the beginning of some program lines to make them serve as a "notebook" or "scratchpad" to hold comments about the program. The REM statement is not executed. Everything on a line beginning with REM is ignored by the computer.

A
N
S
I

Statement

If used in multiple statement lines, those statements preceeding the REM statement will be executed, but everything following a statement beginning with REM is ignored. If the information to be noted requires more than one program line, each such line must begin with REM.

TEST PROGRAM

```
1Ø PRINT "'REM' TEST PROGRAM"
2Ø REM PRINT "REM FAILED THE TEST"
3Ø REM * REM FAILED THE TEST IF LINE 2Ø IS PRINTED*
4Ø PRINT "REM PASSED THE TEST"
99 END
```

SAMPLE RUN

```
'REM' TEST PROGRAM
REM PASSED THE TEST
```

Some computers allow either the REM or REMARK statement, while others accept only one.

VARIATIONS IN USAGE

None known.

ALSO SEE

REMARK, '(apostrophe), !

REMARK is used by some computers as an optional word for REM. Computers that use the REMARK statement may also accept its abbreviation (REM).

For more information see REM.

Statement

TEST PROGRAM

```
10 PRINT "'REMARK' TEST PROGRAM"
20 REMARK PRINT "REMARK FAILED THE TEST"
30 REMARK * REMARK FAILED THE TEST IF LINE 20 IS PRINTED *
40 PRINT "REMARK PASSED THE TEST"
99 END
```

SAMPLE RUN

```
'REMARK' TEST PROGRAM
REMARK PASSED THE TEST
```

VARIATIONS IN USAGE

None known.

ALSO SEE

REM, ' (Apostrophe)

RENUM is used in some computers (e.g. those using versions of Microsoft BASIC) as an abbreviation for the RENUMBER command, which changes program line numbers. For more information see RENUMBER.

RENUM n1,n2,n3 is used to renumber all program lines starting with the original line number n2. Line n2 is assigned line number n1 and the following lines are incremented by the value of n3.

Command

TEST PROGRAM

```
2 REM 'RENUM' TEST PROGRAM
3 X=1
4 PRINT "IF THE PROGRAM LINES ";
5 GOTO 1Ø
6 PRINT "THE RENUM COMMAND ";
7 X=2
8 GOTO 12
1Ø PRINT "ARE RENUMBERED"
12 ON X GOTO 6,14
14 PRINT "PASSED THE TEST."
16 END
```

SAMPLE RUN

Type the command **RENUM 1ØØ,5,5Ø** and RUN.

```
IF THE PROGRAM LINES ARE RENUMBERED
THE RENUM COMMAND PASSED THE TEST.
```

To verify that the program is RENUMbered, LIST the program.

```
2 REM 'RENUM' TEST PROGRAM
3 X=1
4 PRINT "IF THE PROGRAM LINES ";
1ØØ GOTO 3ØØ
15Ø PRINT "THE RENUM COMMMAND ";
2ØØ X=2
25Ø GOTO 35Ø
3ØØ PRINT "ARE RENUMBERED"
35Ø ON X GOTO 15Ø,4ØØ
4ØØ PRINT "PASSED THE TEST."
45Ø END
```

RENUM

If the original line number (n2) is omitted, the computer automatically renumbers each line from the first line to the last. In this case, the computer requires two commas between the values n1 and n3 indicating n2 is omitted. (e.g. RENUM 1∅∅,,5∅.)

Some computers (e.g. DEC-1∅) use the word RESEQUENCE instead of RENUMber.

VARIATIONS IN USAGE

None known.

ALSO SEE

RENUMBER, GOTO, GOSUB, IF-THEN, ON-GOTO, ON-GOSUB, LIST

RENUMBER is used in some computers (e.g. the Cromemco 16K Extended BASIC) to change the program line numbers. The line numbers used in GOTO, GOSUB, IF-THEN, ON-GOTO and ON-GOSUB statements are changed accordingly to maintain the same branching scheme.

If a number is not included in the RENUMBER statement, the computer automatically RENUMBERs each program line starting at line 10, and spacing the lines 10 numbers apart.

Command

TEST PROGRAM

```
2 REM 'RENUMBER' TEST PROGRAM
3 X=1
4 PRINT "IF EACH PROGRAM LINE ";
5 GOTO 10
6 PRINT "THE RENUMBER COMMAND ";
7 X=2
8 GOTO 12
10 PRINT "IS RENUMBERED"
12 ON X GOTO 6,14
14 PRINT "PASSED THE TEST."
16 END
```

RUN, to be sure it works.

Type the command RENUMBER and RUN again.

SAMPLE RUN

```
IF EACH PROGRAM LINE IS RENUMBERED
THE RENUMBER COMMAND PASSED THE TEST.
```

To verify that the program is RENUMBERed, LIST the program. It should appear:

```
10 REM 'RENUMBER' TEST PROGRAM
20 X=1
30 PRINT "IF EACH PROGRAM LINE ";
40 GOTO 80
50 PRINT "THE RENUMBER COMMAND ";
60 X=2
70 GOTO 90
```

```
8Ø PRINT "IS RENUMBERED"
9Ø ON X GOTO 5Ø,1ØØ
1ØØ PRINT "PASSED THE TEST."
11Ø END
```

RENUMBER n is used to renumber each program line starting with line number n and incrementing by 1Ø. To test this feature on the TEST PROGRAM, type RENUMBER 2Ø and LIST the program. It should read:

```
2Ø REM 'RENUMBER' TEST PROGRAM
3Ø X=1
4Ø PRINT "IF EACH PROGRAM LINE ";
5Ø GOTO 9Ø
6Ø PRINT "THE RENUMBER COMMAND ";
7Ø X=2
8Ø GOTO 1ØØ
9Ø PRINT "IS RENUMBERED"
1ØØ ON X GOTO 6Ø,11Ø
11Ø PRINT "PASSED THE TEST."
12Ø END
```

RENUMBER n1,n2 is used to renumber each program line starting with line number n1 and incrementing by the value of n2. To test this feature on the TEST PROGRAM, type RENUMBER 5Ø,2Ø and LIST the program. Now it should read:

```
5Ø REM 'RENUMBER' TEST PROGRAM
7Ø X=1
9Ø PRINT "IF EACH PROGRAM LINE ";
11Ø GOTO 19Ø
13Ø PRINT "THE RENUMBER COMMAND ";
15Ø X=2
17Ø GOTO 21Ø
19Ø PRINT "IS RENUMBERED"
21Ø ON X GOTO 13Ø,23Ø
23Ø PRINT "PASSED THE TEST."
25Ø END
```

RENUMBER n1,n2,n3 is used to renumber each program line starting with the old line number n3. Line number n3 is assigned line number n1, and the remaining line numbers are incremented by the value n2. To test this feature on the last TEST PROGRAM, type RENUMBER 5ØØ,1Ø,9Ø and LIST the program. Does it look like this?

```
5Ø REM 'RENUMBER' TEST PROGRAM
7Ø X=1
5ØØ PRINT "IF EACH PROGRAM LINE ";
```

```
51Ø GOTO 55Ø
52Ø PRINT "THE RENUMBER COMMAND ";
53Ø X=2
54Ø GOTO 56Ø
55Ø PRINT "IS RENUMBERED"
56Ø ON X GOTO 52Ø,57Ø
57Ø PRINT "PASSED THE TEST."
58Ø END
```

RENUMBER n1,n2,n3,n4 is used to renumber the old program lines from line n3 to line n4. Line n3 is assigned line number n1 and those lines following (ending with line n4) are incremented by the value n2. To test this feature on the last TEST PROGRAM, type RENUMBER 6Ø,5,7Ø,51Ø and LIST the program.

```
5Ø REM 'RENUMBER' TEST PROGRAM
6Ø X=1
65 PRINT "IF EACH PROGRAM LINE ";
7Ø GOTO 55Ø
52Ø PRINT "THE RENUMBER COMMAND ";
53Ø X=2
54Ø GOTO 56Ø
55Ø PRINT "IS RENUMBERED"
56Ø ON X GOTO 52Ø,57Ø
57Ø PRINT "PASSED THE TEST."
58Ø END
```

VARIATIONS IN USAGE

None known. [RESEQUENCE is used by some computers (e.g. DEC-1Ø) instead of RENUMBER.]

ALSO SEE

RENUM, REN, GOTO, GOSUB, IF-THEN, ON-GOTO, ON-GOSUB, LIST

RES is used in the PDP-8E as an abbreviation for the RESTORE statement.

For more information see RESTORE.

Statement

TEST PROGRAM

```
10 REM 'RES' TEST PROGRAM
20 FOR X=1 TO 3
30 READ A
40 NEXT X
50 RES
60 READ A
70 IF A=1 THEN 100
80 PRINT "RES FAILED THE TEST"
90 GOTO 999
100 PRINT "RES PASSED THE TEST"
110 DATA 1,2,3,4
999 END
```

SAMPLE RUN

```
RES PASSED THE TEST
```

VARIATIONS IN USAGE

None known.

ALSO SEE

RESTORE, REST., READ, DATA

The RESET statement is used by the TRS-80 Levels I and II as a special feature to "turn off" a graphics block in a predetermined grid on the screen.

RESET

Statement

The block to be "turned off" within the grid is specified by the X,Y coordinates enclosed in parentheses following the RESET statement. For example, RESET (5,8) instructs the computer to turn off a graphics block located in the 5th column and the 8th row of the graphics grid.

To turn on the graphics block, see SET.

TEST PROGRAM

```
1Ø REM 'RESET' TEST PROGRAM
2Ø CLS
3Ø Y=1
4Ø FOR X=1 TO 1ØØ
5Ø SET (X,Y)
6Ø NEXT X
7Ø PRINT
8Ø PRINT "RESET PASSED THE TEST IF THE LINE DISAPPEARS"
9Ø FOR X=1 TO 1ØØ
1ØØ RESET (X,Y)
11Ø NEXT X
999 END
```

SAMPLE RUN

RESET PASSED THE TEST IF THE LINE DISAPPEARS

VARIATIONS IN USAGE

None known.

ALSO SEE

SET, CLS

REST. is used in the TRS-80 Level I as an abbreviation for the RESTORE statement.

For more information see RESTORE.

Statement

TEST PROGRAM

```
1Ø REM 'REST.' TEST PROGRAM
2Ø FOR X=1 TO 3
3Ø READ A
4Ø NEXT X
5Ø REST.
6Ø READ A
7Ø IF A=1 THEN 1ØØ
8Ø PRINT "REST. FAILED THE TEST"
9Ø GOTO 999
1ØØ PRINT "REST. PASSED THE TEST"
11Ø DATA 1,2,3,4
999 END
```

SAMPLE RUN

```
REST. PASSED THE TEST
```

VARIATIONS IN USAGE

None known.

ALSO SEE

RESTORE, RES, READ, DATA

Execution of a RESTORE statement causes the DATA pointer to be "reset" back to the first piece of data in the first DATA line. This enables the computer to use data stored in DATA statements more than once.

RESTORE

A
N
S
I

Statement

TEST PROGRAM

```
1Ø REM 'RESTORE' TEST PROGRAM
2Ø READ X
3Ø IF X=3 THEN 5Ø
4Ø GOTO 2Ø
5Ø RESTORE
6Ø READ X
7Ø IF X=1 THEN 1ØØ
8Ø PRINT "RESTORE FAILED THE TEST"
9Ø GOTO 999
1ØØ PRINT "RESTORE PASSED THE TEST"
11Ø DATA 1,2,3
999 END
```

SAMPLE RUN

```
RESTORE PASSED THE TEST
```

VARIATIONS IN USAGE

Some interpreters will allow resetting only the DATA in a **specific** DATA line by adding that DATA statement line number after a RESTORE statement. See line 1ØØ below.

TEST PROGRAM

```
1Ø REM 'RESTORE (LINE#)' TEST PROGRAM
2Ø READ X
3Ø PRINT X;
4Ø IF X=3 THEN 6Ø
5Ø GOTO 2Ø
6Ø READ X
7Ø PRINT X;
8Ø IF X=6 THEN 1ØØ
9Ø GOTO 6Ø
1ØØ RESTORE 18Ø
11Ø READ X
12Ø IF X=4 THEN 15Ø
```

```
130 PRINT "RESTORE FAILED THE TEST"
140 STOP
150 PRINT "RESTORE PASSED THE TEST"
160 GOTO 999
170 DATA 1,2,3
180 DATA 4,5,6
999 END
```

SAMPLE RUN

```
1  2  3  4  5  6 RESTORE PASSED THE TEST
```

ALSO SEE

DATA, READ

The RESUME statement is used as the last statement in ON-ERROR-GOTO routines, telling the computer to RESUME program execution at a specified line number. The computer does not allow execution of the RESUME statement if it is not preceded by an ON-ERROR-GOTO statement. See ON-ERROR-GOTO for a TEST PROGRAM using RESUME(line number). (Saves space not to duplicate it here.)

RESUME

Statement

RESUME NEXT is used to branch to the line following the error and continues program execution. To test for RESUME NEXT capability in your computer, change line 11∅ in the ON-ERROR-GOTO test program to:

        11∅ RESUME NEXT

SAMPLE RUN (ON-ERROR-GOTO test program using RESUME NEXT) *(using ∅)*

        ENTER A NUMBER AND IT'S INVERSE WILL BE COMPUTED? ∅
        THE INVERSE OF ∅ CANNOT BE COMPUTED - TRY AGAIN
        THE INVERSE OF ∅ IS ∅
        ?

RESUME ∅ and RESUME (without a line number or NEXT) are used to branch to the statement containing the error.

TEST PROGRAM

```
1∅ REM 'RESUME' TEST PROGRAM
2∅ ON ERROR GOTO 1∅∅
3∅ PRINT "ENTER A POSITIVE NUMBER";
4∅ INPUT N
5∅ A=LOG(N)
6∅ PRINT "THE LOG OF";N;"IS";A
7∅ GOTO 3∅
1∅∅ PRINT "A NEGATIVE NUMBER IS NOT ALLOWED"
11∅ N=N*-1
12∅ RESUME ∅
999 END
```

RESUME

SAMPLE RUN *(using 4)*

```
ENTER A POSITIVE NUMBER? -4
A NEGATIVE NUMBER IS NOT ALLOWED
THE LOG OF 4 IS 1.38629
ENTER A POSITIVE NUMBER?
```

To test RESUME (without a line number or NEXT) capability in your computer, change line 120 in the above TEST PROGRAM to:

```
120 RESUME
```

and RUN. The SAMPLE RUN should not change.

VARIATIONS IN USAGE

None known.

ALSO SEE

ON-ERROR-GOTO, ERL, ERR

RET is used in the PDP-8E as an abbreviation for the RETURN statement.

For more information see RETURN.

RET

Statement

TEST PROGRAM

```
10 REM 'RET (RETURN)' TEST PROGRAM
20 PRINT "RET";
30 GOSUB 100
40 PRINT "THE TEST."
50 GOTO 999
100 PRINT " PASSED ";
110 RET
999 END
```

SAMPLE RUN

```
RET PASSED THE TEST.
```

VARIATIONS IN USAGE

None known.

ALSO SEE

RETURN, RET.

RET. is used in the TRS-80 Level I and other variations of Palo Alto Tiny BASIC as an abbreviation for the RETURN statement.

For more information see RETURN.

Statement

TEST PROGRAM

```
10 REM 'RET. (RETURN)' TEST PROGRAM
20 PRINT "RET.";
30 GOSUB 100
40 PRINT "THE TEST."
50 GOTO 999
100 PRINT " PASSED ";
110 RET.
999 END
```

SAMPLE RUN

```
RET. PASSED THE TEST.
```

VARIATIONS IN USAGE

None known.

ALSO SEE

RETURN, RET, GOSUB

The RETURN statement is used in conjunction with the GOSUB statement. It is used as the last statement in a subroutine; it tells the computer to return to the line containing the GOSUB statement and continue program execution from that point.

The computer will not allow execution of the RETURN statement if it was not preceded by a GOSUB statement.

RETURN

A
N
S
I

Statement

TEST PROGRAM

```
10 REM 'RETURN' STATEMENT TEST PROGRAM
20 GOSUB 50
30 PRINT "WAS ACCEPTED."
40 GOTO 99
50 PRINT "THE RETURN STATEMENT ";
60 RETURN
70 PRINT "WAS NOT ACCEPTED."
99 END
```

SAMPLE RUN

```
THE RETURN STATEMENT WAS ACCEPTED.
```

VARIATIONS IN USAGE

None known.

ALSO SEE

GOSUB, ON-GOSUB and IF-GOSUB

The RIGHT(string,n) function is used in some computers (e.g. those using MAX BASIC) to isolate a specific number (n) of string characters, starting from the right most character in the string. For example, **PRINT RIGHT("COMPUSOFT",4)** prints the letters SOFT, which are the right 4 characters in COMPUSOFT, which is a string.

For more information see RIGHT$.

RIGHT

Function

TEST PROGRAM

```
1Ø REM 'RIGHT' TEST PROGRAM
2Ø A$="CONTEST"
3Ø B$=RIGHT(A$,4)
4Ø PRINT "THE 'RIGHT' FUNCTION PASSED THE ";B$
99 END
```

SAMPLE RUN

THE 'RIGHT' FUNCTION PASSED THE TEST

VARIATIONS IN USAGE

None known.

ALSO SEE

RIGHT$

The RIGHT$(string,n) function is used to isolate a specific number (n) of string characters, starting from the right-most character in the string.

For example, **PRINT RIGHT$("COMPUSOFT",4)** prints the letters SOFT, which are the right 4 characters in COMPUSOFT, which is a string.

The string must be enclosed in quotes or assigned to a string variable. The number (n) of characters can be expressed as a variable, number or arithmetic operation. A comma must separate the string from the number.

RIGHT$

Function

If the value of (n) is a decimal, the computer automatically finds its integer value.

TEST PROGRAM

```
10 REM 'RIGHT$' TEST PROGRAM
20 A$="CONTEST"
30 B$=RIGHT$(A$,4)
40 PRINT "THE ";RIGHT$("ALRIGHT",5);"$ FUNCTION PASSED THE ";B$
99 END
```

SAMPLE RUN

```
THE RIGHT$ FUNCTION PASSED THE TEST
```

VARIATIONS IN USAGE

None known.

ALSO SEE

PRINT, LEFT$, MID$, CHR$, SPACE$, STR$, STRING$, INKEY$

RND is used to generate a random number greater than
$\emptyset$ and less than 1.

RND

Function

TEST PROGRAM

```
1Ø REM 'RND' TEST PROGRAM
2Ø FOR X=1 TO 8
3Ø PRINT RND,
4Ø NEXT X
99 END
```

SAMPLE RUN *(Typical)*

.627633	.358479	.137551	.127641
.125Ø54	.8Ø9923	.888Ø76	.787762

RND($\emptyset$) is used by many computers to specify the same operation as RND.

TEST PROGRAM

```
1Ø REM 'RND(Ø)' TEST PROGRAM
2Ø FOR X=1 TO 8
3Ø PRINT RND(Ø),
4Ø NEXT X
99 END
```

SAMPLE RUN *(Typical)*

.862675	.735285	.476Ø59	.55141
.2457Ø8	.242171	.968336	.721Ø14

While RND(n) generates a random number, in some computers RND($\emptyset$) repeats the last
number generated by the random number generator.

RND(n) is used by some computers to create a random number greater than $\emptyset$ and less
than 1 when n is any number greater than zero.

TEST PROGRAM

```
1Ø REM 'RND(Ø) AS A REPEAT' TEST PROGRAM
2Ø PRINT "RND(1)"
3Ø FOR X=1 TO 4
4Ø PRINT RND(1),
5Ø NEXT X
6Ø PRINT "RND(Ø)"
7Ø FOR Y=1 TO 4
8Ø PRINT RND(Ø),
9Ø NEXT Y
99 END
```

RND

SAMPLE RUN *(Typical)*

```
RND(1)
 .592453            .245804            .118263            .961308
RND(0)
 .961308            .961308            .961308            .961308
```

A few computers create a random integer between 1 and the value of n when n is greater than 1 (e.g. TRS-80).

RND(n) automatically integers the value of n.

TEST PROGRAM

```
10 REM 'RND' TEST PROGRAM
20 N=10
30 FOR X=1 TO 4
40 PRINT RND(N),
50 NEXT X
99 END
```

SAMPLE RUN *(Typical)*

```
    8               7               2               9
```

Some computers reset the internal (seed) number and create a random number greater than 0 and less than 1 when the n in RND(n) is negative. See RANDOM or RANDOMIZE for details.

A TRICK

If your computer is one that generates random numbers > 0 and < 1 and you need a random integer number from 0 to 9, then try this trick.

```
PRINT INT(10*RND)
```

A random number from 1 to 10 can be printed with this trick.

```
PRINT INT(10*RND+1)
```

ALSO SEE

RAND, RANDOM, RANDOMIZE

RU is used by some computers (e.g. the T.I. 99Ø) as an abbreviation for the RUN command.

For more information see RUN.

Command

TEST PROGRAM

```
1Ø REM 'RU (RUN)' TEST PROGRAM
2Ø PRINT "THIS LINE COURTESY OF THE RU COMMAND."
99 END
```

SAMPLE RUN

After entering the RU command, the computer should print

THIS LINE COURTESY OF THE RU COMMAND.

VARIATIONS IN USAGE

None known.

ALSO SEE

RUN, R.

The RUN command instructs the computer to execute the program or programs held in memory, starting with the lowest line number. With many computers, a line number may be included after the RUN command to specify a starting line other than the first one (e.g. **RUN 4Ø**).

RUN

Command

TEST PROGRAM

```
1Ø REM 'RUN' TEST PROGRAM
2Ø PRINT "THIS PRINTING STARTED AT LINE 2Ø."
3Ø GOTO 99
4Ø PRINT "THIS PRINTING STARTED AT LINE 4Ø."
99 END
```

SAMPLE RUN

After entering the RUN Command, the computer should display:

```
THIS PRINTING STARTED AT LINE 2Ø.
```

By adding the number 4Ø to the RUN command, RUN4Ø or RUN 4Ø, the computer should start at line 4Ø and print the following message:

```
THIS PRINTING STARTED AT LINE 4Ø.
```

The RUN command is used only at the monitor or command level and is never accepted in program statements. If you want to RUN a program using a program statement, see CHAIN.

ALSO SEE

R., RU, CHAIN

S. is used in the TRS-80 Level I and other variations of Palo Alto Tiny BASIC as an abbreviation for the STEP statement and the graphics SET statement. Most versions of Palo Alto Tiny BASIC (but not the TRS-80 Level I) use S. to abbreviate the STOP statement and SIZE command.

S. is recognized as STEP when preceeded by the NEXT statement, and as SET when followed by two values enclosed in parenthesis and separated by a comma [e.g. S.(X,Y)]. S. replaces STOP when it is used alone as a statement, and as SIZE when used as a command.

**Command
Function
Statement**

The following program uses S. as the STEP statement. For more information see STEP.

TEST PROGRAM

```
1Ø REM 'S. (STEP)' TEST PROGRAM
2Ø FOR X=1 TO 1Ø S.2
3Ø PRINT X;
4Ø NEXT X
5Ø PRINT "'S.' PASSED THE TEST"
99 END
```

SAMPLE RUN

```
1 3 5 7 9 'S.' PASSED THE TEST
```

The next program uses S. as the graphics SET statement. For more information see SET.

TEST PROGRAM

```
1Ø REM 'S. (SET)' TEST PROGRAM
2Ø PRINT "'S.' PASSES THE TEST IF A HORIZONTAL LINE APPEARS."
3Ø FOR X=Ø TO 127
4Ø S.=(X,21)
5Ø NEXT X
99 END
```

SAMPLE RUN

```
'S.' PASSES THE TEST IF A HORIZONTAL LINE APPEARS.
```

The next program uses S. as a STOP command. For more information see STOP.

S.

TEST PROGRAM

```
10 REM 'S. (STOP)' TEST PROGRAM
20 PRINT "THE S. STATEMENT IN ACTION"
30 S.
40 PRINT "THE S. STATEMENT FAILED THE TEST"
99 END
```

SAMPLE RUN

```
THE S. STATEMENT IN ACTION
BREAK AT LINE 30
```

This next program uses S. as a SIZE function.

TEST PROGRAM

```
10 REM 'S. (SIZE)' TEST PROGRAM
20 PRINT "THIS PROGRAM SIZE CAN BE CHECKED WITH THE S. COMMAND"
99 END
```

SAMPLE RUN

Type the command PRINT S. and the computer should print the number of bytes of memory occupied by this TEST PROGRAM.

VARIATIONS IN USAGE

None known.

ALSO SEE

STEP, SET, STOP, STO, ST.

SAVE is used in a few computers (e.g. the APPLE II BASIC and the Commodore PET) to record programs from computer memory to cassette tape.

For more information see CSAVE.

Command

TEST PROGRAM

```
10 REM 'SAVE' TEST PROGRAM
20 PRINT "THIS PROGRAM TESTS THE SAVE FEATURE"
99 END
```

Set up the cassette recorder for recording and type the command SAVE. The computer should control the operation of the cassette recorder by turning the motor on and off (at the beginning and end of the record cycle).

Once the program is recorded on cassette tape, type "NEW" (or whatever is required) to erase the program from memory. Load the program from tape back into the computer (see LOAD). List the program to verify that the program held in the computer's memory is identical to that originally entered (see LIST).

SAMPLE RUN

THIS PROGRAM TESTS THE SAVE FEATURE

VARIATIONS IN USAGE

Some computers with disc storage capability use SAVE to copy programs in computer memory to disc memory.

ALSO SEE

LOAD, CSAVE, CLOAD, LIST

The SET statement is used as a special feature by the TRS-80 Level I and II BASICs to "turn on" or "light up" a graphics block in a predetermined grid on the screen.

Statement

The block to be lit, within the grid, is specified by the X,Y coordinates enclosed in parentheses following the SET statement. For example, **SET (5,8)** instructs the computer to SET a graphics block located in the 5th column and the 8th row of the graphics grid.

To turn off the graphics block, see RESET.

TEST PROGRAM

```
10 REM 'SET' TEST PROGRAM
20 PRINT "ENTER X COORDINATE";
30 INPUT X
40 PRINT "ENTER Y COORDINATE"
50 INPUT Y
60 SET(X,Y)
70 PRINT "SET PASSED THE TEST"
80 PRINT "IF A LIGHT APPEARED AT (X,Y) COORDINATE (";X;",";Y;")."
99 END
```

SAMPLE RUN *(Using 65 and 40)*

```
ENTER X COORDINATE? 65
ENTER Y COORDINATE? 40
SET PASSED THE TEST
IF A LIGHT APPEARED AT (X,Y) COORDINATE ( 65, 40 ).
```

VARIATIONS IN USAGE

None known.

ALSO SEE

RESET

SCRN is used by the APPLE II BASIC as a special feature to indicate the color of a graphics block on the screen. The computer has the capability of displaying 16 colors (numbered from Ø to 15). For a complete color listing, see COLOR.

Function

The graphics block is specified by the X,Y coordinates enclosed in parentheses following SCRN. The X value represents the column number and the Y value represents the row number. These values may range from Ø to 39.

TEST PROGRAM

```
1Ø REM 'SCRN' TEST PROGRAM
2Ø GR
3Ø COLOR=11
4Ø PLOT 2Ø,1Ø
5Ø IF SCRN(2Ø,1Ø)=11 THEN 8Ø
6Ø PRINT "THE SCREN FUNCTION FAILED THE TEST"
7Ø GOTO 99
8Ø PRINT "THE SCRN FUNCTION PASSED THE TEST"
99 END
```

SAMPLE RUN

```
THE SCRN FUNCTION PASSED THE TEST
```

VARIATIONS IN USAGE

None known.

ALSO SEE

COLOR, PLOT, GR, POINT

The SIN(A) function computes the Sine of the angle A, when that angle is expressed **in Radians, (not in degrees!).** One radian = approximately 57 degrees.

Function

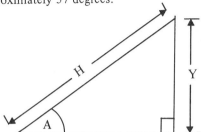

Sine (SIN) is defined as the ratio of the length of the side opposite the angle in question to the length of the hypotenuse. This formula applies only to right triangles: $SIN(A)=Y/H$

The opposite of SIN is ARCSIN. ARCSIN finds the value of the angle when its SIN, or ratio of sides (Y/H), is known.

TEST PROGRAM

```
1Ø REM 'SINE' TEST PROGRAM
2Ø PRINT "ENTER AN ANGLE (EXPRESSED IN RADIANS)";
3Ø INPUT R
4Ø Y=SIN(R)
5Ø PRINT "THE SINE OF A";R;"RADIAN ANGLE IS";Y
3Ø999 END
```

SAMPLE RUN *(using 1)*

```
ENTER AN ANGLE (EXPRESSED IN RADIANS)? 1
THE SINE OF A 1 RADIAN ANGLE IS .841471
```

To convert angles from degrees to radians, multiply the angle in degrees times .Ø174533.

For example, R=SIN(A*.Ø174533)

To convert angles from radians to degrees, multiply radians times 57.29578.

IF YOUR COMPUTER DOES NOT HAVE IT

If your interpreter does not have the SINe capability, the following subroutine can be substituted.

```
3ØØØØ GOTO 3Ø999
3Ø370 REM * SINE SUBROUTINE * INPUT X IN RADIANS, OUTPUT Y
3Ø372 REM ALSO USES Z INTERNALLY
3Ø374 X=X*57.29578
```

```
30376 Z=ABS(X)/X
30378 X=Z*X
30380 IF X>=360 THEN 30388
30382 IF X>90 THEN 30394
30384 X=X/57.29578
30385 IF ABS(X)<2.48616E-4 THEN 30437
30386 GOTO 30420
30388 X=X/360
30390 X=(X-INT(X))*360
30392 GOTO 30382
30394 X=X/90
30396 Y=INT(X)
30398 X=(X-Y)*90
30400 ON Y GOTO 30402,30406,30410
30402 X=90-X
30404 GOTO 30384
30406 X=-X
30408 GOTO 30384
30410 X=X-90
30415 GOTO 30384
30420 Y=X-X*X*X/6+X*X*X*X*X/120-X*X*X*X*X*X*X/5040
30425 Y=Y+X*X*X*X*X*X*X*X*X/362880
30430 IF Z=-1 THEN 30440
30435 GOTO 30445
30437 Y=0
30438 GOTO 30445
30440 Y=—Y
30445 RETURN
```

To use this subroutine with the TEST PROGRAM to find the SINE of an angle (expressed in Radians), make the following TEST PROGRAM changes:

```
35 X=R
40 GOSUB 30370
```

To find the SINE of an angle (expressed in Degrees) either delete line 30372 or change line 40 to:

```
40 GOSUB 30376
```

VARIATIONS IN USAGE

Some (rare) interpreters convert everything to degrees automatically.

ALSO SEE

TAN, COS, ATN

SLEEP is used by the HARRIS BASIC-V to suspend program execution for a specified number of tenths of seconds.

For example, **SLEEP 3ØØ** causes the computer to pause 3Ø seconds before continuing program execution.

Statement

TEST PROGRAM

```
1Ø REM 'SLEEP' TEST PROGRAM
2Ø PRINT "THE COMPUTER SHOULD PRINT THE FOLLOWING LINE"
3Ø SLEEP 15Ø
4Ø PRINT "AFTER SLEEPING 15 SECONDS"
99 END
```

SAMPLE RUN

```
THE COMPUTER SHOULD PRINT THE FOLLOWING LINE
            (15 second pause)
AFTER SLEEPING 15 SECONDS
```

IF YOUR COMPUTER DOESN'T HAVE IT

Insert a FOR-NEXT loop to "burn up" computer time. Test your computer to see how many loops it executes per second. A micro-computer may perform as few as several hundred, while a big mainframe may execute 5Ø,ØØØ or more. Replace line 3Ø in the TEST PROGRAM (assuming your computer executes 1ØØØ loops per second) with:

```
3Ø FOR L=1 TO 15ØØØ
35 NEXT L
```

VARIATIONS IN USAGE

None known.

ALSO SEE

WAIT

The SPA(n) function is used in the Hewlett-Packard 2000 BASIC to insert a specified number (n) of spaces (blank positions).

For example, **PRINT SPA(1Ø);"HELLO"** prints 1Ø spaces followed by the word HELLO.

Function

TEST PROGRAM

```
1Ø REM 'SPACE' TEST PROGRAM
2Ø PRINT "IF THE FOLLOWING LINE CONTAINS 1Ø LEADING SPACES"
3Ø PRINT SPA(1Ø);"THE SPA FUNCTION PASSED THE TEST"
99 END
```

SAMPLE RUN

```
IF THE FOLLOWING LINE CONTAINS 1Ø LEADING SPACES
          THE SPA FUNCTION PASSED THE TEST
```

IF YOUR COMPUTER DOESN'T HAVE IT

In most cases, SPAces can be inserted by careful use of the TAB function.

For example, **3Ø PRINT TAB(1Ø);"THE SPA FUNCTION PASSED THE TEST"** will accomplish the same thing, and a variable could have been used instead of the number 1Ø.

Where a variable isn't needed, simple enclosure of spaces between quotes will also work.

For example, **3Ø PRINT "   THE SPA FUNCTION PASSED THE TEST"**

VARIATIONS IN USAGE

None known.

ALSO SEE

SPACE, SPACE$, SPC, TAB

The SPACE(n) function is used in a few computers (e.g. those using MAX BASIC) to print a specified number (n) of spaces (blank positions).

For example, **PRINT SPACE(1Ø);"HELLO"** prints 1Ø spaces followed by the word HELLO.

Function

TEST PROGRAM

```
1Ø REM 'SPACE' TEST PROGRAM
2Ø PRINT "IF THE FOLLOWING LINE CONTAINS 1Ø LEADING SPACES"
3Ø PRINT SPACE(1Ø);"THE SPACE FUNCTION PASSED THE TEST"
99 END
```

SAMPLE RUN

```
IF THE FOLLOWING LINE CONTAINS 10 LEADING SPACES
          THE SPACE FUNCTION PASSED THE TEST
```

IF YOUR COMPUTER DOESN'T HAVE IT

In most cases, SPACEs can be inserted by careful use of the TAB function.

For example, **3Ø PRINT TAB(1Ø);"THE SPACE FUNCTION PASSED THE TEST"** will accomplish the same thing, and a variable could have been used instead of the number 1Ø.

Where a variable isn't needed, simple enclosure of spaces between quotes will also work.

For example, **3Ø PRINT "   THE SPACE FUNCTION PASSED THE TEST"**

VARIATIONS IN USAGE

Some computers require a $ sign following the SPACE function.

ALSO SEE

SPACE$, SPA, SPC, TAB

The SPACE$(n) function is used to insert a specified number (n) of spaces.

For example, **PRINT SPACE$(2∅);"HELLO"** prints 2∅ spaces followed by the word HELLO.

Most computers with SPACE$(n) capability require the value (n) to be greater than ∅ and less than 256.

Function

TEST PROGRAM

```
1∅ REM 'SPACE$' TEST PROGRAM
2∅ A$=SPACE$(1∅)
3∅ PRINT "IF THE FOLLOWING LINE CONTAINS 1∅ LEADING SPACES"
4∅ PRINT A$;"THE SPACE$ FUNCTION PASSED THE TEST"
99 END
```

SAMPLE RUN

```
IF THE FOLLOWING LINE CONTAINS 1∅ LEADING SPACES
          THE SPACE$ FUNCTION PASSED THE TEST"
```

IF YOUR COMPUTER DOESN'T HAVE IT

In most cases, SPACEs can be inserted by careful use of the TAB function.

For example, **3∅ PRINT TAB(1∅);"THE SPACE$ FUNCTION PASSED THE TEST"** will accomplish the same thing, and a variable could have been used instead of the number 1∅.

Where a variable isn't needed, simple enclosure of spaces between quotes will also work.

For example, **3∅ PRINT "   THE SPACE$ FUNCTION PASSED THE TEST"**

VARIATIONS IN USAGE

None known.

ALSO SEE

SPACE, SPA, SPC, TAB

The SPC(n) function is used to insert a specified number (n) of spaces (blank positions).

For example, **PRINT SPC(1Ø);"HELLO"** prints 1Ø spaces followed by the word HELLO.

Function

TEST PROGRAM

```
1Ø REM 'SPC' TEST PROGRAM
2Ø PRINT "IF THE FOLLOWING LINE CONTAINS 1Ø LEADING SPACES"
3Ø PRINT SPC(1Ø);"THE SPC FUNCTION PASSED THE TEST"
99 END
```

SAMPLE RUN

```
IF THE FOLLOWING LINE CONTAINS 1Ø LEADING SPACES
          THE SPC FUNCTION PASSED THE TEST
```

IF YOUR COMPUTER DOESN'T HAVE IT

In most cases, SPACEs can be inserted by careful use of the TAB function.

For example, **3Ø PRINT TAB(1Ø);"THE SPC FUNCTION PASSED THE TEST"** will accomplish the same thing, and a variable could have been used instead of the number 1Ø.

Where a variable isn't needed, simple enclosure of spaces between quotes will also work.

For example, **3Ø PRINT "   THE SPC FUNCTION PASSED THE TEST"**

VARIATIONS IN USAGE

None known.

ALSO SEE

SPACE, SPACE$, SPA, TAB

The SQR(n) function returns the square root of any positive number ($\sqrt{n}$).

TEST PROGRAM

SQR

Function

N
S
I

```
10 REM 'SQR' TEST PROGRAM
20 PRINT "THE SQUARE ROOT OF 225 IS";
30 PRINT SQR(225)
40 PRINT "'SQR' PASSED THE TEST IF THE RESULT IS 15"
30999 END
```

SAMPLE RUN

```
THE SQUARE ROOT OF 225 IS 15
'SQR' PASSED THE TEST IF THE RESULT IS 15
```

IF YOUR COMPUTER DOESN'T HAVE IT

If the computer failed the Test Program substitute the following subroutine:

```
30000 GOTO 30999
30010 REM * SQUARE ROOT SUBROUTINE * INPUT X, OUTPUT Y
30020 REM USES W AND Z INTERNALLY
30025 IF X=0 THEN 30085
30030 IF X>0 THEN 30045
30035 PRINT "ROOT OF NEGATIVE NUMBER?"
30040 STOP
30045 Y=X/4
30050 Z=0
30055 W=(X/Y—Y)/2
30060 IF W=0 THEN 30090
30065 IF W=Z THEN 30090
30070 Y=Y+W
30075 Z=W
30080 GOTO 30055
30085 Y=0
30090 RETURN
```

To use this subroutine in the TEST PROGRAM, make these Test Program changes:

```
25 X=225
30 GOSUB 30010
35 PRINT Y
50 GOTO 30999
```

SQR

VARIATIONS IN USAGE

None known.

ALSO SEE

SQRT

The SQRT(n) function computes the square root of any positive number ($\sqrt{n}$).

Function

TEST PROGRAM

```
10 REM 'SQRT' TEST PROGRAM
20 PRINT "THE SQUARE ROOT OF 225 IS";
30 PRINT SQRT(225)
40 PRINT "'SQRT' PASSED THE TEST IF THE RESULT IS 15"
30999 END
```

SAMPLE RUN

```
THE SQUARE ROOT OF 225 IS 15
'SQRT' PASSED THE TEST IF THE RESULT IS 15
```

If your computer failed the TEST PROGRAM, try the TEST PROGRAM in SQR. If it fails, substitute the subroutine found under SQR.

To use the SQR subroutine in the TEST PROGRAM, make these TEST PROGRAM changes:

```
25 X=225
30 GOSUB 30010
35 PRINT Y
```

VARIATIONS IN USAGE

None known.

ALSO SEE

SQR

ST is used by some computers (e.g. the TI 990) as an abbreviation for the STEP statement.

For more information see STEP.

Function

TEST PROGRAM

```
10 REM 'ST (STEP)' TEST PROGRAM
20 FOR X=1 TO 10 ST 2
30 PRINT X;
40 NEXT X
50 PRINT "'ST' PASSED THE TEST"
99 END
```

SAMPLE RUN

```
1  3  5  7  9 'ST' PASSED THE TEST
```

VARIATIONS IN USAGE

None known.

ALSO SEE

STEP, STE, S.

ST. is used in the TRS-80 Level I as an abbreviation for the STOP statement.

For more information see STOP.

Statement

TEST PROGRAM

```
10 REM 'ST. (STOP)' TEST PROGRAM
20 PRINT "THE PROGRAM SHOULD 'STOP' AFTER THIS LINE"
30 ST.
40 PRINT "'ST.' FAILED THE TEST IF THIS LINE IS PRINTED"
99 END
```

SAMPLE RUN

```
THE PROGRAM SHOULD 'STOP' AFTER THIS LINE
BREAK AT 30
```

VARIATIONS IN USAGE

None known.

ALSO SEE

STOP, STO, S., END, CONT

STE is used in the PDP-8E as an abbreviation for the STEP statement.

For more information see STEP.

Function

TEST PROGRAM

```
1Ø REM 'STE' TEST PROGRAM
2Ø FOR X=1 TO 1Ø STE 2
3Ø PRINT X;
4Ø NEXT X
5Ø PRINT "'STE' PASSED THE TEST"
99 END
```

SAMPLE RUN

```
1   3   5   7   9   'STE' PASSED THE TEST
```

VARIATIONS IN USAGE

None known.

ALSO SEE

STEP, S., ST

The STEP function is used to specify the size of the step incremented in a FOR-NEXT statement. The STEP value can be positive, negative or sometimes even a non-integer decimal value. When a STEP value is not specified, the value of +1 is automatically assumed.

STEP

A N S I

Function

TEST PROGRAM #1

```
10 REM 'STEP' TEST PROGRAM
20 PRINT "WHEN THE STEP VALUE IS 2, X=";
30 FOR X=1 TO 10 STEP 2
40 PRINT X;
50 NEXT X
99 END
```

SAMPLE RUN

```
WHEN THE STEP VALUE IS 2,X=   1  3  5  7  9
```

The following program tests the interpreter's ability to handle negative STEP values.

TEST PROGRAM #2

```
10 REM 'NEGATIVE STEP' TEST PROGRAM
20 PRINT "WHEN THE STEP VALUE IS —2, X=";
30 FOR X=10 TO 1 STEP -2
40 PRINT X;
50 NEXT X
99 END
```

SAMPLE RUN

```
WHEN THE STEP VALUE IS -2, X=10   8   6   4   2
```

Test program #3 checks the interpreter's ability to handle non-integer decimal STEP values.

TEST PROGRAM #3

```
10 REM 'NON-INTEGER STEP' TEST PROGRAM
20 PRINT "WHEN THE STEP VALUE IS .5, X=";
30 FOR X=1 TO 5 STEP .5
40 PRINT X;
50 NEXT X
99 END
```

STEP

SAMPLE RUN

WHEN THE STEP VALUE IS .5, X=1   1.5   2   2.5   3   3.5   4   4.5   5

A variable is accepted as the STEP value by some interpreters. For example, **FOR X=1 TO 3Ø STEP A** causes the value of X to be incremented by the value of variable A each time the corresponding NEXT statement is executed.

TEST PROGRAM #4

```
1Ø REM 'VARIABLE STEP' TEST PROGRAM
2Ø PRINT "ENTER A STEP VALUE (BETWEEN 1 AND 1Ø)"
3Ø INPUT S
4Ø PRINT "THE VALUE OF X=";
5Ø FOR X=1 TO 1Ø STEP S
6Ø PRINT X;
7Ø NEXT X
99 END
```

SAMPLE RUN *(Using 3)*

```
ENTER A STEP VALUE (BETWEEN 1 AND 1Ø)
? 3
THE VALUE OF X=1   4   7   1Ø
```

IF YOUR COMPUTER DOESN'T HAVE IT

If STEP is not intrinsic, or not powerful enough, it can be easily simulated in ascending FOR-NEXT statements. Omit 'STEP S' from line 5Ø in the last test program, and add the following lines:

```
65 X=X+S-1
67 IF X<Ø THEN 99
```

Inserting these lines immediately before the corresponding NEXT statement allows incrementing X by any integer or decimal fraction you wish.

ALSO SEE

FOR-NEXT,S., ST, STE

STO is used in the Tektronix 4051 and PDP-8E as an abbreviation for the STOP statement.

For more information see STOP.

Statement

TEST PROGRAM

```
1Ø REM 'STO (STOP)' TEST PROGRAM
2Ø PRINT "THE PROGRAM SHOULD 'STOP' AFTER PRINTING THIS LINE"
3Ø STO
4Ø PRINT "'STO' FAILED THE TEST IF THIS LINE IS PRINTED"
99 END
```

SAMPLE RUN

THE PROGRAM SHOULD 'STOP' AFTER PRINTING THIS LINE

VARIATIONS IN USAGE

None known.

ALSO SEE

STOP, END, CONT

The STOP statement is used to STOP execution of the program and place the computer in the monitor or immediate mode. It can be placed at any point within a program, but is not usually used in place of the END statement.

STOP

Statement

Some computers will stop the program at the line which contains the STOP statement, while others jump to the line containing the END statement.

Many computers with interpreters (but not compilers) print the line number where the program stopped, and allow continuation of program execution via the CONTINUE command (see CONT).

TEST PROGRAM

```
1Ø REM 'STOP' TEST PROGRAM
2Ø PRINT "SEE THE STOP STATEMENT IN ACTION"
3Ø STOP
4Ø PRINT "THE STOP STATEMENT FAILED THE TEST"
99 END
```

SAMPLE RUN

```
SEE THE STOP STATEMENT IN ACTION
BREAK AT LINE 3Ø
```

VARIATIONS IN USAGE

Trying to both STOP and END in the same program can be unusually frustrating unless you know your machine's capabilities. Some machines (e.g. Varian) require physical intervention (push a button) before RUNning, after hitting a program STOP.

Others (mostly large machines) allow an unlimited number of STOP's, but no END. Others allow an unlimited number of END's, but no STOP's. Most micros allow mixing of STOP's and END's.

With care, the STOP/END problem can almost always be resolved and programs can be converted quite easily.

ALSO SEE

S., ST., STO, CONT, END

The STR$(n) function is used to convert a numeric value (n) into a string. The value (n) may be expressed as a number or a numeric variable.

For example,

Function

```
1Ø A$ = STR$(35)
2Ø PRINT A$
```

prints the number 35 as a string. The computer automatically inserts a space before the number to allow for the sign (−).

Conversion of a number to a string via the STR$ function allows its manipulation using string modifiers (e.g. LEFT$, RIGHT$, MID$, ASC, etc.).

TEST PROGRAM

```
1Ø REM 'STR$' TEST PROGRAM
2Ø A = 123456
3Ø A$ = STR$(A)
4Ø PRINT "IF THE NUMBER";A;"IS CONVERTED TO THE STRING";A$
5Ø PRINT "THEN THE STR$ FUNCTION PASSED THE TEST."
99 END
```

SAMPLE RUN

```
IF THE NUMBER 123456 IS CONVERTED TO THE STRING 123456
THEN THE STR$ FUNCTION PASSED THE TEST.
```

VARIATIONS IN USAGE

None known.

ALSO SEE

ASC, CHR$, LEN, LEFT$, MID$, RIGHT$, STRING$, VAL

The STRING$(n,ASCII code) function is used with the PRINT statement to print an ASCII character (n) number of times.

For example, **PRINT STRING$(1ø,65)** prints the ASCII character A (ASCII code 65) ten times.

STRING$

Function

TEST PROGRAM

```
1ø REM 'STRING$' TEST PROGRAM
2ø PRINT STRING$(23,42);
3ø PRINT "STRING$ FUNCTION ";
4ø PRINT STRING$(23,42)
99 END
```

SAMPLE RUN

```
*********************** STRING$ FUNCTION***********************
```

VARIATIONS IN USAGE

Some computers (e.g. the TRS-80 Level II) allow string characters (enclosed in quotes) or string variables in the STRING$ function.

For example, **1ø PRINT STRING$(1ø,"A")**

prints the letter A ten times.

```
1ø A$="B"
2ø PRINT STRING$(5,A$)
```

prints the letter B five times.

TEST PROGRAM

```
1ø REM 'STRING$' TEST PROGRAM
2ø PRINT "ENTER ANY LETTER, NUMBER OR SYMBOL";
3ø INPUT A$
4ø PRINT STRING$(2ø,".");
5ø PRINT STRING$(2ø,A$)
99 END
```

STRING$

SAMPLE RUN

```
ENTER ANY LETTER, NUMBER OR SYMBOL? X
. . . . . . . . . . . . . . . . . .XXXXXXXXXXXXXXXXXXXX
```

IF YOUR COMPUTER DOES NOT HAVE IT

If your computer does not accept the STRING$ function, it can be simulated by finding the ASCII character in the ASCII table (see Appendix A) which matches the ASCII code listed in the STRING$ function. Then place that character in a PRINT statement the number of times specified by the first number in the STRING$ function.

For example:

```
1Ø PRINT STRING$(12,45)
```

can be entered as:

```
1Ø PRINT "———————————"
```

ALSO SEE

PRINT, ASC, CHR$, LEN, MID$, LEFT$, RIGHT$, STR$, VAL

STUFF is used in the Digital Group Opus 1 and Opus 2 BASIC to insert integer values between Ø and 255 into specified memory locations.

STUFF

For example, STUFF 3ØØØ,65 places the decimal value 65 in memory address 3ØØØ.

The FETCH function can be used with STUFF to check what STUFF has stored into memory. (Some computers use PEEK or EXAM instead.)

Statement

Computers vary in the amount of available memory and memory addresses that can be STUFFed without erasing memory dedicated to other purposes. Check your computer's manual before running this TEST PROGRAM to determine that addresses 15ØØ1 to 15Ø1Ø are non-critical memory locations. If they are not, select 1Ø other consecutive addresses.

TEST PROGRAM

```
1Ø REM 'STUFF' TEST PROGRAM
2Ø FOR X=1 TO 1Ø
3Ø STUFF 15ØØØ+X,X
4Ø NEXT X
5Ø FOR X=15ØØ1 TO 15Ø1Ø
6Ø Y=FETCH(X)
7Ø PRINT Y;
8Ø NEXT X
9Ø PRINT
1ØØ PRINT "'STUFF' PASSED THE TEST IF #1 THRU #1Ø ARE PRINTED"
999 END
```

SAMPLE RUN

```
1 2 3 4 5 6 7 8 9 1Ø
'STUFF' PASSED THE TEST IF #1 THRU #1Ø ARE PRINTED
```

IF YOUR COMPUTER DOESN'T HAVE IT

If your computer failed the TEST PROGRAM, try the Test Programs found in POKE and FILL.

VARIATIONS IN USAGE

None known.

ALSO SEE

POKE, FILL, PEEK, FETCH, EXAM

SYS is used by a few computers (e.g. the Commodore PET and the Sperry Univac System/9 BASIC) as an abbreviation for the SYSTEM command.

For more information see SYSTEM.

Command

To test the computer's SYS capability, type the command SYS. The computer accepted the SYS command if the computer changed to the monitor mode and prints an asterisk followed by a question mark (*?), (or some other appropriate monitor response).

This feature can be activated on some terminals by pressing the escape (ESC) key.

The SYSTEM command is used in some computers to allow machine language data (object file) to be loaded from cassette tape or disc into the computer. These computers may also use SYSTEM as a program statement.

SYSTEM

**Command
Statement**

When the computer executes the line containing the SYSTEM statement, or when SYSTEM is typed on the terminal, the computer changes to the monitor mode and prints an asterisk followed by a question mark (*?) or some other cryptic symbol. This signal indicates the computer is ready to accept the object file from disc or tape.

Place an object file tape in the cassette player and set it to the PLAY mode. Type the object file name and RETURN. The cassette recorder's motor is controlled by the computer, which turns it on and off before and after the load cycle. The cassette should "play back" the data into the computer. When the data is loaded in the computer, another *? is displayed.

To execute the object file routine, type a slash (/) followed by a memory decimal starting address. If the / is entered without the starting address, then execution begins at the address specified in the object file.

The TRS-80 Level I-to-Level II CONVersion cassette tape is a typical example of how SYSTEM is used.

VARIATIONS IN USAGE

Some computers use the SYSTEM command similar to the ESC (escape) key on many keyboards to place the computer in the System, Executive or monitor mode.

ALSO SEE

SYS, PEEK, POKE

T. is used in the TRS-80 Level I BASIC as an abbreviation for the TAB function and the THEN statement.

The computer's interpreter recognizes T. as a TAB function when it is followed by a number enclosed in parentheses [e.g. T.(2Ø)]. It is recognized as a THEN statement when **not** followed by a number enclosed in parentheses and the computer has previously executed the IF statement (e.g. IF X=2Ø T.1ØØ).

Function Statement

The first test program uses T. as the function TAB. For more information see TAB.

TEST PROGRAM

```
1Ø REM 'T. (TAB)' TEST PROGRAM
2Ø PRINT T.(15);" 'T.' PASSED THE TAB FUNCTION TEST"
99 END
```

SAMPLE RUN

```
               'T.' PASSED THE TAB FUNCTION TEST''
```

This next test program uses T. as a THEN statement. For more information see THEN or IF-THEN.

TEST PROGRAM

```
1Ø REM 'T. (THEN)' TEST PROGRAM
2Ø X=1Ø
3Ø IF X=1Ø T.6Ø
4Ø PRINT " 'T. FAILED THE TEST"
5Ø GOTO 99
6Ø PRINT "'T.' PASSED THE TEST"
99 END
```

SAMPLE RUN

```
'T.' PASSED THE TEST
```

VARIATIONS IN USAGE

None other known.

ALSO SEE

TAB, THEN, IF-THEN, THE, IF-THE, IF-T.

The TAB function is used with PRINT statements in a manner similar to the TAB key on a typewriter. When the PRINT statement is followed by TAB( ) the computer inserts a number of spaces (enclosed in parenthesis) before the statement to be printed. The TAB value must always be positive and should be less than the number of spaces allowed per line.

TAB

A
N
S
I

Function

If more than one TAB statement is used in one line, the numerical values must get progressively larger and allow room inbetween for that which is to be printed. If insufficient room is allowed between TABs, they will be overrun, just like on a typewriter.

The value may be expressed as a number, **PRINT TAB(5)**; a variable, **PRINT TAB(X)**; or an expression, **PRINT TAB(2X+Y)**. TAB( ) must be followed by a semicolon or comma, depending upon the interpreter.

TEST PROGRAM

```
1Ø REM 'TAB' FUNCTION TEST PROGRAM
2Ø PRINT TAB(5); "TAB 5"
3Ø X = 1Ø
4Ø PRINT TAB(X); "TAB 1Ø"
5Ø PRINT TAB(6*X/5+8); "TAB 2Ø"
999 END
```

SAMPLE RUN

```
TAB 5
      TAB 1Ø
            TAB 2Ø
```

The maximum value of the TAB on your computer can be quickly determined by adding the following lines to the test program:

```
6Ø PRINT "TYPE IN A TAB VALUE";
7Ø INPUT T
8Ø PRINT TAB(T);  "TAB";T
9Ø GOTO 6Ø
```

The TAB value entered in line 7Ø will cause line 8Ø to print the TAB value following the same number of spaces.

VARIATIONS IN USAGE

None known.

TAB

IF YOUR COMPUTER DOESN'T HAVE IT

There is no totally satisfactory replacement for TAB, but there are several ways to obtain printouts which may be acceptable. Assume an original PRINT series:

```
2ØØ PRINT TAB(1Ø);"THE";TAB(2Ø);"QUICK";TAB(3Ø);"BROWN";
21Ø PRINT TAB(4Ø);"FOX"
```

The TAB values are simple numbers and could be replaced by:

```
2ØØ PRINT "          THE          QUICK          BROWN          FOX"
```

or, less accurately:

```
2ØØ PRINT "THE","QUICK","BROWN","FOX"
```

or

A combination of inserting spaces and automatic zone spacing.

A third, and generally less satisfactory, method of arriving at a usable printout involves combining the carriage return suppressing ability of the semicolon (;), the automatic zoning of the comma (,), and inserted spaces. In some interpreters (compilers) however this can create a remarkably messy situation.

ALSO SEE

PRINT, PRINT AT, ,(comma), ;(semicolon)

The TAN(A) function computes the Tangent of the angle A when that angle is expressed **in radians** *(not in degrees!)*. One radian = approximately 57 degrees.

Function

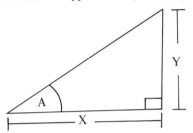

Tangent (TAN) is defined as the ratio of the length of the side opposite the angle being investigated to the length of the side adjacent to it.

TAN(A)=Y/X

The opposite of TAN is ARCTAN (ATN). ARCTAN finds the value of the angle when its TAN, or ratio of sides (Y/X) is known.

TEST PROGRAM

```
10 REM 'TAN' TEST PROGRAM
20 PRINT "ENTER AN ANGLE (EXPRESSED IN RADIANS)";
30 INPUT R
40 Y=TAN(R)
50 PRINT "THE TANGENT OF A";R;"RADIAN ANGEL IS";Y
30999 END
```

SAMPLE RUN *(using 1)*

```
ENTER AN ANGLE (EXPRESSED IN RADIANS)? 1
THE TANGENT OF A 1 RADIAN ANGLE IS 1.55741
```

To convert values from degrees to radians, multiply the angle in degrees times .0174533. For example, **R=TAN(A*.0174533)** To convert values from radians to degrees, multiply the angle in radians times 57.29578.

IF YOUR COMPUTER DOESN'T HAVE IT

If your interpreter has the SINe and COSine capability but not TANgent, substitute SIN(A)/COS(A) for TAN(A).

If your interpreter does not have SINe, COSine or TANgent capability, the following subroutine can be substituted.

The subroutine programs found under SIN and COS **must** be added to this one to make it work (saves space not to duplicate them here).

```
30000 GOTO 30999
30300 REM * TANGENT SUBROUTINE * INPUT X IN RADIANS, OUTPUT Y
30302 REM ALSO USES A,C,W AND Z INTERNALLY
30304 X=X*57.29578
30306 A=X
30308 GOSUB 30356
30310 IF ABS(Y) < 1E -6 THEN 30320
30312 PRINT "TANGENT UNDEFINED"
30315 STOP
30320 C=Y
30325 X=A
30330 GOSUB 30376
30335 Y=Y/C
30340 RETURN
```

To use this subroutine with the TEST PROGRAM to find the TANGENT of an angle (expressed in RADIANS), make the following TEST PROGRAM changes:

```
35 X=R
40 GOSUB 30300
```

To find the TANGENT of an angle (expressed in DEGREES), either delete line 30304 or change line 40 to:

```
40 GOSUB 30306
```

VARIATIONS IN USAGE

Some (rare) interpreters convert everything to **degrees** automatically.

ALSO SEE

SIN, COS, ATN

TEXT is used in the APPLE II BASIC as both a command and a program statement to change the computer's operation from the graphics mode to the normal TEXT (narrative) mode.

**Command
Statement**

TEST PROGRAM

```
1Ø REM 'TEXT' TEST PROGRAM
2Ø TEXT
3Ø PRINT "THE 'TEXT' STATEMENT DID NOT CRASH"
4Ø END
```

SAMPLE RUN

```
THE 'TEXT' STATEMENT DID NOT CRASH
```

VARIATIONS IN USAGE

TEXT is used in computers with MAXBASIC to specify designated variables as string variables. For example, TEXT A,F,M defines variables A,F and M as string variables.

ALSO SEE

GR, DEFSTR

THE is used in the PDP-8E as an abbreviation for the THEN statement.

For more information see THEN.

Statement

TEST PROGRAM

```
1Ø REM 'THE (THEN)' TEST PROGRAM
2Ø X=1Ø
3Ø IF X=1Ø THE 6Ø
4Ø PRINT "'THE' FAILED THE TEST"
5Ø GOTO 99
6Ø PRINT "'THE' PASSED THE TEST"
99 END
```

SAMPLE RUN

```
'THE' PASSED THE TEST
```

VARIATIONS IN USAGE

None known.

ALSO SEE

THEN, IF-THEN, T., IF-T.

THEN is used with the IF statement to indicate the next operation the computer is to perform when the condition of the IF statement is met.

For more information see IF-THEN.

A N S I

Statement

TEST PROGRAM

```
1Ø REM 'THEN' TEST PROGRAM
2Ø X=1Ø
3Ø IF X=1Ø THEN 6Ø
4Ø PRINT "'THEN' FAILED THE TEST"
5Ø GOTO 99
6Ø PRINT "'THEN' PASSED THE TEST"
99 END
```

SAMPLE RUN

```
'THEN' PASSED THE TEST
```

VARIATIONS IN USAGE

None known.

ALSO SEE

IF-THEN, THE, T.

TI is used in the Commodore PET as an abbreviation for the TIME function.

For more information see TIME.

Function

TEST PROGRAM

```
1Ø REM 'TI' TEST PROGRAM
2Ø A=TI
3Ø FOR X=1 TO 2ØØØ
4Ø NEXT X
5Ø B=TI
6Ø IF B > A THEN 9Ø
7Ø PRINT "THE TI FUNCTION FAILED THE TEST"
8Ø GOTO 99
9Ø PRINT "'TI' PASSED — ELAPSED TIME = ";B-A
99 END
```

SAMPLE RUN *(typical)*

```
'TI' PASSED — ELAPSED TIME = 167
```

VARIATIONS IN USAGE

None known.

ALSO SEE

TI$, TIME, TIME$, TIM, CLK, CLK$

TIM is used by some computers (e.g. the DEC 10 BASIC and the Sperry Univac System/9 BASIC) to indicate the elapsed program run time in seconds.

For example, **PRINT TIM** may print a number (such as 1∅, indicating the computer program ran 1∅ seconds) before executing the PRINT statement.

The Univac System/9 BASIC requires a variable (enclosed in parenthesis) following TIM, although the variable has no effect on the TIM function.

Function

TEST PROGRAM

```
1∅ REM 'TIM' TEST PROGRAM
2∅ A=TIM
3∅ PRINT "TIME IS MARCHING ON"
4∅ FOR X=1 TO 2∅∅∅
5∅ NEXT X
6∅ B=TIM
7∅ IF B > A THEN 1∅∅
8∅ PRINT "THE TIM FUNCTION FAILED THE TEST"
9∅ GOTO 999
1∅∅ PRINT "'TIM' PASSED THE TEST — ELAPSED TIME = ";B-A
999 END
```

SAMPLE RUN *(typical)*

```
TIME IS MARCHING ON
'TIM' PASSED THE TEST — ELAPSED TIME = 6
```

The Hewlett Packard 2∅∅∅ BASIC uses TIM(n) to indicate the current time in minutes, hours, days and years, depending on the TIM number (n). The TIM number (n) must be an integer from ∅ to 3, as follows:

TIM(∅) indicates the current minute (∅ to 59)
TIM(1) indicates the current hour (∅ to 23)
TIM(2) indicates the current day (∅ to 366)
TIM(3) indicates the current year (∅ to 99)

TIM

TEST PROGRAM

```
10 REM 'TIM(N)' TEST PROGRAM
20 PRINT "THE CURRENT TIME IS"
30 PRINT TIM(0);"MINUTES"
40 PRINT TIM(1);"HOURS"
50 PRINT TIM(2);"DAYS"
60 PRINT TIM(3); "YEARS"
99 END
```

SAMPLE RUN *(typical)*

```
THE CURRENT TIME IS
43 MINUTES
16 HOURS
194 DAYS
78 YEARS
```

ALSO SEE

TIME, TIME$, TI, TI$, CLK, CLK$

TIME is used as a special feature in some computers to indicate the elapsed time in seconds or fractions of seconds from a known reference point in time.

Command Function

Most "time-shared" machines start the time count from 12:00 midnight until the following midnight, while "stand-alone" machines start the count from the moment the computer is turned on until it is turned off.

For example, **PRINT TIME** may print a number similar to Ø17230 indicating the total computer run time in some units.

Computers are not consistent in the unit of time used to increment the TIME counter. For example, the Commodore PET increments the TIME value at a rate of 60 times per second, those using MAX BASIC increment at a rate of 1ØØØ times per second, and the DEC BASIC-PLUS-2 increments at a rate of one count per second.

Some computers (e.g. the Commodore PET) process the elapsed TIME value as a six-digit number, and this value cannot be changed or reset to zero except by turning the computer off.

TEST PROGRAM

```
1Ø REM 'TIME' TEST PROGRAM
2Ø A=TIME
3Ø PRINT "TIME IS MARCHING ON"
4Ø FOR X=1 TO 2ØØØ
5Ø NEXT X
6Ø B=TIME
7Ø IF B > A THEN 1ØØ
8Ø PRINT "THE TIME FUNCTION FAILED THE TEST"
9Ø GOTO 999
1ØØ PRINT "'TIME' PASSED THE TEST - ELAPSED TIME = ";B-A
999 END
```

SAMPLE RUN *(typical)*

```
'TIME' PASSED THE TEST - ELAPSED TIME = 27Ø
```

VARIATIONS IN USAGE

The DEC BASIC-PLUS-2 uses the following TIME variations:

TIME(Ø) indicates the total elapsed time in seconds since midnight.

TIME

For example, 1ØØ **PRINT TIME(Ø)** may print a value similar to 25128 indicating 25,128 seconds have elapsed since midnight.

TIME(1%) indicates the total elapsed program time in tenths of seconds.

For example, 1ØØ **PRINT TIME(1%)** may print a value similar to 85 indicating the program ran 8.5 seconds before printing TIME(1%).

TIME(2%) indicates the total elapsed time in minutes that a terminal was connected to a time share system.

For example, 1Ø **PRINT TIME(2%)** may print a value similar to 13Ø indicating 13Ø seconds have elapsed since the terminal was connected to the time share system.

The Hewlett Packard 2ØØØF TIME-SHARED BASIC uses TIME as a command to print the elapsed time since the terminal was logged onto the system, and the total accumulated account time.

For example, if the command TIME is typed, it will print a report similar to this;

> **CONSOLE TIME = 5 MINUTES. TOTAL TIME = 2Ø45 MINUTES.**

ALSO SEE

TIME$, TIM, TI, TI$, CLK$

TIME$ is used as a special feature by some computers (e.g. the Commodore PET and the DEC BASIC-PLUS-2) to indicate the time of day.

Function

The PET stores the TIME$ value in hours (∅ -24), minutes, and seconds as a six digit number (hhmmss). The TIME$ value can be "set" by assigning a six digit number (enclosed in quotes) to TIME$.

For example, `TIME$="1445∅∅"` sets the TIME$ at 1445∅∅ (which is the same as 2:45 p.m.). The TIME$ continues advancing each second from the time the computer is turned on (the TIME$ value is initialized at ∅∅∅∅∅∅), or from the moment it is assigned a new value.

TEST PROGRAM

```
1∅ REM 'TIME$' TEST PROGRAM
2∅ PRINT "THE CURRENT TIME IS ";TIME$
3∅ PRINT "THE TIME$ FUNCTION PASSED THE TEST"
4∅ PRINT "IF A SIX DIGIT NUMBER IS PRINTED"
99 END
```

SAMPLE RUN *(typical)*

```
THE CURRENT TIME IS ∅12536
THE TIME$ FUNCTION PASSED THE TEST
IF A SIX DIGIT NUMBER IS PRINTED
```

VARIATIONS IN USAGE

The DEC BASIC-PLUS-2 uses TIME$(∅%) to indicate the time of day in hours and minutes.

For example, `PRINT TIME$(∅%)` will print a time similar to 14:32. The computer automatically inserts the colon between the hours and minutes. Also, DEC BASIC-PLUS-2 uses TIME(n%) to indicate the time (n) minutes before midnight.

ALSO SEE

TIME, TI, TI$, CLK$

TI$ is used in the Commodore PET as an abbreviation for the TIME$ function.

For more information see TIME$.

Function

TEST PROGRAM

```
1Ø REM 'TI$' TEST PROGRAM
2Ø PRINT "THE CURRENT TIME IS ";TI$
3Ø PRINT "'TI$' PASSED THE TEST"
4Ø PRINT "IF A SIX DIGIT NUMBER IS PRINTED"
99 END
```

SAMPLE RUN *(typical)*

```
THE CURRENT TIME IS 171307
'TI$' PASSED THE TEST
IF A SIX DIGIT NUMBER IS PRINTED
```

VARIATIONS IN USAGE

None known.

ALSO SEE

TIME$, TIME, TIM, CLK

The TRACE command is used in the APPLE II BASIC to activate a feature which prints program line numbers as each one is executed by the computer. It is used as a trouble-shooting aid. This execution tracing feature is disabled by the NOTRACE command.

TRACE may also be used as a program statement to trace only specific sections of programs.

**Command
Statement**

TEST PROGRAM

```
10 REM 'TRACE' TEST PROGRAM
20 PRINT "'TRACE' TRACES EACH LINE"
30 TRACE
40 GOTO 90
50 PRINT "UNTIL TURNED OFF BY"
60 NOTRACE
70 PRINT "THE 'NOTRACE' STATEMENT"
80 GOTO 110
90 PRINT "THAT FOLLOWS THE 'TRACE' STATEMENT"
100 GOTO 50
110 PRINT "AS ILLUSTRATED BY THIS LINE"
999 END
```

SAMPLE RUN

```
'TRACE' TRACES EACH LINE
#40#90 THAT FOLLOWS THE 'TRACE' STATEMENT
#100#50 UNTIL TURNED OFF BY
#60 THE 'NOTRACE' STATEMENT
AS ILLUSTRATED BY THIS LINE
```

VARIATIONS IN USAGE

None known.

ALSO SEE

NOTRACE, TRON, TRACE ON, TROFF

The TRACE OFF command is used in the Motorola BASIC to disable the trace function (see TRACE ON). TRACE OFF may be used as a program statement to turn the trace off at specified areas in the program.

**Command
Statement**

TEST PROGRAM

```
10 REM 'TRACE OFF' TEST PROGRAM
20 TRACE ON
30 PRINT "EACH LINE SHOULD BE TRACED"
40 TRACE OFF
50 PRINT "BY THE 'TRACE ON' STATEMENT"
60 PRINT "UNTIL TURNED OFF BY THE 'TRACE OFF' STATEMENT"
99 END
```

SAMPLE RUN

```
<30> EACH LINE SHOULD BE TRACED
<40> BY THE 'TRACE ON' STATEMENT
UNTIL TURNED OFF BY THE 'TRACE OFF' STATEMENT
```

VARIATIONS IN USAGE

None known.

ALSO SEE

TRACE ON, TRACE, NOTRACE, TROFF, TRON

The TRACE ON command is used in the Motorola BASIC to activate a feature which prints program line numbers as each one is executed by the computer. It is used as a trouble-shooting aid. This tracing feature is disabled by the TRACE OFF command.

TRACE ON may be used as a program statement to trace only specified sections of a program.

**Command
Statement**

TEST PROGRAM

```
10 REM 'TRACE ON' TEST PROGRAM
20 PRINT "'TRACE ON' TRACES EACH LINE"
30 TRACE ON
40 GOTO 90
50 PRINT "UNTIL TURNED OFF BY"
60 TRACE OFF
70 PRINT "THE 'TRACE OFF' STATEMENT"
80 GOTO 110
90 PRINT "THAT FOLLOWS THE 'TRACE ON' STATEMENT"
100 GOTO 50
110 PRINT "AS ILLUSTRATED BY THIS LINE"
999 END
```

SAMPLE RUN

```
'TRACE ON' TRACES EACH LINE
  <40>   <90>  THAT FOLLOWS THE 'TRACE ON' STATEMENT
  <100>   <50>  UNTIL TURNED OFF BY
  <60>  THE 'TRACE OFF' STATEMENT
AS ILLUSTRATED BY THIS LINE
```

VARIATIONS IN USAGE

None known.

ALSO SEE

TRACE OFF, TRACE, TRON, NOTRACE, TROFF

TROFF (trace off) is a command which disables the trace feature found in many interpreters (e.g. TRS-80 Level II). TROFF may also be used as a program statement to turn the trace off at specific areas in the program.

**Command
Statement**

TEST PROGRAM

Type the TRON command, then RUN this test program:

```
1Ø REM 'TROFF' TEST PROGRAM
2Ø PRINT "THE FIRST TWO LINES OF THIS PROGRAM"
3Ø TROFF
4Ø PRINT "ARE PRINTED WITH THE TRACE TURNED ON."
5Ø PRINT "THIS LINE IS PRINTED WITH THE TRACE TURNED OFF."
99 END
```

SAMPLE RUN

```
<1Ø><2Ø>THE FIRST TWO LINES OF THIS PROGRAM
<3Ø>ARE PRINTED WITH THE TRACE TURNED ON.
THIS LINE IS PRINTED WITH THE TRACE TURNED OFF.
```

VARIATIONS IN USAGE

None known.

ALSO SEE

TRON, NOTRACE

The TRON (trace on) command is used to activate an analytical tool which prints program line numbers as each line is executed by the computer. This trace feature is disabled by the TROFF or NEW commands. TRON is intended to be used as a program tracing and trouble-shooting aid.

TRON

Command
Statement

TEST PROGRAM

```
1Ø REM 'TRON' TEST PROGRAM
2Ø GOTO 5Ø
3Ø PRINT "OF THIS TEST PROGRAM."
4Ø GOTO 7Ø
5Ø PRINT "TRON TRACES EACH LINE"
6Ø GOTO 3Ø
7Ø PRINT "END OF TEST PROGRAM."
99 END
```

SAMPLE RUN

Type TRON before running the test program.

```
<1Ø><2Ø><5Ø > TRON TRACES EACH LINE
<6Ø><3Ø>OF THIS TEST PROGRAM.
<4Ø><7Ø>END OF TEST PROGRAM.
<99>
```

TRON may also be used as a program statement to trace specific sections of programs. To test this feature, type TROFF to be sure the "trace" is off, then add the following line to the test program and RUN it.

```
35 TRON
```

SAMPLE RUN

```
TRON TRACES EACH LINE
OF THIS TEST PROGRAM.
<4Ø><7Ø>END OF TEST PROGRAM.
<99>
```

VARIATIONS IN USAGE

None known.

ALSO SEE

TROFF, NEW

The USR function executes a machine language routine stored in the computer's memory. The machine language routine can be entered into memory from the keyboard using the POKE statement or from cassette tape using a SYSTEM command.

Function

The USR function can be used in programs similar to any other "built in" function.

For example, 1Ø PRINT USR(N) If a
If a machine language routine which computes the square root of N, is stored in the computer's memory, then the computer will print the square root of the number N.

To test for the USR function, you must load a machine language routine into the computer (at appropriate addresses) using the POKE statement or SYSTEM command. Refer to your computer's Manual for correct use of this special function.

ALSO SEE

POKE, SYSTEM

The VAL function is used to convert numbers which are written as strings, back into numeric notation. VAL has the effect of stripping off the strings or dollar sign.

Function

For example:

```
1Ø A$="35"
2Ø PRINT VAL(A$)
```

prints the number 35 as a numeric value.

TEST PROGRAM

```
1Ø REM 'VAL' TEST PROGRAM
2Ø A$="45.12"
3Ø A=VAL(A$)
4Ø PRINT "IF THE STRING ";A$;" IS CONVERTED TO THE NUMBER";A
5Ø PRINT "THEN THE VAL FUNCTION PASSED THE TEST."
99 END
```

SAMPLE RUN

```
IF THE STRING 45.12 IS CONVERTED TO THE NUMBER 45.12
THEN THE VAL FUNCTION PASSED THE TEST.
```

VARIATIONS IN USAGE

Some computers (e.g. the TRS-80 Level II and other Microsoft variations) allow the use of combinations of numbers and letters with the VAL function, but the numbers must precede the letters. If they don't, the VAL function produces a Ø indicating it did not find a number as the first character.

For example, **PRINT VAL("123ABC")** prints the number 123.

TEST PROGRAM

```
1Ø REM 'VAL WITH MIXED STRING' TEST PROGRAM
2Ø A$="12 O'CLOCK"
3Ø A=VAL(A$)
4Ø PRINT "IF THE STRING ";A$;" IS CONVERTED TO THE NUMBER";A
5Ø PRINT "THE VAL FUNCTION ACCEPTED NUMBERS MIXED WITH LETTERS."
99 END
```

SAMPLE RUN

IF THE STRING 12 O'CLOCK IS CONVERTED TO THE NUMBER 12
THE VAL FUNCTION ACCEPTED NUMBERS MIXED WITH LETTERS.

ALSO SEE

STR$, ASC, CHR$, LEN, LEFT$, MID$, RIGHT$, STRING$

VLIN-AT is used in the APPLE II BASIC as a special feature to display a Vertical LINe AT a specified column on the screen.

Statement

The vertical line length is determined by two numbers following the VLIN statement. These numbers indicate the bounds between which the line will extend. The line may extend any length between rows 0 to 39.

The number following the AT function represents the column number which the line must occupy. This number may range from 0 to 39.

For example, **VLIN 10,30 AT 20** tells the computer to draw a vertical line from row 10 to row 30 AT column 20.

The **GR**aphics statement must be executed before the computer can accept the VLIN-AT statement (see GR). The line's color is determined by the COLOR statement (see COLOR).

TEST PROGRAM

```
10 REM 'VLIN-AT' TEST PROGRAM
20 GR
30 Y=0
40 FOR X=0 TO 39
50 COLOR = Y
60 VLIN 0,39 AT X
70 Y=Y+1
80 IF Y 16 THEN 100
90 Y=0
100 NEXT X
999 END
```

SAMPLE RUN

If the computer accepted the VLIN-AT statement, the screen should be filled with 39 vertical lines of various colors.

VARIATIONS IN USAGE

None known.

ALSO SEE

GR, COLOR, PLOT, HLIN-AT, TEST

VTAB (vertical tab) is used by the APPLE II BASIC to specify the starting line location on the screen for a PRINT statement. VTAB values from 1 to 24, representing the screen's 24 lines, are accepted.

For example, **VTAB 12** specifies the PRINT starting point as the 12th line down on the screen.

Statement

TEST PROGRAM

```
1Ø REM 'VTAB' TEST PROGRAM
2Ø PRINT "ENTER A VTAB VALUE FROM 1 TO 24";
3Ø INPUT N
4Ø VTAB N
5Ø PRINT "VTAB PASSED THE TEST IF THIS IS PRINTED ON LINE ";N
99 END
```

SAMPLE RUN *(using 5)*

```
ENTER A VTAB VALUE FROM 1 TO 24? 5




VTAB PASSED THE TEST IF THIS IS PRINTED ON LINE 5
```

IF YOUR COMPUTER DOESN'T HAVE IT

The easiest way to cause printing to start a certain number of lines down the screen is to first clear it [by a long series of PRINT statements in succession, or with a series of ASCII "line feeds" or CLS (clear screen)]. Check your ASCII chart to find your proper "N" for PRINT CHR$(N).

Then, again using PRINTs or an ASCII character, move down the screen the desired number of lines before printing.

VARIATIONS IN USAGE

None known.

ALSO SEE

TAB, PRINT-AT, PRINT, ASC, CHR$

WAIT is used in some computers (e.g. those using MAX-BASIC) to suspend program execution for a specified time.

Command Statement

For example, **WAIT 3Ø** tells the computer to wait 3Ø seconds before executing the next statement.

A few computers WAIT a fractional value (e.g. 1/1Ø or 1/1ØØØ) of the specified time.

For example, **WAIT 1ØØØØ** requires computers with ADDS BASIC to WAIT 1ØØØ seconds while the VARIAN 62Ø will WAIT 1Ø seconds.

This program allows you to check your computer's WAIT capability.

TEST PROGRAM #1

```
1Ø REM 'WAIT TIME PERIOD' TEST PROGRAM
2Ø PRINT "ENTER A UNIT OF TIME FOR THE COMPUTER TO WAIT";
3Ø INPUT T
4Ø PRINT "THE COMPUTER IS WAITING FOR";T;"UNITS OF TIME"
5Ø WAIT T
6Ø PRINT "THE WAIT STATEMENT PASSED THE TEST"
99 END
```

SAMPLE RUN *(using 6Ø)*

```
ENTER A UNIT OF TIME FOR THE COMPUTER TO WAIT? 6Ø
THE COMPUTER IS WAITING FOR 6Ø UNITS OF TIME

THE WAIT STATEMENT PASSED THE TEST
```

For a time delay alternative, substitute the following FOR-NEXT loop for WAIT in TEST PROGRAM #1. The value of T will require adjustment for your computer to produce the same amount of delay as the WAIT statement.

```
5Ø FOR X=1 TO T
55 NEXT X
```

WAIT is used by some other computers (e.g. those using variations of the Microsoft BASIC) to suspend program execution until the byte value at a specified computer port meets the conditions established by two byte values listed after WAIT.

WAIT

For example, **WAIT 3Ø, 6, 4** tells the computer to WAIT until a non-zero value is produced when the byte value at port 3Ø is exclusive ORed with the byte value 4, and the resultant value is logically ANDed with the byte value of 6. (Oh well . . . back to bird watching.) When this condition is met, program execution continues at the next statement. If this condition is not met, the keyboard BREAK, MONITOR, ESCAPE (or whatever works) key can be pressed to get out of the WAIT condition.

Each value listed in the WAIT statement must be between Ø and 255 (the range of values that can be held in an 8 bit memory cell). When the last byte value (4 in the above example) is omitted from the WAIT statement, the computer assumes its value to be Ø.

In the above example, port 3Ø must equal 2 before the computer continues program execution as illustrated by this "truth table".

PORT VALUE		3rd BYTE VALUE				2nd BYTE VALUE		
2	*OR*	5	=	7	*AND*	2	=	2
0		1		1		0		0
1		0		1		1		1
0		1		1		0		0
0		0		0		0		0
0		0		0		0		0
0		0		0		0		0
0		0		0		0		0
0		0		0		0		0

Some computers (e.g. the Processor Technology Extended Cassette BASIC) WAIT until the byte value at the specified computer port, ANDed with the second byte value, is equal to the third byte value.

For example, **WAIT 12Ø, 5, 5** the computer WAITS until the byte value at port 12Ø is equal to 5 as shown in this truth table.

PORT VALUE		2nd BYTE= VALUE		3rd BYTE VALUE
5	*AND*	5	=	5
1		1		1
0		0		0
1		1		1
0		0		0
0		0		0
0		0		0
0		0		0

WAIT

TEST PROGRAM #2

```
1Ø REM 'WAIT FOR PORT CONDITION' TEST PROGRAM
2Ø PRINT "THE COMPUTER IS WAITING FOR ONLY BIT 1 TO BE SET"
3Ø PRINT "IN PORT 2Ø (THE DECIMAL VALUE OF 2)"
4Ø WAIT 2Ø,253,2
5Ø PRINT "BIT 1 IN PORT 2Ø IS SET"
99 END
```

SAMPLE RUN

```
THE COMPUTER IS WAITING FOR ONLY BIT 1 TO BE SET
IN PORT 2Ø (THE DECIMAL VALUE OF 2)
BIT 1 IN PORT 2Ø IS SET
```

If you are unable to set bit 1 in port 2Ø, then press the keyboard BREAK key (or whatever works) to escape from this condition.

Some computers can use WAIT as a command.

IF YOUR COMPUTER DOESN'T HAVE IT

If your computer has the INP capability, but does not have WAIT, substitute INP for WAIT in TEST PROGRAM #2, using these changes:

```
4Ø IF INP(2Ø)=2 THEN 5Ø
45 GOTO 4Ø
```

ALSO SEE

INP, FOR-NEXT

Operators

Since the Operators defy logical organization, we've arbitrarily put the "punctuation-type" operators first, then miscellaneous and ended up with all the math-type operators. Since there are relatively few operators, we won't attempt to index them (might take you just as long to search through an index anyway).

Pairs of quotation marks (") are used in PRINT statements to enclose letters, numbers or characters to be printed. If the quotes are omitted, the computer recognizes the letters as variables and prints whatever values may be assigned to them.

Operator

For example, PRINT "A" prints the letter "A". While PRINT A prints the value assigned to variable A.

Quotes can be used to print numbers without the usual space for their + or − sign. It can insert extra spaces by enclosing them.

For example,

```
1Ø PRINT "        THE NUMBER";
2Ø PRINT "1Ø"
```

will print

```
        THE NUMBER1Ø
```

Quotes **cannot** be "nested" inside other quotes. (The computer is unable to distinguish which one is the end of the actual PRINT statement.)

For example, PRINT "I SAID "HELLO" TO HIM" will not work. An apostrophy is usually substituted for the inside quotes in these cases.

For example, PRINT "I SAID 'HELLO' TO HIM"

TEST PROGRAM

```
1Ø REM 'QUOTED ('') ' PRINT STATEMENT TEST PROGRAM
2Ø A=5
3Ø B=1Ø
4Ø PRINT "A+B =";A+B
5Ø PRINT "THE QUOTATION MARKS PASSED THE PRINT TEST."
99 END
```

SAMPLE RUN

```
A+B = 15
THE QUOTATION MARKS PASSED THE PRINT TEST.
```

Quotes can be used with most recent computers to allow the INPUT statement to serve in both a PRINT and INPUT capacity.

TEST PROGRAM

```
1Ø REM 'QUOTED (") ' INPUT STATEMENT TEST PROGRAM
2Ø INPUT "ASSIGN A VALUE TO VARIABLE X";X
3Ø PRINT "THE VALUE F X IS";X
99 END
```

SAMPLE RUN *(using 5)*

```
ASSIGN A VALUE TO VARIABLE X? 5
THE VALUE OF X IS 5
```

Some computers require quotes around strings in DATA statements, while others require them only when the string is preceded by, encloses, or is followed by a blank, comma or colon. For more information see DATA.

TEST PROGRAM

```
1Ø REM 'QUOTED (") ' DATA STATEMENT TEST PROGRAM
2Ø DATA " DATA STATEMENT "
3Ø READ A$
4Ø PRINT "QUOTES IN";A$;"PASSED THE TEST"
99 END
```

SAMPLE RUN

```
QUOTES IN DATA STATEMENT PASSED THE TEST
```

Quotes are used with CSAVE and CLOAD in the TRS-80 Level II (and other versions of MICROSOFT) BASIC to assign a specific name to the program recorded on cassette tape.

For example,

```
CSAVE "A"
CLOAD "A"
```

will record a program on cassette tape, naming it "A", and will load only the program named "A" back into the computer. For more information and test procedures see CLOAD and CSAVE.

The TRS-80 Level I BASIC uses quotes in the PRINT# statement to record data on cassette tape.

For example, `PRINT#A;",";B;",";C` will store the values assigned to variables A, B and C on cassette tape. For more information and TEST PROGRAMS see PRINT.

ALSO SEE

PRINT, TAB, ;(semicolon), ,(comma), DATA, READ, CSAVE, CLOAD

The Comma is an operator with a wide range of uses. One of the more common is with the PRINT statement, where it causes individual items to be printed in pre-established horizontal zones. For example, **PRINT 1,2,3,4** prints each number in a separate zone.

Each zone usually allows a maximum of sixteen characters. The number of zones allowed on each line varies from 4 to 8, depending on screen (or printer) line width.

A
N
S
I

Operator

TEST PROGRAM # 1

```
1∅ REM TEST PROGRAM USING 'COMMA' FOR ZONING
2∅ PRINT "THE FOLLOWING LINE WILL PRINT IN 4 ZONES"
3∅ PRINT 1,2,3,4
4∅ PRINT "THE FOLLOWING LINES SHOW YOUR AVAILABLE ZONES"
5∅ PRINT 1,2,3,4,5,6,7,8,9,1∅,11,12,13,14,15,16
99 END
```

SAMPLE RUN *(4 zone per line display, 64 characters maximum per line)*

```
THE FOLLOWING LINE WILL PRINT IN 4 ZONES
1               2               3               4
THE FOLLOWING LINES WILL SHOW YOUR AVAILABLE ZONES
1               2               3               4
5               6               7               8
9               1∅              11              12
13              14              15              16
```

The COMMA is also used to separate elements in array fields. Example, **A(I,J,K)**. The COMMA separates I,J, and K into individual elements within this three-dimension array.

TEST PROGRAM #2

```
1∅ REM TEST PROGRAM USING 'COMMA' IN 2 DIMENSION ARRAY
2∅ A(1,1)=5
3∅ PRINT "A(1,1)  =";A(1,1)
4∅ PRINT "LINE 2∅ PASSED THE TEST IF A(1,1) = 5."
99 END
```

SAMPLE RUN

```
A(1,1)=5
LINE 2∅ PASSED THE TEST IF A(1,1) = 5.
```

The COMMA is used in a similar manner in the DATA, DIM, INPUT, ON-GOTO, and READ statements to separate items of data.

This program tests the COMMA capability in the INPUT and PRINT statements.

TEST PROGRAM #3

```
10 REM 'COMMA' TEST PROGRAM
50 PRINT "ENTER THREE NUMBERS";
60 INPUT A,B,C
100 PRINT "NUMBER 1 =";A,2;"="; B,3;"=";C
999 END
```

SAMPLE RUN *(using 11,12,13)*

```
ENTER THREE NUMBERS? 11,12,13
NUMBER 1 = 11     2 = 12          3 = 13
```

To test the COMMA capability in the READ and DATA statements, add these lines to the last TEST PROGRAM.

```
80 READ D,E,F
100 PRINT "NUMBER";D;"=";A,E;"=";B,F;"=";C
110 DATA 1,2,3
```

Run the program. The SAMPLE RUN should remain the same.

To test the COMMA capability in the ON-GOTO statement, add these lines:

```
30 FOR X=1 TO 3
40 ON X GOTO 50,80,100
70 NEXT X
90 NEXT X
```

Run the program, and again the sample run should remain the same.

The computer's COMMA capability in DIM statements can be checked by adding this line:

```
20 DIM A(1),B(2),C(3)
```

The addition of this line should not change the SAMPLE RUN.

For other applications of the COMMA see PRINT USING, AT and @.

VARIATIONS IN USAGE

Some computers (e.g. those with Palo Alto Tiny BASIC) use the COMMA in LET statements similar to the way most computers use the COLON, and it's use in the PRINT and INPUT statements can be modified with the # and − operators.

ALSO SEE

DATA, DIM, INPUT, ON-GOTO, AT, @, PRINT USING, READ

The Period is used in the TRS-80 Level II BASIC (and others) to cause the computer to LIST or EDIT the last program line entered, listed or which caused an error in the computer.

TEST PROGRAM

Operator

```
10 REM '. (PERIOD)' TEST PROGRAM
20 PRINT "THE PERIOD FOLLOWING THE LIST COMMAND"
30 PRINT "SHOULD LIST THE LAST LINE YOU ENTER"
99 END
```

SAMPLE RUN

Type the command: LIST. (if you omit the period following LIST, the entire program will of course be LISTed). The computer should print:

```
99 END
```

Add the following line to the TEST PROGRAM:

```
40 PRINT "THE PERIOD PASSED THE TEST"
```

Type the command: EDIT. (including the period).

If the computer has this EDIT capability, the computer will print the number 40 followed by a cursor. This indicates the computer is in the EDIT mode and is ready to modify line 40 (the last line entered).

VARIATIONS IN USAGE

Several computers (e.g. the TRS-80 Level I and other variations of Tiny BASIC) use the period as part of word abbreviations.

For example, the letter I is normally used as a variable, but I. can be used as an abbreviation for INPUT or INTeger depending on how it is used in the program (for more Information see I.). In addition, P.=PRINT, R.=RUN, L.=LIST, etc.

ALSO SEE

EDIT, LIST, I., INPUT, INT

A **semicolon** is used in PRINT statements to allow several printed sections to be joined together (concatenized) onto one line. For example, PRINT "H";"I" is printed as HI.

A
N
S
I

Operator

TEST PROGRAM

```
1Ø REM 'SEMICOLON' STRING TEST PROGRAM
2Ø PRINT "IF THIS SENTENCE IS PRINTED ";
3Ø PRINT "ON ONE LINE, THE TEST PASSED."
99 END
```

SAMPLE RUN

```
IF THIS SENTENCE IS PRINTED ON ONE LINE, THE TEST PASSED.
```

When a SEMICOLON is used to separate the printing of numeric values or numeric variables, a space is automatically inserted before each number to make room for its + or − sign. An additional space is automatically inserted after the number since it's assumed that such a space is always required. This feature can cause programming difficulties when trying to get a special print format.

For example, PRINT 1;2;3 is printed with two spaces inserted between each number.

TEST PROGRAM

```
1Ø REM 'SEMICOLON' TEST PROGRAM WITH NUMERICS
2Ø A=5
3Ø PRINT "STUDY THE SPACING BETWEEN EACH OF THE NUMBERS."
4Ø PRINT 1;"2";"3";4;A;"6"; −7
5Ø PRINT "12345678901234567890"
99 END
```

SAMPLE RUN

```
STUDY THE SPACING BETWEEN EACH OF THE NUMBERS.
 1 23  4  5 6-7
12345678901234567890
```

VARIATIONS IN USAGE

A few interpreters insert a space between strings being concatenized. Such a (rare) feature eliminates the need for the space after the letter "D" in line 2Ø of the first TEST.

ALSO SEE

COMMA, PRINT USING, TAB

The COLON allows placing more than one statement on a single program line.

For example, **1Ø PRINT "SAMPLE LINE" :LET A=1Ø: GOTO 99** holds three separate statements ... PRINT, LET and GOTO in one program line, number 1Ø.

Operator

SAMPLE RUN

```
1Ø REM 'COLON (:) OPERATOR' TEST PROGRAM
2Ø PRINT "THIS TEST";:FOR X=1 TO 5ØØØ: NEXT X: PRINT " IS COMPLETE"
99 END
```

SAMPLE RUN

THIS TEST *(PAUSE)* IS COMPLETE

GOTO, IF-GOTO, IF-THEN, ON-GOTO and other branching statements must be the last statement on a multiple statement line to prevent branching out of it before the entire line is executed.

For example, in the line

1Ø FOR X=1 TO 1Ø:NEXT X:GOTO 1ØØ:PRINT "THE LOST WORDS"

The computer executes the GOTO statement and branches to line 1ØØ before it has a chance to execute the PRINT statement. There is no way to PRINT the "LOST WORDS".

Most computers do not allow DATA statements in multiple statement lines. Others (e.g. IMSAI) do not execute statements on the same line if they follow a GOSUB statement even though a RETURN directs execution back to that line.

Be especially careful to put IF-THEN statements only at the end of multiple statement lines. If one fails, execution will fall to the next **numbered** line, *not to the next statement in the same line.*

1Ø IF A=1Ø THEN B=A:PRINT "A IS NOT EQUAL TO 1Ø"
2Ø END

If the value of A is not equal to 1Ø, the condition of the IF-THEN statement is not met, and the program ENDs without initializing the value of B to A or executing the PRINT statement. When IF-THEN statements can't be placed last on a multi-statement line, they must be given a "private line."

IF YOUR COMPUTER DOESN'T HAVE IT

Many computers have no provision for writing more than one program statement on a numbered line. Others that do however, may use a backslash (\) instead of a colon. A very few use a semicolon.

VARIATIONS IN USAGE

None known.

ALSO SEE

\, ;, GOTO, IF-THEN, IF-GOTO, ON-GOTO, etc.

Parentheses are used in arithmetic operations to determine the order in which math operations are performed. Math operations enclosed within parentheses are performed before those outside the parentheses. If a math operation is enclosed in parentheses which is in turn enclosed within another set of parentheses (and so on), the computer first performs those operations "buried the deepest". When there is a "tie", the operation to the left is executed first.

Operator

For example, `A=5+(((2*4)-2)*3)` The computer performs this math operation in the following sequence:

$$A = 5+((8-2)*3) = 5+(6*3) = 5+18 = 23$$

TEST PROGRAM

```
1Ø REM '( ) PARENTHESES' TEST PROGRAM
2Ø A=(10*(5-3))/2
3Ø PRINT "A =";A
4Ø PRINT "THE PARENTHESES PASSED THE TEST IF A = 1Ø"
99 END
```

SAMPLE RUN

```
A = 1Ø
THE PARENTHESES PASSED THE TEST IF A = 1Ø
```

PARENTHESES are required with "logical math" operators to identify the two statements being compared.

For example, `IF (A=8) * (B=6) THEN 8Ø`
For more information see * and AND.

PARENTHESES are also used to enclose the elements in DIM statements and array variables. For more information see DIM.

TEST PROGRAM

```
1Ø REM '( ) PARENTHESES' TEST PROGRAM USING DIM AND ARRAYS
2Ø DIM A(5,5)
3Ø A(1,1)=2Ø
4Ø PRINT "( ) PASSED THE TEST IN LINES";A(1,1);"AND";A(1,1)+1Ø
99 END
```

SAMPLE RUN

Most computers with built in functions use PARENTHESES to enclose the numbers or letters to be manipulated.

For example, LOG(1Ø)

Most computers that use parentheses but not brackets ([ ]) allow parentheses to substitute for brackets without ill effect. In most cases, parentheses can be used instead of brackets.

For example,

[(A*B)/C]

can be written

((A*B)/C)

ALSO SEE

*, +, AND, OR, DIM

The @ Operator is used by a few computers (e.g. TRS-80 Level II) to specify a PRINT statement starting location on the video screen. Its value should be from 0 to 1023 and must be followed by a comma. For example, **PRINT @ 475,"HELLO"** prints the word HELLO on the CRT starting at grid position 475.

Operator

TEST PROGRAM

```
10 REM "@" PRINT MODIFIER TEST PROGRAM
20 PRINT @ 128, "2. IF THIS LINE IS PRINTED AFTER LINE 1."
30 PRINT @ 0, "1. THE @ OPERATOR PASSED THE TEST"
40 GOTO 40
99 END
```

SAMPLE RUN

```
1. THE @ OPERATOR PASSED THE TEST
2. IF THIS LINE IS PRINTED AFTER LINE 1.
```

IF YOUR COMPUTER DOESN'T HAVE IT

If your computer does not use the @ operator as a PRINT modifier, this feature can be simulated by using an appropriate number of PRINT statements (to activate line feeds) and spaces to arrive at the same location on the CRT.

VARIATIONS IN USAGE

The @ (AT) operator is used by some computers (e.g. TRS-80 Level II) to erase the last line displayed on the screen and execute a carriage return. For example, type **10 REM LINE DELETION TEST** (but don't hit the ENTER or RETURN key) and press the @ key. The line should be erased and the cursor should return to the left margin.

The same operation can be accomplished on some computers by pressing the RUB (rub out), SCR (scratch), ← (left arrow) or SND (send) key, or by pressing the ENTER (or RETURN) key before and after typing the number of the line to be deleted.

ALSO SEE

PRINT, AT, PRINT AT

The # sign is used to specify individual variables as being of "double-precision". Double precision variables are capable of storing numbers containing 17 digits (only 16 digits are printed). Single-precision variables are accurate to 6 digits.

Operator

The # sign must be placed after a variable for it to be defined as having double-precision, each time that variable is used in the program. If the # sign is found with a variable that is listed in DEFSNG or DEFINT statements (within the same program), the double precision character (#) over-rides their action and declares the variable to be of double-precision.

TEST PROGRAM

```
10 REM '#' DOUBLE PRECISION OPERATOR TEST PROGRAM
20 DEFSNG A,B
30 A=1.234567890123456
40 B#=1.234567890123456
50 IF A=B# THEN 100
60 PRINT "A  =";A
70 PRINT "B#  =";B#
80 PRINT "THE # SIGN PASSED THE DOUBLE PRECISION TEST"
90 GOTO 999
100 PRINT "THE # SIGN FAILED THE DOUBLE PRECISION TEST"
999 END
```

SAMPLE RUN

```
A = 1.23457
B# = 1.234567890123456
THE # SIGN PASSED THE DOUBLE PRECISION TEST
```

The # (number sign) is used by a few computers as a shorthand symbol for the PRINT statement. For more information see PRINT.

TEST PROGRAM #1

```
10 REM '#' TEST PROGRAM
20 #"THE # SIGN PASSED THE PRINT TEST"
99 END
```

# #

SAMPLE RUN

THE # SIGN PASSED THE PRINT TEST

The # operator is used by a few computers as the relational operator "not-equal-to" (< >).

For example, **IF A#B THEN 1ØØ** tells the computer to branch to line 1ØØ if the value of variable A is **not** equal to variable B.

The # operator is used in the PRINT USING statement by most computers using a Microsoft BASIC to indicate the PRINT position for each digit in a number or numeric variable. If the PRINT USING statement contains more # signs than the number of digits in a number, the computer prints a space for each unused # sign to the **left** of the decimal point, and a zero for each unused # sign to the **right** of the decimal point.

For example, **1Ø PRINT USING "#####.###";1 2.5** will print the number 12.5ØØ with 3 blank spaces printed to the left of the number 1 in place of the 3 unused # signs.

For more information see PRINT USING.

TEST PROGRAM #2

```
1Ø REM '#' PRINT USING TEST PROGRAM
2Ø PRINT "ENTER A VALUE FOR VARIABLE N";
3Ø INPUT N
4Ø PRINT "THE NUMBER";N;"IS PRINTED AS";
5Ø PRINT USING "####.##" ;N
99 END
```

SAMPLE RUN *(using 12.5)*

ENTER A VALUE FOR VARIABLE N? 12.5
THE NUMBER 12.5 IS PRINTED AS 12.5Ø

Computers with file handling capability use the # operator in such statements as INPUT#, PRINT#, READ#, CLOSE#, and others to indicate a device number to store data and retrieve data from external memory such as disc and cassette tape.

TEST PROGRAM #3 *(stores data on cassette tape TRS-80 Level II)*

Set the cassette recorder to the RECORD mode and RUN this program.

```
10 REM 'PRINT#' TEST PROGRAM
20 PRINT "DATA SHOULD BE RECORDING ON CASSETTE TAPE"
30 PRINT#-1, "TEST" ,1,2,3
40 PRINT "PRINT# HAS COMPLETED THE DATA TRANSFER"
99 END
```

SAMPLE RUN

```
DATA SHOULD BE RECORDING ON CASSETTE TAPE
PRINT# HAS COMPLETED THE DATA TRANSFER
```

To test the computer's READ# capability, rewind the cassette tape, set the recorder to the PLAY mode, erase memory and RUN the next TEST PROGRAM.

TEST PROGRAM #4 *(enters data from cassette into the computer)*

```
10 REM 'INPUT#' TEST PROGRAM
20 PRINT "THE COMPUTER SHOULD NOW READ DATA FROM CASSETTE"
30 INPUT#-1,A$,A,B,C
40 PRINT "THE INPUT# STATEMENT PASSED THE TEST IF"
50 PRINT A$;A;B;C;"IS PRINTED"
99 END
```

SAMPLE RUN

```
THE COMPUTER SHOULD NOW READ DATA FROM CASSETTE
THE INPUT# STATEMENT PASSED THE TEST IF
TEST 1 2 3 IS PRINTED
```

In large time-sharing systems (e.g. the DEC-10), one program can access a number of different data files, each of which is given a name and stored on disc. A statement in the program gives a number to each file it will be using, and that file will be referred to by number, not name. The # sign then literally means "number" — — — the file number(name) from which DATA is to be READ, INPUT, PRINTed or otherwise processed.

Example:

```
30 FILE #1,"TESTING"
80 READ #1,A,B,C,D,E
```

etc.

ALSO SEE

DEFDBL, DEFSNG, DEFINT, !, %, PRINT, REM, PRINT USING, READ#, FILE#,< >

The $ symbol following a letter or letter/number combination is used to declare a variable to be a string variable.

Information declared a string variable in a program statement must usually be enclosed in quotation marks. For example, **A$ = "THE BASIC HANDBOOK."** If an INPUT statement is used to assign the information entered to a string variable, then quotes are not usually required. (See INPUT and READ.)

A
N
S
I

Operator

TEST PROGRAM #1

```
10 REM '$' TEST PROGRAM WITH STRING STATEMENT
20 A$ =" LINE 20"
30 PRINT "THIS COMPUTER PASSED THE '$' TEST IN";A$
99 END
```

SAMPLE RUN

```
THIS COMPUTER PASSED THE '$' TEST IN LINE 20
```

The number of characters that can be assigned to a string variable is limited by the computer's interpreter. Most computers with string capability accept at least 16 characters, and some can accept as many as 255.

Some computers (e.g.Hewlett-Packard) require you to reserve memory space for each separate string with a DIM statement [e.g. **10 DIM A$(50)**]. (See DIM and CLEAR.)

The following program demonstrates the assignment of characters to the variable A$ (pronounced "A string"):

TEST PROGRAM #2

```
10 REM '$' INPUT STRING WITH LENGTH TEST PROGRAM
20 PRINT "ENTER A KNOWN QUANTITY OF CHARACTERS"
30 INPUT A$
40 PRINT "COUNT THE NUMBER OF CHARACTERS PRINTED BELOW"
50 PRINT A$
99 END
```

SAMPLE RUN *(Typical)*

The "character string" shown in the sample run is 10 characters long:

```
ENTER A KNOWN QUANTITY OF CHARACTERS
? 1234567890
COUNT THE NUMBER OF CHARACTERS PRINTED BELOW
1234567890
```

If all the characters were printed and no error message appeared, RUN again and add perhaps 1Ø more characters. If that prints, continue the process until characters start being chopped off the end, or an error message appears.

Most computers which can handle strings allow all the letters of the alphabet to serve as string variable designators. A few computers allow only a few. (e.g. Radio Shack TRS-80 LEVEL I allows only two strings, A$ and B$ and they cannot be compared against each other.)

The next program tests the full range (A and Z) of alphabet characters allowed by your computer.

TEST PROGRAM #3

```
1Ø REM '$' (STRING) VARIABLE TEST PROGRAM
2Ø A$="LINE 2Ø, "
3Ø PRINT "A$ PASSED THE TEST IN ";A$;
4Ø Z$="AND Z$ IN LINE 4Ø"
5Ø PRINT Z$
99 END
```

SAMPLE RUN

```
A$ PASSED THE TEST IN LINE 2Ø, AND Z$ IN LINE 4Ø
```

Many string handling computers allow combinations of letters, numbers and symbols to specify string and numeric variables. Each variable must start with a letter, but only the first several (usually 2) alphanumeric characters are recognized and processed by the interpreter. For example, **AB34K$** and **ABYN8$** (if accepted), are usually processed as the same string variable (AB$) since the first two letters are identical. A little experimenting will quickly show your machine's capability.

TEST PROGRAM #4

```
1Ø REM '$' (STRING NAME) TEST PROGRAM
2Ø ABCDE$="TEST STRING"
3Ø PRINT "ABXYZ$ = ";ABXYZ$
4Ø PRINT "AB123$ = ";AB123$
5Ø PRINT "ONLY THE FIRST TWO LETTERS OF THE STRING NAME"
6Ø PRINT "WERE RECOGNIZED IF THE TWO STRINGS ARE IDENTICAL"
99 END
```

$

ABXYZ$ = TEST STRING
AB123$ = TEST STRING
ONLY THE FIRST TWO LETTERS OF THE STRING NAME
WERE RECOGNIZED IF THE TWO STRINGS ARE IDENTICAL

Words that are intrinsic Statements or Functions cannot be used as string or numeric variables. For example, SPRINTS$ may be an illegal string variable because it contains the word "PRINT". Refer to your owner's manual for a list of "reserved words" that cannot be used in your computer's programs.

Most computers that accommodate strings, permit string comparison. That is, one string or string variable can be compared character by character against another string or string variable using relational operators. Strings must be enclosed in quotation marks when compared to a string variable.

TEST PROGRAM #5

```
10 REM '$' (STRING) COMPARISON TEST PROGRAM
20 READ A$
30 IF A$="WHOA" THEN 60
40 PRINT A$,
50 GOTO 20
60 PRINT "STRINGS CAN BE COMPARED."
70 DATA ONE, TWO, WHOA
99 END
```

SAMPLE RUN

ONE   TWO   STRINGS CAN BE COMPARED.

VARIATIONS IN USAGE

None known in the BASIC language.

ALSO SEE

DEFSTR, CHR$, FRE(string), INKEY$, LEN, LEFT$, MID$, RIGHT$, STR$, STRING$, VAL, LET, DATA, READ, DIM and CLEAR

The ! (exclamation mark) is used to specify individual variables as being of "single-precision". Single precision variables are capable of storing numbers containing no more than 7 digits (only 6 digits are printed). Double-precision means having 16 digit precision.

Operator

Since variables are automatically single precision, the ! operator is used in programs to change a variable back to single precision after it has been declared double-precision by a previous DEFDBL statement or # operator.

TEST PROGRAM

```
1Ø REM 'I' SINGLE PRECISION OPERATOR TEST PROGRAM
2Ø DEFDBL X,N
3Ø N=1234.5678ØØ12345
4Ø X=N
5Ø PRINT "DOUBLE PRECISION VARIABLE X =";X
6Ø X!=N
7Ø PRINT "SINGLE PRECISION VARIABLE X! =";X!
8Ø PRINT "THE '!' SINGLE PRECISION OPERATOR PASSED THE TEST"
99 END
```

SAMPLE RUN

```
DOUBLE PRECISION VARIABLE X = 1234.5678ØØ12345
SINGLE PRECISION VARIABLE X! = 1234.57
THE '!' SINGLE PRECISION OPERATOR PASSED THE TEST
```

The ! operator is also used by some computers (e.g. those using the Microsoft BASIC) in the PRINT USING statement to allow only the left-most character in a string to be printed.

For example, **PRINT USING"!";"COMPUSOFT"** should print the letter "C".

For more information see PRINT USING and the next Test Program.

TEST PROGRAM

```
1Ø REM '! STRING SPECIFIER' TEST PROGRAM
2Ø PRINT "ENTER A SAMPLE WORD";
3Ø INPUT A$
4Ø PRINT "THE FIRST LETTER IN THE WORD ";A$;" IS ";
5Ø PRINT USING "!";A$
99 END
```

SAMPLE RUN *(using HANDBOOK)*

ENTER A SAMPLE WORD? HANDBOOK
THE FIRST LETTER IN THE WORD HANDBOOK IS H

VARIATIONS IN USAGE

Some interpreters (e.g. the COMPUMAX BASIC) use ! as an abbreviation for the REMark statement.

TEST PROGRAM

```
10 PRINT "'! (REMARK) ' TEST PROGRAM"
20 ! PRINT " THE ! SIGN FAILED THE REM TEST"
30 ! THE ! SIGN FAILED THE REMARK TEST IF LINE 20 IS PRINTED"
40 PRINT "THE ! SIGN PASSED THE TEST"
99 END
```

SAMPLE RUN

'! (REMARK) ' TEST PROGRAM
THE ! SIGN PASSED THE TEST

ALSO SEE

DEFDBL, DEFSNG, #, PRINT USING

% is used by some computers (e.g. those using Microsoft BASIC) to define variables as integers. When the % sign is placed to the right of a variable, that variable is then only capable of storing integer values.

For more information on the use of the INTeger function see INT.

Operator

TEST PROGRAM #1

```
1Ø REM '% INTEGER OPERATOR' TEST PROGRAM
2Ø I%=2.864
3Ø IF I%=2 THEN 6Ø
4Ø PRINT "THE % INTEGER OPERATOR FAILED THE TEST"
5Ø GOTO 99
6Ø PRINT "THE % INTEGER OPERATOR PASSED THE TEST"
99 END
```

SAMPLE RUN

```
THE % INTEGER OPERATOR PASSED THE TEST
```

The % operator is used by some computers (e.g. those using Microsoft BASIC) in the PRINT USING statement. It causes the printing of as many left-most characters in a string as there are spaces between two % signs. The computer also counts the two % signs, therefore no less than two characters can be specified. (To specify one character in the string, see the ! operator.)

For example, **PRINT USING "%   %";"ABCDEFGHI"** should print the first four letters "ABCD" because two spaces were included between the % signs (2 spaces + 2 % signs = 4 letters). For more information see PRINT USING.

TEST PROGRAM #2

```
1Ø REM '%' STRING SPECIFIER TEST PROGRAM
2Ø A$"TESTIMONIAL"
3Ø PRINT "THE % OPERATOR PASSED THE STRING SPECIFIER ";
4Ø PRINT USING "%   %";A$
99 END
```

%

SAMPLE RUN

THE % OPERATOR PASSED THE STRING SPECIFIER TEST

Some computers use the % sign in the PRINT USING statement to "flag" a number as having exceeded the field specifier (#).

For example, **PRINT USING** "###.#";**1234.56** should print the number %1234.6. The entire number on the left side of the decimal point is printed when it exceeds the field specifier limits. If the number on the right side of the decimal point exceeds the field specifier, it is rounded up. For more information see PRINT USING.

TEST PROGRAM #3

```
10 REM '%' PRINT USING OVERFLOW TEST PROGRAM
20 A=123.45
30 PRINT "THE PRINT USING STATEMENT CHANGED #";A;"TO ";
40 PRINT USING "##.#" ;A
99 END
```

SAMPLE RUN

THE PRINT USING STATEMENT CHANGED # 123.45 TO %123.5

ALSO SEE

INT., I., PRINT USING, #

The ? (question mark) is used by many computers (e.g. those with variations of Microsoft BASIC) as an abbreviation for PRINT. Most (but not all) automatically change the ? sign to the word "PRINT" when the program is LISTed.

For more information see PRINT.

Operator

TEST PROGRAM

```
10 REM '? (PRINT)' TEST PROGRAM
20 ? "THE ? SIGN PASSED THE PRINT TEST"
99 END
```

SAMPLE RUN

```
THE ? SIGN PASSED THE PRINT TEST
```

Most computers print a ? when it executes the INPUT statement, indicating it is waiting for you to enter some data or an answer. Execution resumes when the ENTER or RETURN key is pressed.

For more information see INPUT.

TEST PROGRAM

```
10 REM '?' (INPUT REQUEST) TEST PROGRAM
20 PRINT "THE ? SIGN PASSED THE TEST"
30 PRINT "IF THE FOLLOWING LINE CONTAINS THE ? SIGN"
40 INPUT A
99 END
```

SAMPLE RUN

```
THE ? SIGN PASSED THE TEST
IF THE FOLLOWING LINE CONTAINS THE ? SIGN
?
```

Some computers (e.g. those with a Microsoft BASIC) use the ? sign with the CLOAD command to compare a program stored in the computer's memory with a program stored on cassette.

To test this feature, see the test procedures under CLOAD.

ALSO SEE

PRINT, #, INPUT, CLOAD, LIST

The \ operator is used by a few computers to allow multiple statements in one program line.

For example, `1Ø A=1Ø\B=5\C=A-B\PRINT C` combines four operations in one line.

For more information see: (Colon).

TEST PROGRAM

Operator

```
1Ø REM '\OPERATOR' TEST PROGRAM
2Ø PRINT "THIS TEST ";\FOR X=1 TO 5ØØ\NEXT X\PRINT "IS COMPLETE"
99 END
```

SAMPLE RUN

```
THIS TEST IS COMPLETE
```

VARIATIONS IN USAGE

The back-slash is sometimes seen separating letters and numbers as they are being erased or "rubbed out" on some terminals. This is often done when correcting typing errors.

ALSO SEE

: (COLON)

The ∗∗ (double asterisk) is used as an arithmetic exponentiation sign in some computers (e.g. the DEC-10, DEC-17D, DEC-BASIC-PLUS-2, H.P. 3000, and those using the MAXBASIC) to compute the value of a base number to a specified power.

For example, 2∗∗3 is the same as the cube of 2 or 2^3. For more information see ↑.

Operator

TEST PROGRAM

```
10 REM '** (EXPONENTIATION)' TEST PROGRAM
20 PRINT "ENTER A BASE NUMBER";
30 INPUT B
40 PRINT "NEXT, ENTER THE EXPONENT";
50 INPUT E
60 A=B**E
70 PRINT "THE NUMBER";B;"TO THE";E;"POWER IS";A
30999 END
```

SAMPLE RUN *(using 4 and 3)*

```
ENTER A BASE NUMBER? 4
NEXT, ENTER THE EXPONENT? 3
THE NUMBER 4 TO THE 3 POWER IS 64
```

The ∗∗ (double asterisk) is also used by some computers (e.g. those using Microsoft BASIC) in the PRINT USING statement. An asterisk (∗) is printed in all unused spaces to the left of a specified number's decimal point. The primary purpose for doing this is to prevent someone from increasing the size of a check printed by computer.

For example, **PRINT USING"∗∗######.##";456.25** will print ∗∗∗∗456.25

The # sign represents the spaces set aside for the numeric value to be printed. The unused spaces are filled by a ∗ sign.

For more information see PRINT USING.

TEST PROGRAM

```
10 REM '** PRINT SPECIFIER' TEST PROGRAM
20 PRINT "ENTER A SAMPLE NUMBER";
30 INPUT N
40 PRINT USING "**#######";N
50 PRINT "THE ** SIGN PASSED THE PRINT USING TEST"
99 END
```

SAMPLE RUN *(using 468)*

```
ENTER A SAMPLE NUMBER? 468
****468
THE ** SIGN PASSED THE PRINT USING TEST
```

ALSO SEE

PRINT USING, ↑, !, ∧ and ⌐

The ⌒ (circumflex) is an arithmetic exponentiation sign used to compute the value of a base number to a specified power.

For example, $2 ⌒ 3$ is the same as the cube of 2 or 2^3

For more information see ↑.

Operator

TEST PROGRAM

```
10 REM '⌒(EXPONENTIATION)' TEST PROGRAM
20 PRINT "ENTER A BASE NUMBER";
30 INPUT B
40 PRINT "NEXT, ENTER THE EXPONENT";
50 INPUT E
60 A=B⌒E
70 PRINT "THE NUMBER";B;"TO THE";E;"POWER IS";A
30999 END
```

SAMPLE RUN *(using 4 and 3)*

```
ENTER A BASE NUMBER? 4
NEXT, ENTER THE EXPONENT 3
THE NUMBER 4 TO THE 3 POWER IS 64
```

VARIATIONS IN USAGE

None known.

ALSO SEE

↑, ∧, !, and **

The most common use of the + sign is in arithmetic addition. Example, **PRINT A+B** prints the sum of variables A and B.

Operator

TEST PROGRAM

```
10 REM '+' MATH OPERATOR TEST PROGRAM
20 PRINT "ENTER A VALUE FOR VARIABLE A";
30 INPUT A
40 PRINT "ENTER A VALUE FOR VARIABLE B";
50 INPUT B
60 C=A+B
70 PRINT "THE SUM OF";A;"+";B;"IS";C
99 END
```

SAMPLE RUN *(using 6 and 14)*

```
ENTER A VALUE FOR VARIABLE A? 6
ENTER A VALUE FOR VARIABLE B? 14
THE SUM OF 6 + 14 IS 20
```

Some computers use the + sign as a logical "OR" operator in an IF-THEN statement.

For example, **10 IF (A=8)+(B=6) THEN 80** reads: if the value of A equals 8 OR the value of B equals 6 the IF-THEN condition is met and execution continues at line 80.

Note that both (A=8) and (B=6) are enclosed in parenthesis. Since there is no other apparent reason to enclose such simple equations in parenthesis, they are the tip-off in determining if the + is used for addition or as a logical OR.

TEST PROGRAM

```
10 REM '+' LOGICAL OPERATOR TEST PROGRAM
20 PRINT "ENTER A VALUE FOR VARIABLE A";
30 INPUT A
40 PRINT "ENTER A VALUE FOR VARIABLE B";
50 INPUT B
60 PRINT "A =";A,"B=";B
70 IF (A=8)+(B=6) THEN 100
80 PRINT "NEITHER A = 8 NOR B = 6"
90 GOTO 999
100 PRINT "EITHER A = 8 OR B = 6"
999 END
```

SAMPLE RUN *(using 4 and 6)*

```
ENTER A VALUE FOR VARIABLE A? 4
ENTER A VALUE FOR VARIABLE B? 6
A = 4                    B = 6
EITHER A = 8 OR B = 6
```

VARIATIONS IN USAGE

Many computers use the + sign to join (concatenize) separate strings into one. For example, PRINT "H"+"I" concatenizes the strings "H" and "I" to form the word HI.

TEST PROGRAM

```
10 REM '+' CONCATENATION TEST PROGRAM
20 A$="PASSED THE CON"
30 B$="CATENATION TEST"
40 PRINT "THE + SIGN ";
50 PRINT A$+B$
99 END
```

SAMPLE RUN

```
THE + SIGN PASSED THE CONCATENATION TEST
```

The + sign is used by some computers in PRINT USING statements to automatically insert a + sign before positive numbers.

ALSO SEE

AND, *, $, PRINT USING

The — symbol is used as an arithmetic subtraction sign to find the arithmetic difference between two numbers or numeric variables. For example, **PRINT A-B** prints the value of variable A minus the value of variable B.

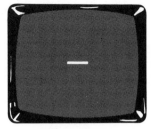

Operator

The — sign is also used for negation in arithmetic operations. Negation means simply "changing the sign from what it is to the opposite".

Example, **PRINT -(3-8)** subtracts 8 from 3 which results in a negative 5. The first - (negation) sign reverses the sign within the parentheses and prints 5 (the + sign is implied).

TEST PROGRAM

```
1Ø REM '-SIGN' TEST PROGRAM
2Ø A=3
3Ø B=6
4Ø C=B-A-(B-A)
5Ø PRINT "C =";C
6Ø PRINT "THE - SIGN PASSED THE TEST IF C = Ø
99 END
```

SAMPLE RUN

```
C = Ø
THE - SIGN PASSED THE TEST IF C = Ø
```

VARIATIONS IN USAGE

None known.

The / sign is used as an arithmetic division sign to find the quotient of two numbers or numeric variables.

Example, 8/4 is the same as 8÷4

A
N
S
I

Operator

TEST PROGRAM

```
10 REM '/ DIVISION SIGN' TEST PROGRAM
20 A=8
30 B=4
40 C=A/B
50 PRINT "C =";C
60 PRINT "THE / SIGN PASSED THE TEST IF C = 2"
99 END
```

SAMPLE RUN

```
C = 2
THE / SIGN PASSED THE TEST IF C = 2
```

VARIATIONS IN USAGE

None known.

The * symbol (asterisk) is used as an arithmetic multiplication sign (instead of the letter "X") to find the product of two numbers or numeric variables.

A
N
S
I

Operator

TEST PROGRAM

```
10 REM '*' MATH OPERATOR TEST PROGRAM
20 A=5
30 B=A*6
40 PRINT "* PASSED THE TEST IN LINE";B
99 END
```

SAMPLE RUN

```
* PASSED THE TEST IN LINE 30
```

VARIATIONS IN USAGE

Some computers also use the * sign as the "lotical math" operator for "AND". For example:

```
IF (A=8) * (B=6) THEN 80
```

reads, if the value of A equals 8 **AND** the value of B equals 6 then the IF-THEN condition is met and execution continues at line 80.

Note that both (A=8) and (B=6) are enclosed in parenthesis. This is the tip to look for when determining if an * is being used for multiplication or as a logical AND.

TEST PROGRAM

```
10 REM '*' LOGICAL 'AND' TEST PROGRAM
20 A=8
30 B=6
40 IF (A=8) * (B=6) THEN 70
50 PRINT "* FAILED THE TEST AS AND OPERATOR"
60 GOTO 99
70 PRINT "* PASSED THE AND OPERATOR TEST"
99 END
```

SAMPLE RUN

```
* PASSED THE AND OPERATOR TEST
```

The * asterisk is used by some computers to specify a format for printing numeric values or strings in the PRINT USING statement. See PRINT USING for details.

ALSO SEE

AND, PRINT USING

MATH OPERATOR

The = symbol is used as a mathematical equal sign. For example, A=3+5 assigns the value 8 to variable A.

TEST PROGRAM

Operator

```
1Ø REM TEST PROGRAM USING = AS MATH OPERATOR
2Ø A=4
3Ø B=6
4Ø C=A+B
50 PRINT "C =";C
6Ø PRINT "THE = SIGN PASSED THE TEST IF C = 1Ø"
99 END
```

SAMPLE RUN

```
C = 1Ø
THE = SIGN PASSED THE TEST IF C = 1Ø
```

RELATIONAL OPERATOR

The = sign is also used by most computers as a relational operator to compare two numeric values for equality. For example, **IF A=B THEN 1ØØ** tells the computer to branch to line 1ØØ when then numeric variable A is equal to numeric variable B. If the condition of the = sign is not met (i.e. A≠B), the test "falls through" and program execution continues on the next line.

Most computers also use the = sign for **string** comparisons. This feature allows one string or string variable to be compared character-by-character against another string or string variable. In the example, **IF A\$ = "ABCD" THEN 1ØØ** the interpreter compares the ASCII code of each character (from left-to-right) stored in string variable A\$ against the characters enclosed in quotation marks. If the ASCII code of all characters is found equal, the computer branches or "jumps" to line 1ØØ. If the ASCII code of all characters is not found equal, the test "falls through" and program execution continues on the next line.

TEST PROGRAM

```
1Ø REM TEST OF = SIGN AS NUMERIC COMPARISON OPERATOR
2Ø A=5
3Ø IF A=5 THEN 6Ø
4Ø PRINT "= SIGN FAILED NUMERIC COMPARISON TEST"
5Ø GOTO 99
6Ø PRINT "= SIGN PASSED NUMERIC COMPARISON TEST"
99 END
```

SAMPLE RUN

```
= SIGN PASSED NUMERIC COMPARISON TEST
```

TEST PROGRAM

```
10 REM TEST PROGRAM USING = FOR STRING COMPARISON
20 A$ = "ABCDE"
30 IF A$ = "ABCDE" THEN 60
40 PRINT "THE = SIGN FAILED THE STRING COMPARISON TEST"
50 GOTO 99
60 PRINT "THE = SIGN PASSED THE STRING COMPARISON TEST"
99 END
```

SAMPLE RUN

THE = SIGN PASSED THE STRING COMPARISON TEST

VARIATIONS IN USAGE

Different interpreters allow different length character strings to be compared. Some allow only one letter to be compared against another single letter, while others allow enough characters to compare an entire name and address, or more.

The combination of > or < with = is very common. Sometimes only numerics can be so compared, but in most cases the ASCII values of strings are automatically derived and those values compared.

ALSO SEE

>, <, $, < =, > =

The ∧ (carat) is an arithmetic exponentiation sign used to compute the value of a base number to a specified power.

For example, 2 ∧ 3 is the same as the cube of 2 or 2^3

For more information see ↑.

Operator

TEST PROGRAM

```
1∅ REM ' ∧ (EXPONENTIATION)' TEST PROGRAM
2∅ PRINT "ENTER A BASE NUMBER";
3∅ INPUT B
4∅ PRINT "NEXT, ENTER THE EXPONENT";
5∅ INPUT E
6∅ A=B ∧ E
7∅ PRINT "THE NUMBER";B;"TO THE";E;,,POWER IS";A
3∅999 END
```

SAMPLE RUN *(using 4 and 3)*

```
ENTER A BASE NUMBER? 4
NEXT, ENTER THE EXPONENT? 3
THE NUMBER 4 TO THE 3 POWER IS 64
```

VARIATIONS IN USAGE

None known.

ALSO SEE

↑, ⌢, and **

The ↑ (up-arrow) is used as an arithmetic exponentiation sign to compute the value of a base number to a specified power.

For example, **2↑3** is the same as the cube of 2 or 2^3.

Operator

TEST PROGRAM

```
10 REM '↑ (EXPONENTIATION)' TEST PROGRAM
20 PRINT "ENTER A BASE NUMBER";
30 INPUT D
40 PRINT "NEXT ENTER A POWER NUMBER";
50 INPUT F
60 P=D↑F
70 PRINT "THE NUMBER";D; "TO THE";F;"POWER IS";P
30999 END
```

SAMPLE RUN *(using 4 and 3)*

```
ENTER A BASE NUMBER? 4
NEXT ENTER A POWER NUMBER? 3
THE NUMBER 4 TO THE 3 POWER IS 64
```

The ↑ sign is also used to compute a number's root value by enclosing the inverse of the index number in parenthesis (1/n).

For example, **8↑(1/3)** is the same as the cube root of 8, or $\sqrt[3]{8}$.

TEST PROGRAM

```
10 REM '↑ (USED AS A RADICAL SIGN)' TEST PROGRAM
20 PRINT "ENTER A BASE NUMBER";
30 INPUT B
40 PRINT "NEXT ENTER A ROOT NUMBER";
50 INPUT N
60 R=B↑(1/N)
70 PRINT "THE";N;"ROOT OF";B;"IS";R
30999 END
```

SAMPLE RUN *(using 64 and 3)*

```
ENTER A BASE NUMBER? 64
NEXT ENTER A ROOT NUMBER? 3
THE 3 ROOT OF 64 IS 4
```

DIFFERENT OPERATORS FOR ↑

See **, ∧ and ⌒

IF YOUR COMPUTER DOESN'T HAVE IT

If they all fail, substitute the following subroutine:

The subroutine programs found under LOG and EXP **must** be added to this one to make it work (saves space not to duplicate them here).

```
30000 GOTO 30999
30100 REM * EXPONENTIATION SUBROUTINE * INPUT X,Y; OUTPUT P
30102 REM ALSO USES E,L,A,B,C INTERNALLY
30104 P=1
30106 E=0
30108 IF Y=0 THEN 30120
30110 IF X < 0 THEN 30114
30112 GOTO 30116
30114 IF INT(Y)=Y THEN 30122
30116 IF X <> 0 THEN 30130
30118 P=P*E
30120 RETURN
30122 P=1-2*Y+4*INT(Y/2)
30125 X=-X
30130 GOSUB 30170
30135 X=Y*L
30140 GOSUB 30240
30145 P=P*E
30150 RETURN
```

To use this subroutine in the TEST PROGRAM, make these program changes:

```
35 X=D
55 Y=F
60 GOSUB 30100
```

VARIATIONS IN USAGE

None known.

ALSO SEE

EXP, LOG, **, ∧ , ⌒

The < sign is used as a "less-than" relational operator to compare two numeric values in IF-THEN statements. For example, IF A<B THEN 1ØØ tells the computer to branch to line 1ØØ if the value of variable A is less than variable B.

A
N
S
I

Operator

TEST PROGRAM

```
1Ø REM '<RELATIONAL OPERATOR' TEST PROGRAM
2Ø A=1Ø
3Ø IF A< 2Ø THEN 6Ø
4Ø PRINT "THE< SIGN FAILED THE TEST"
5Ø GOTO 99
6Ø PRINT "THE< SIGN PASSED THE TEST"
99 END
```

SAMPLE RUN

```
THE< SIGN PASSED THE TEST
```

VARIATIONS IN USAGE

The < sign can be used by most computers to compare strings. The < sign compares the ASCII code of each character (from left-to-right) in two strings. The first difference in equality encountered determines the relationship. For example, string ABCDEF is less than string ABD even though the first string has more characters. Since the ASCII code for C (decimal 67) in the first string is less than, or precedes, the ASCII code for D (decimal 68) in the second string, it passes the < test.

If each string has the same sequence of characters, then the longer·string is considered larger. For example, string ABCD is larger than string ABC.

TEST PROGRAM

```
1Ø REM '< STRING OPERATOR' TEST PROGRAM
2Ø A$="ABC"
3Ø B$="ABCD"
4Ø C$="B"
5Ø IF A$ < B$ THEN 8Ø
6Ø PRINT "THE < SIGN FAILED THE TEST IN LINE 5Ø"
7Ø GOTO 999
8Ø IF B$< C$ THEN 11Ø
9Ø PRINT "THE< SIGN FAILED THE TEST IN LINE 8Ø"
1ØØ GOTO 999
11Ø PRINT "THE< SIGN PASSED THE TEST"
999 END
```

SAMPLE RUN

THE < SIGN PASSED THE TEST

< is frequently combined with = to make the < = operator and combined with > to make "inequal" operators <>or ><. Some interpreters limit the number of characters which can be specifically compared in a string.

ALSO SEE

>, <>, ><, =, $, IF-THEN

The > sign is used as a "greater-than" relational operator to compare two numeric values in IF-THEN statements. For example, **IF A > B THEN 1ØØ** tells the computer to branch to line 1ØØ if the value of variable A is greater than variable B.

Operator

TEST PROGRAM

```
1Ø REM '>RELATIONAL OPERATOR' TEST PROGRAM
2Ø A=2Ø
3Ø IF A >1Ø THEN 6Ø
4Ø PRINT "THE>SIGN FAILED THE TEST"
5Ø GOTO 99
6Ø PRINT "THE>SIGN PASSED THE TEST"
99 END
```

SAMPLE RUN

```
THE>SIGN PASSED THE TEST
```

VARIATIONS IN USAGE

The > sign can be used by most computers to compare strings. The > sign compares the ASCII code of each character (from left-to-right) between two strings. The first difference in equality encountered determines the relationship. For example, string ABD is greater than string ABCDEF even though the first string has fewer characters. Since the ASCII code for D (decimal 68) in the first string is greater than, or follows the ASCII code for C (67) in the second string, it passes the > test.

If each string has the same sequence of characters, the longer string is considered larger. For example, string ABCD is larger than string ABC.

TEST PROGRAM

```
1Ø REM '>STRING OPERATOR' TEST PROGRAM
2Ø A$="ABCD"
3Ø B$="ABC"
4Ø C$="B"
5Ø IF A$ > B$ THEN 8Ø
6Ø PRINT "THE >SIGN FAILED THE TEST IN LINE 50"
7Ø GOTO 999
8Ø IF C$ >B$ THEN 11Ø
9Ø PRINT "THE >SIGN FAILED THE TEST IN LINE 8Ø"
1ØØ GOTO 999
11Ø PRINT "THE >SIGN PASSED THE TEST"
999 END
```

SAMPLE RUN

THE >SIGN PASSED THE TEST

\> is commonly combined with = to make the >=operator and combined with < to make "inequal" operators <>or >< . Some interpreters limit the number of characters which can be specifically compared in a string.

ALSO SEE

<, <>, ><, =, GT, LT, NE, $, IF-THEN

The $<>$ sign is used as a "not-equal" relational operator to compare two numeric values in IF-THEN statements for inequality. For example, IF A$<>$B THEN 1ØØ tells the computer to branch to line 1ØØ if the value of variable A is **not** equal to variable B.

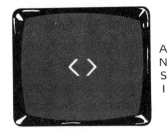

A
N
S
I

Operator

TEST PROGRAM

```
1Ø REM ' < > RELATIONAL OPERATOR' TEST PROGRAM
2Ø A=1Ø
3Ø IF A < > 2Ø THEN 6Ø
4Ø PRINT "THE < > SIGN FAILED THE TEST"
5Ø GOTO 99
6Ø PRINT "THE < >SIGN PASSED THE TEST"
99 END
```

SAMPLE RUN

```
THE< >SIGN PASSED THE TEST
```

VARIATIONS IN USAGE

The $<>$ sign can be used by most computers to compare strings. The $<>$ sign compares the ASCII code of each character (from left-to-right) in two strings. The first difference in equality encountered determines the relationship. In the example, IF A$$<>$"ABC" THEN 1ØØ the interpreter compares the ASCII code of each character (from left-to-right) stored in string variable A$ against the characters enclosed in quotation marks. If a difference in equality is encountered, or one string is longer than the other, the condition of the $<>$ sign is met and the computer branches to line 1ØØ.

TEST PROGRAM

```
1Ø REM ' < > STRING OPERATOR' TEST PROGRAM
2Ø A$="ABCDE"
3Ø IF A$ < > "ABCD" THEN 6Ø
4Ø PRINT "THE < > SIGN FAILED THE TEST IN LINE 3Ø"
5Ø GOTO 999
6Ø IF A$ < > "ABCDE" THEN 8Ø
7Ø GOTO 1ØØ
8Ø PRINT "THE < > SIGN FAILED THE TEST IN LINE 6Ø"
9Ø GOTO 999
1ØØ PRINT "THE < > SIGN PASSED THE TEST"
999 END
```

SAMPLE RUN

Some computers use the operator >< or #. Some interpreters limit the number of characters which can be specifically compared in a string.

ALSO SEE

#, ><, <, >, IF-THEN, $

The $><$ sign is used by a few computers (e.g. those using MAX BASIC) as a "not-equal" relational operator.

For more information see $<>$.

Operator

TEST PROGRAM

```
10 REM '>< RELATIONAL OPERATOR' TEST PROGRAM
20 A=10
30 IF A >< 20 THEN 60
40 PRINT "THE >< SIGN FAILED THE TEST"
50 GOTO 99
60 PRINT "THE >< SIGN PASSED THE TEST"
99 END
```

SAMPLE RUN

```
THE >< SIGN PASSED THE TEST
```

VARIATIONS IN USAGE

None known.

ALSO SEE

$<>$, #, NE, IF-THEN

The $\leq$ sign is used as a "less than or equal to" relational operator to compare two numeric values in IF-THEN statements. For example, IF A$\leq$=B THEN 1ØØ tells the computer to branch to line 1ØØ if the value of variable A is **less than or equal to** variable B.

Operator

A N S I

TEST PROGRAM

```
1Ø REM '<=RELATIONAL OPERATOR' TEST PROGRAM
2Ø A=1Ø
3Ø IF A<=2Ø THEN 6Ø
4Ø PRINT "THE<=SIGN FAILED THE TEST IN LINE 3Ø"
5Ø GOTO 999
6Ø IF A<=1Ø THEN 9Ø
7Ø PRINT "THE<=SIGN FAILED THE TEST IN LINE 6Ø"
8Ø GOTO 999
9Ø PRINT "THE<=SIGN PASSED THE TEST"
999 END
```

SAMPLE RUN

```
THE<= SIGN PASSED THE TEST
```

VARIATIONS IN USAGE

The $\leq$ sign can be used by most computers to compare strings. The $\leq$ sign compares the ASCII code of each character (from left-to-right) in two strings. The first difference in equality encountered determines the relationship.

If both strings have identical characters and are the same length, then they satisfy the $\leq$ relationship. For example, string ABCDEF is $<$ string ABD even though the first string has more characters. Since the ASCII code for C (decimal 67) in the first string is less than, or precedes the ASCII code for D (68) in the second string, it passed the $\leq$ test.

If each string has the same sequence of characters, then the longer string is considered larger. For example, string ABCD is larger than string ABC.

TEST PROGRAM

```
10 REM '<=STRING OPERATOR' TEST PROGRAM
20 A$="ABC"
30 B$="ABCD"
40 C$="B"
50 IF A$<=B$ THEN 80
60 PRINT "THE<= SIGN FAILED THE TEST IN LINE 50"
70 GOTO 999
80 IF A$<= "ABC" THEN 110
90 PRINT "THE<= SIGN FAILED THE TEST IN LINE 80"
100 GOTO 999
110 IF B$<= C$ THEN 140
120 PRINT "THE<= SIGN FAILED THE TEST IN LINE 110"
130 GOTO 999
140 PRINT "THE <= SIGN PASSED THE TEST"
999 END
```

SAMPLE RUN

```
THE <= SIGN PASSED THE TEST
```

Some computers use the = < sign instead. Others allow it as an option. Some interpreters limit the number of characters which can be specifically compared in a string.

ALSO SEE

IF-THEN, < , =, = < , > , >=, >< , < > , $, LE, LT, EQ, GT, GE

$>=$ is used as a "greater-than or equal-to" relational operator to compare two numeric (or string, when allowed) values in IF-THEN statements.

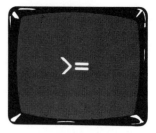

For example, IF A $>=$B THEN 1ØØ tells the computer to branch to line 1ØØ if the value of variable A is greater-than **or** equal to variable B.

Operator

TEST PROGRAM

```
1Ø REM ' >= RELATIONAL OPERATOR' TEST PROGRAM
2Ø A=2Ø
3Ø IF A >=1Ø THEN 6Ø
4Ø PRINT "THE >= SIGN FAILED THE TEST IN LINE 3Ø"
5Ø GOTO 999
6Ø IF A >=2Ø THEN 9Ø
7Ø PRINT "THE >= SIGN FAILED THE TEST IN LINE 6Ø"
8Ø GOTO 999
9Ø PRINT "THE >= SIGN PASSED THE TEST"
999 END
```

SAMPLE RUN

```
THE >= SIGN PASSED THE TEST
```

The $>=$ operator is allowed by some computers for string comparison. It compares the ASCII code of each character (from left-to-right) in two strings. The first difference in equality encountered determines the relationship. If both strings have identical characters and are the same length, then they satisfy the $>=$ relationship.

For example, string ABD is greater than string ABCDEF even though the first string has has fewer characters. Since the ASCII code for D (decimal 68) in the first string is greater than the ASCII code for C (decimal 67) in the second string, it passed the $>=$ test.

If each string has the same sequence of characters, then the longer string is considered larger. String ABCD is larger than string ABC.

TEST PROGRAM

```
10 REM ' >=STRING OPERATOR' TEST PROGRAM
20 A$="ABCD"
30 B$="ABC"
40 C$="B"
50 IF A$ >=B$ THEN 80
60 PRINT "THE >= SIGN FAILED THE TEST IN LINE 50"
70 GOTO 999
80 IF A$ >="ABCD" THEN 110
90 PRINT "THE >= SIGN FAILED THE TEST IN LINE 80"
100 GOTO 999
110 IF C$ >= B$ THEN 140
120 PRINT "THE >= SIGN FAILED THE TEST IN LINE 110"
130 GOTO 999
140 PRINT "THE >= SIGN PASSED THE TEST"
999 END
```

SAMPLE RUN

```
THE >= SIGN PASSED THE TEST
```

Some computers use the = > sign instead (or interchangeably).

VARIATIONS IN USAGE

None known.

ALSO SEE
IF-THEN, > , < , < =, < > , ><

=< is used as an "equal to or less than" relational operator to compare two numeric (or string, when allowed) values in IF-THEN statements. For example, IF A=<B THEN 1ØØ tells the computer to branch to line 1ØØ if the value of variable A is equal to **or** less than variable B.

For more information see <=

Operator

TEST PROGRAM

```
1Ø REM '=< RELATIONAL OPERATOR' TEST PROGRAM
2Ø A=1Ø
3Ø IF A=< 2Ø THEN 6Ø
4Ø PRINT "THE=< SIGN FAILED THE TEST IN LINE 3Ø"
5Ø GOTO 999
6Ø IF A=< 1Ø THEN 9Ø
7Ø PRINT "THE=< SIGN FAILED THE TEST IN LINE 6Ø"
8Ø GOTO 999
9Ø PRINT "THE=< SIGN PASSED THE TEST"
999 END
```

SAMPLE RUN

```
THE =< SIGN PASSED THE TEST
```

VARIATIONS IN USAGE

None known.

ALSO SEE

IF-THEN, <=

=> is used as an "equal to or greater than" relational operator to compare two numeric (or string, when allowed) values in IF-THEN statements. For example, IF A=> B THEN 1ØØ tells the computer to branch to line 1ØØ if the value of variable A is equal to or greater than variable B.

For more information see >=

Operator

TEST PROGRAM

```
1Ø REM '=> RELATIONAL OPERATOR' TEST PROGRAM
2Ø A=2Ø
3Ø IF A=> 1Ø THEN 6Ø
4Ø PRINT "THE => SIGN FAILED THE TEST IN LINE 3Ø"
5Ø GOTO 999
6Ø IF A=>2Ø THEN 9Ø
7Ø PRINT "THE => SIGN FAILED THE TEST IN LINE 6Ø"
8Ø GOTO 999
9Ø PRINT "THE => SIGN PASSED THE TEST"
999 END
```

SAMPLE RUN

THE => SIGN PASSED THE TEST

VARIATIONS IN USAGE

None known.

ALSO SEE

IF-THEN, >=

The ≤ sign is used in the IBM 5100 and 5110 BASIC as an "equal to or less than" relational operator to compare two numeric values in IF-GOTO statements.

For example, IF A ≤ B GOTO 1ØØ tells the computer to branch to line 1ØØ if the value of variable A is equal to or less than variable B.

For more information see <=

Operator

TEST PROGRAM

```
1Ø REM ' ≤ RELATIONAL OPERATOR' TEST PROGRAM
2Ø A=1Ø
3Ø IF A ≤ 2Ø GOTO 6Ø
4Ø PRINT "THE ≤ SIGN FAILED THE TEST IN LINE 3Ø"
5Ø GOTO 999
6Ø IF A ≤ 1Ø GOTO 9Ø
7Ø PRINT "THE ≤ SIGN FAILED THE TEST IN LINE 6Ø"
8Ø GOTO 999
9Ø PRINT "THE ≤ SIGN PASSED THE TEST"
999 END
```

SAMPLE RUN

```
THE ≤ SIGN PASSED THE TEST
```

VARIATIONS IN USAGE

None known.

ALSO SEE

<=, =<

The $\geq$ sign is used in the IBM 5100 and 5110 BASIC as an "greater than or equal to" relational operator to compare two numeric values in IF-GOTO statements.

For example, IF A $\geq$ B GOTO 1ØØ tells the computer to branch to line 1ØØ if the value of variable A is greater than or equal to variable B.

For more information see   >=

Operator

TEST PROGRAM

```
1Ø REM ' ≥ RELATIONAL OPERATOR' TEST PROGRAM
2Ø A=2Ø
3Ø IF A ≥ 1Ø GOTO 6Ø
4Ø PRINT "THE ≥ SIGN FAILED THE TEST IN LINE 3Ø"
5Ø GOTO 999
6Ø IF A ≥ 2Ø GOTO 9Ø
7Ø PRINT "THE ≥ SIGN FAILED THE TEST IN LINE 6Ø"
8Ø GOTO 999
9Ø PRINT "THE ≥ SIGN PASSED THE TEST"
999 END
```

SAMPLE RUN

```
THE ≥ SIGN PASSED THE TEST
```

VARIATIONS IN USAGE

None known.

ALSO SEE

>=, =>

The ≠ sign is used in the IBM 5100 and 5110 BASIC as a "not-equal" relational operator to compare two numeric values in IF-GOTO statements.

For example, IF A ≠ B GOTO 1ØØ tells the computer to branch to line 1ØØ if the value of variable A is **not** equal to variable B.

For more information see < > .

Operator

TEST PROGRAM

```
1Ø REM '≠ RELATIONAL OPERATOR' TEST PROGRAM
2Ø A=1Ø
3Ø IF A≠2Ø GOTO 6Ø
4Ø PRINT "THE ≠ SIGN FAILED THE TEST"
5Ø GOTO 99
6Ø PRINT "THE ≠ SIGN PASSED THE TEST"
99 END
```

SAMPLE RUN

```
THE ≠ SIGN PASSED THE TEST
```

VARIATIONS IN USAGE

None known.

ALSO SEE

< > , >< , #

The ' (apostrophe) is used by many computers as an abbreviation for the REMark statement.

For more information see REM.

A
N
S
I

Statement

TEST PROGRAM

```
1Ø REM '(APOSTROPHE) TEST PROGRAM
2Ø 'PRINT "THE APOSTROPHE FAILED THE REM TEST"
3Ø "THE APOSTROPHE FAILED THE TEST IF LINE 2Ø IS PRINTED"
4Ø PRINT "THE APOSTROPHE PASSED THE REM TEST"
99 END
```

SAMPLE RUN

```
THE APOSTROPHE PASSED THE REM TEST
```

VARIATIONS IN USAGE

A few computers use the apostrophe in PRINT statements to enclose strings instead of using quotation marks.

TEST PROGRAM

```
1Ø REM '(APOSTROPHE) * USED AS QUOTES * TEST PROGRAM
2Ø PRINT 'THE APOSTROPHE PASSED THE QUOTATION MARK TEST'
99 END
```

SAMPLE RUN

```
THE APOSTROPHE PASSED THE QUOTATION MARK TEST
```

ALSO SEE

REM, PRINT

NOTES

NOTES

NOTES